Corporations

Origin and
Development

Corporations

A Study of the Origin and Development of Great Business Combinations and of their Relation to the Authority of the State

By
JOHN P. DAVIS

Volume II

BeardBooks
Washington, D.C.

CONTENTS

AN INTRODUCTORY STUDY OF CORPORATIONS

I

EDUCATIONAL AND ELEEMOSYNARY CORPORATIONS
(Continued)

VI—The Universities from 1550 to 1850

WHEN the first period of the history of the English universities came to an end with the general historical period of the Middle Ages, their constitution was in most respects fully established. During the second period of their history their structure was not modified sufficiently to bring them into complete harmony with the new movements of modern history; they yielded only so much as was unavoidable and retained enough to assure the conservation of their principal elements in the presence of wide-spread change. From the sixteenth to the nineteenth century, through all the political changes caused by the despotism of the new Tudor monarchy, the imperious tyranny of the Stuarts, the leading iconoclasm of the Commonwealth and the constitutional kingship of the Hanoverians, through all the religious shifting of Roman Catholicism, Anglicanism, Puritanism, Presbyterianism, non-conformity and dissent, and through all the great intellectual movements from the Renaissance and

the Reformation to the beginning of the liberal development of the present day, the English universities, as
institutions, remained substantially intact. Serious modifications of their mediæval structure have been mostly
temporary. The Middle Ages were characterized by
the rearing of imposing institutions rather than by the
development of ideas to find expression in them; the
Catholic Church was greater than Catholicism; feudalism
was greater than kings or barons. Modern history, on
the contrary, has been distinguished by the growth of
ideas rather than of institutions; Protestantism is greater
than the Protestant Churches; liberty and equality are
greater than parliaments and constitutional kingships.
Even abstract thought, in the limited field that it occupied before the Reformation, was cast in the imposing
and symmetrical form of the scholastic philosophy. The
great movement of civilization in the Middle Ages was
one of reabsorption, of regaining the body of knowledge
left by the ancient world and providing institutions for it;
the most effective force in Christianity had to lie dormant until the Reformation should arouse it, because
humanity had not yet absorbed the product of Greek and
Roman life. The work of humanity in the modern era
has been that of expansion in ideas within the structural
framework left by the Middle Ages, and the vexatious side
of the problem of civilization has been not in the incapacity to generate and develop ideas, but in the inability to
provide an adequate social structure for them. The aim
of the present day is not to get men to do — they do
enough and do it well,—but so to regulate their relations
in the doing that it may not be wanting in effect. The
recently renewed interest in mediæval institutions can be
explained only by a renewed appreciation of the need of
developing an organization of present society that will
allow present social forms the degree of activity necessary
to their effectiveness. Of all the institutions that the

Middle Ages bequeathed to the modern world those of the English universities have proved to be most enduring, have suffered the least change in response to the demands of modern life. The study of university history on its formal side is therefore less difficult after than before the end of the fifteenth century and may be disposed of with some degree of brevity. For the sake of convenience, the second period may be considered under the three heads already used in connection with other subjects: (1) Relations to the State, (2) Relations to the Church and (3) Internal relations,—though the facts included under the second heads were more or less completely merged with those under the first head after the Reformation and may not always be easily distinguished or distributed.

1. The attitude of the new Tudor monarchy towards the universities was characterized by the same element of despotism that pervaded its relations to all other national institutions. They had been promoted largely for the sake of learning itself; they were now used to subserve the interests of the monarchy. Though Henry VIII. was a true friend of learning, its exponents, like the Church, the courts and Parliament, must support his pretensions. When he was seeking a divorce from Catherine, in 1530, he demanded that the University of Oxford unite its sanction with those that had been obtained from continental universities. Though with reluctance and only after some of the younger masters of arts had been persuaded to withdraw from convocation and withhold their adverse votes, the University yielded. So, too, in 1534, when separation from Rome was about to be consummated by the royal assumption of the title of "Supreme Head of the Church of England," the University, all its charters having four years earlier been delivered into the king's hands, there to remain for thirteen years, was found compliant in approving the step

even before it had been taken. When James I. had found the theory of the "divine right of kings" a sufficient basis for the imperious tyranny of the Stuarts, he found in the Arminian party in the University his strongest adherents and accordingly favored their control of the institution, though he had brought with him from Scotland predilections for Presbyterianism. When the doctrine of "passive obedience" needed support, the University convocation almost eagerly passed a resolution in condemnation of all resistance, whether offensive or defensive, to a reigning sovereign.

On the other hand, the University, while it had been able in the fourteenth century to rely on the Crown for protection against other powers in the state, found it necessary after the beginning of the sixteenth century to protect itself by humility, conciliation and obsequiousness, against the Crown itself. The chancellor, originally the representative of the Church in its control of learning, but long the active head of the University and resident in Oxford, became its ambassador or advocate, almost the royal minister of higher education, and resident at court, leaving his active work as administrative head to be done by a resident vice-chancellor; he must now be a courtier or courtly prelate, a Leicester or a Laud. Every radical change of policy, whether political or religious, was accompanied by a demand for a revision of the statutes of the University involving, at least in theory, even its constitution; whether the new code of statutes in answer to the demand emanated from the Crown directly, or indirectly through the subservient chancellor or a royal commission, they were properly known as the "Edwardine," the "Marian," or the "Caroline" statutes, though the University might in form have asserted the right to perfunctorily approve them or pass them at the dictation of their actual makers. While the new codes were in process of compilation, the constitution of the

University was frequently suspended. So dependent was it in the reign of Henry VIII. that it humbly surrendered all its charters into the hands of Cardinal Wolsey with the request that he should use his own pleasure in amending them; when they were returned five years later, with a new one from the King, they were received with the greatest obsequiousness; even later in the reign they were again in the King's hands for a period of thirteen years. The spoliation of the monastic houses by Henry VIII. and Edward VI. made the University and its component colleges tremble for their own revenues, and when fear of spoliation was past the desire of sharing with the courtiers in the spoils was fully as destructive of independence. With the increasing power of Parliament in the government came the necessity of securing its recognition of the corporate status in an enactment, in 1570 (or 1571),

"that the . . . chancellor of the University of Oxford, and his successors forever, and the masters and scholars of the . . . University of Oxford for the time being, shall be incorporated and have a perpetual succession in fact, deed, and name, by the name of 'the Chancellor, Masters and Scholars of the University of Oxford.' "

In 1604, in the first year of the reign of James I., the University was given the right to elect two burgesses to Parliament who should inform that body "of the true state of the university and of each particular college." Even in the reign of Elizabeth, at the time of the statutory incorporation of the University, Parliament had not hesitated to interfere by legislation in its internal affairs. In two acts of the thirteenth and eighteenth years of her reign it was provided, by the earlier, that college estates should be leased for twenty-one years or not to exceed three lives, and by the later, that one third of the rentals reserved in such leases should be rendered in corn or malt estimated at 6s. 8d. and 5s. per quarter; in 1589 followed an act to prevent the sale and collusory resignation of fellowships and corrupt election to them.

The University and the Anglican Church became as dependent on the Crown as the Crown on them. When the civil war broke out the University was more than loyal to the Stuarts; though for other reasons in addition to that of the loyalty of the University, Oxford became the base of Charles's military operations and virtually his capital, the schools and halls being converted into barracks, mints and storehouses, as well as into royal palaces and courts, until the city was captured by the Parliamentary army. When James II., by his Declaration of Indulgence, in 1687, sought to confer on Roman Catholics the right of admission to corporations, and began the enforcement of his policy in the place where his arbitrary will would be most likely to meet with no opposition, he very consistently chose the University of Oxford; on the resistance of Magdalen College to his mandate to elect Parker to its presidency, already filled by a candidate of their own choice, a royal commission expelled the president and twenty-five fellows, though James afterwards reinstated them when the loss of his throne was threatened by the nation. Yet such an affinity seems to exist between corporations enjoying special privileges and the arbitrary rulers upon whom the possession of the privileges depends, that the University of Oxford, notwithstanding the arbitrariness of James II., continued for eighty years to be the stronghold of Jacobitism; not until the accession of George III. were the results of the revolution of 1688 accepted in Oxford otherwise than as an unavoidable calamity. The University had become so dependent on the Crown and had left so little of its spirit of fourteenth-century independence that in 1759 its power to repeal any of the Caroline statutes without the royal consent was denied by the proctors, though they were not sustained in their opposition; the power had certainly not been exercised in an important matter for a century.

In the reign of Henry VIII. began the succession of royal and parliamentary commissions and boards of visitors, so frequent in time and so comprehensive in purpose during the sixteenth and seventeenth centuries that they threatened at times to form a permanent part of the University constitution. A commission appointed by Edward VI. under the great seal was designed chiefly to eliminate popery from Oxford and in effecting its purpose destroyed "superstitious" emblems, and after expelling all Catholic masters and scholars, introduced Protestants (some of them aliens) in their places; it eventually provided a complete code of new statutes, afterwards known as the "Edwardine statutes." When Mary ascended the throne, the tables were turned. Most of the Protestants fled from Oxford, but such as remained were burned at the stake or expelled by a board of visitors deputed in 1556 by Cardinal Pole, the new Catholic chancellor; English Bibles and Protestant books in the libraries were burned; the code of "Marian statutes" was the work of the visitors. Elizabeth had no sooner succeeded Mary on the throne than she suspended all academical elections at Oxford and appointed a board of visitors for the purpose of enforcing compliance with the act of supremacy on the University; nine heads of colleges and many fellows and others were expelled for non-compliance. With such a chancellor as Laud, Charles I. hardly needed to resort to commissions; a delegacy of convocation spent four years in codifying the University statutes; the code was then corrected and amended by Laud, and, after a year for the suggestion of further amendments by the University and colleges, was finally promulgated by him in 1636 with the confirmation of the king; the new statutes were called the "Caroline" or "Laudian" statutes and remained in force (except during the interregnum of the Commonwealth) until the middle of the nineteenth century. When Oxford had been captured, in 1646, during the civil war, by the insurgent forces, Parliament at once suspended academical elections and the renewal of leases of college estates "until the pleasure of Parliament be made known therein." In the following year an ordinance was enacted "for the visitation and reformation of the University of Oxford and the several colleges and halls therein," by a board of twenty-four visitors, of whom fourteen were laymen and ten were clergy. It was intended at first largely as an inquisitorial body, having actual power to act in lesser matters, to provide information for a standing committee of lords and commons and to submit reports and appeals to it; the board of visitors, however, soon acquired all necessary powers and used them to depose ten heads of colleges and many professors and fellows, filling many of their places at once with their own nominees; they further supervised and directed the administration of the University and colleges in all its details. Cromwell himself became chancellor in 1650, and in 1652 the board of visitors was merged in a resident commission consisting of the vice-chancellor, three heads of colleges and a prebendary of Christ Church, which should put into permanent effect the more fundamental changes made by the original board of visitors; in 1654, the commission was again changed, but not essentially, and continued to govern the University for four years. The commission exercised substantially all the powers formerly exercised by the chancellor and visitors of the University and colleges; the degree of permanence enjoyed by it had threatened to convert the University into a state institution. When weakness developed in the government of the Commonwealth, the University resumed many of the powers that it formerly exercised and the restoration of the monarchy completed the change. Soon after Charles II. had reached London, he appointed

a new board of visitors to undo the work of Cromwell,
but its changes were almost entirely personal, and not
constitutional; a few heads and fellows of colleges were
replaced by others and little else occurred. The numerous other commissions cannot be examined in detail;
the general result of their activity, however, was to reduce the independence of the University and to bring it
into greater harmony with the state and with the changes
in the Church caused by the interference of the state.

After the Revolution of 1688, the state seemed to sustain a somewhat modified attitude towards the University
largely because religious questions had lost their previous
importance in national politics and because the University
itself had declined in importance. The century following the revolution is rightly called by Brodrick "the Dark
Age of academical history." [1] Only when a rebellion in
behalf of the Pretender was threatened, early in the reign
of George I., did the government consider the strong
Jacobite sentiment worthy of notice. On that occasion,
it was proposed that the king be empowered for seven
years

" to nominate and appoint all and every the Chancellor, Vice-
Chancellor, Proctors, and other officers of the [two] universities, and all heads of houses, fellows, students, chaplains,
scholars, and exhibitioners, and all members of and in all and
every the college and colleges, hall and halls in the said universities or either of them upon all and every vacancy and
vacancies ";

another plan suggested contemplated the election of heads
of colleges by certain officers of state and the distribution of other positions and the management and disposition of college revenues by a commission. Neither
plan, however, was adopted.

2. Much that might be said of the relations of the

[1] G. C. Brodrick, *History of the University of Oxford*, page 174.

University of Oxford to the Church after the Reformation
has been placed under the head of its relations to the
state; the state acted through the Church and usually
treated the University as a part of the ecclesiastical system. But some of the more intimate relations must be
considered. For two centuries the contest between the
secular church, which tended to become nationalized, and
the monasteries, which had adhered closely to Rome, had
been bitter in the University; the suppression of religious
houses at the Reformation ended the contest and left the
national church in control, while some of the colleges
profited by the diversion to them of the property of the
suppressed bodies, and Christ Church and some professorships were endowed from it. The University was now
dominated by the Anglican Church and opposed Catholics, non-conformists and dissenters, as the Catholic
Church (in England) had formerly opposed the monks
and friars and Lollards. The University was narrower
under the Church of England than it had been before the
Reformation. The continual weeding out of Catholics at
one time and of Protestants at another left it thoroughly
lifeless, except as a seminary for the clergy, to whom its
fellowships were almost all confined. When the policy
of the state was sufficiently liberal, as in Elizabeth's
reign, to admit any but adherents of the Anglican Church,
the University simply became the battle-ground of theo-
logical controversy to the exclusion of everything else.
It shared to only a slight extent in the revival of the
brilliant Elizabethan era. After the Reformation, too,
more avenues had been opened to the energetic man of
education than the career in the Church that had formerly
been all that he could hope for, not so much as a result
of the Reformation as of the broader movement against
tradition and in favor of individual development of which
it properly formed a part. Under James I. and Charles
I., the University was brought into closer connection

with the Church not only by restricting the membership more closely through the imposition of test-oaths but by opening benefices more numerously to graduates. The intimacy of the dependence of the University on the Established Church appears most clearly in a petition of the resident graduates to Parliament in 1641 when it was threatening the exclusion of the bishops from the House of Lords; the petition prayed for the maintenance of the bishops and their Cathedral churches, as, among other things,

"the principal outward motive of all students, especially in divinity, and the fittest reward of some deep and eminent scholars; as affording a competent portion in an ingenious way to many younger brothers of good parentage who devote themselves to the ministry of the gospel; . . . and as funds by which many of the learned professors in our university are maintained."[1]

The University was not widened at the Revolution and continued thereafter, during its dismal eighteenth century, the narrow seminary of the Anglican Church that it had become. Subscription to the Thirty-nine Articles at matriculation and declaration of conformity to the liturgy of the Established Church on acceptance of a fellowship and the obligation of entering holy orders continued to be exacted until the middle of the nineteenth century.

3. At the end of the fifteenth century the crystallization of University activity in the colleges had been quite complete. The colleges suffered so little internal modification until the middle of the ninteenth century that they need no consideration; a lesser proportion of the fellows in the post-Reformation foundations were required to be in holy orders, and the old group of theology, canon law and civil law was not so generally imposed on fellows,—

[1] Quoted by G. C. Brodrick, *History of the University of Oxford*, pp. 123, 124.

in fact, the study of the canon law was abolished; laxity in the enforcement of the minor regulations of daily life and of the more important requirement of residence by heads of houses and fellows might be a subject of complaint; many minute regulations of living and study like those of the Laudian statutes were provided, but they would hardly change one's general impression of a college or its inmates when compared with that of the college at the beginning of the sixteenth century.

The "college monopoly" expanded during the sixteenth and seventeenth century until it controlled not only the membership of the University but also its government. After the chancellor became habitually nonresident and rather the University's "friend at court" than its head, the vice-chancellor, appointed by him, became the acting head; in 1569, he was required by the Edwardine statutes to be elected by the congregation; twenty years later his nomination was again vested in the chancellor and has since so remained. By the same statute of 1569, passed under the influence of Leicester, the Black Congregation as far as concerned its power to give preliminary consideration to measures to be brought before convocation was abolished, and in its place was substituted a body consisting of the vice-chancellor, doctors, heads of colleges and proctors. In 1629, the older methods of electing proctors, either by vote of the entire academic body or by vote of congregation, were discontinued and cycles of twenty-three years were settled during each of which, in future, each college, according to its size and importance, should elect a definite number of proctors. Some years later the Laudian (or Caroline) statutes confirmed the use of the proctorial cycles and further provided that in each college the proctors should be elected by the doctors and masters of a given rank. By the Laudian statutes the administration of the University was given to the Hebdomadal Board, composed of the vice-chancellor, heads of colleges and proctors; the vice-chancellor, moreover, was to be nominated annually by the chancellor from the heads of colleges in rotation with the approval of convocation.

But while the college monopoly seems to have been complete in 1636 and to have been formally maintained until the nineteenth century, some movements in the history of the University of Oxford plainly tended in the opposite direction—to the ultimate restoration of the University unit. Wolsey is said to have had in contemplation the establishment of University professorships and of University lecture-rooms at the time of the foundation of his Cardinal College. Henry VIII. afterwards founded his five Regius professorships of Divinity, Civil Law, Medicine, Hebrew and Greek, though he provided them only with a meagre endowment of £40 annually. Some such professorships had previously been established and others were afterwards added, even during the dismal eighteenth century. The establishment of professorships and lectureships in separate colleges but open to the whole University must have had a similar tendency; Henry VIII. stipulated with the colleges that such lectureships should be established at the expense of the five wealthiest colleges and that they should be attended daily not only by the scholars of the colleges in which they were maintained but also by the scholars of all the other colleges. One of the effects of the closer supervision of the universities and colleges by the state through the agency of ministerial chancellors and boards of visitation was to introduce a considerable degree of uniformity into the conditions prevalent in all of them, for it was inclined to treat them rather as one body. According to the Edwardine statutes, the retention of a fellowship was made conditional on six months' residence, lectures were to be followed by examinations and matriculation examinations were to be held,—rules apparently enforceable

in all colleges, whatever their previous custom may
have been; likewise the limitation of fellowships to a
term of years, enforced in a few periods, appears to have
been applicable to all and not to only a part of the colleges.[1]   The commissioners appointed by Edward VI.
were given power to consolidate several colleges into one,
but did not exercise it; they had also projected the plan
of having separate colleges devoted to special branches
of study, as New College to arts and All Souls' to civil
law, but did not execute it.   The University also acquired
some new functions or more effectual organs for the exercise of those that it already possessed.   In 1581 a statute
passed by convocation provided that all tutors should
submit to be examined and licensed by a board composed
of the vice-chancellor and six doctors or bachelors of
divinity.   Representation in Parliament, conferred by
James I. in 1604, was conferred on the University without reference to its colleges.[2]   The cheapening of books
after the sixteenth century may have operated to decrease
the corporate spirit of the colleges by permitting the
scholar to study with less dependence on the books owned
by the college and used in common.   The Laudian statutes provided for a system of public oral examinations
for the degrees of Bachelor of Arts and Master of Arts,
to "be conducted, in rotation, by all the regent masters,
under the orders of the senior proctor," and covering
branches of study in which, by the statutes, the candidate should be required to have heard lectures.   Whatever centripetal forces of University activity were effective

---

[1] A similar course seems to have been pursued towards the two Universities of Oxford and Cambridge ; the policy applied in one was likely to be
applied in the other at the same time. *E. g.*, two commissioners were appointed by Edward VI. in 1549, one for Oxford and one for Cambridge, to
bring them into harmony with the changes wrought by the Reformation.
The statutes for both were made substantially the same " in order that each
eye of the nation might be set in motion by similar muscles."

[2] J. Bass Mullinger, *History of the University of Cambridge*, p. 140.

in overcoming the centrifugal forces of college activity, the principle was still severely applicable in 1770, that no single one of the heads of colleges, or all of them together, "could dispense with statutable rules, independently of Convocation "

VII—The Universities after 1850

In 1850 a new period in the constitutional history of the English universities began, though some preliminary reforms had taken place between 1800 and 1830. The Laudian statutes had provided that in the University of Oxford examinations for the degrees of Bachelor of Arts and Master of Arts should be conducted in rotation by all the regent masters, under the orders of the senior proctor,[1] but during the eighteenth century the system had fallen into decay; no responsibility rested on the examiners, they received no compensation, and their positions lacked permanence. In 1800, the system was amended by the division of candidates into two classes, to whom "pass " and "honor " examinations were respectively given; the candidates for honors were subdivided into two classes according to the degrees of merit attained by them; the examiners, moreover, were given responsibility and standing by being made appointive officers, receiving salaries and serving for definite terms. Even as amended, the system suffered much further modification in the course of thirty years, the principal changes being the substitution of written for the oral examinations required by the original Laudian statutes, as well as by the amendatory statute of 1800; the candidates for honors were divided into three instead of two classes; the system of honor schools was also given a beginning by placing mathematics in a school separate from the classical school. In 1850, however, the system of

[1] See page 14, *supra.*

examinations was amplified so that they should be held at the end of the second, third and fourth years, the last being the final examination for the degree of Bachelor of Arts; two "pass" examinations were to be held each year in the several branches of study; the honor schools were increased to four by the addition of one for natural science and one for law and modern history to the classical school and the school of mathematics; the number was later increased to six by the division of that of law and modern history into one for jurisprudence and one for modern history and by the addition of one for theology. But such changes, great as they were, demanded only slight constitutional changes; to the extent that they exerted an influence, they served to magnify the importance of the University in comparison with its component colleges. The University was exercising its power to determine to what candidates it should grant degrees by setting a higher standard or at least by insisting on a more rigid adherence to the standard formerly too loosely maintained. The inevitable reaction was certain to have an appreciable effect on the colleges, the organs of the University by which almost all its work of instruction was done. The colleges, however, were so heavily encumbered by the mass of mediæval restrictions under which they worked that the national government, it was generally agreed, had to be appealed to for the initiation of fundamental reforms.

In 1850, accordingly, and largely at the instance of the authorities of the University and colleges themselves, a royal commission was appointed for an investigation of the state of the University and colleges, and of their discipline and revenues. After a thorough investigation, the commission made many recommendations, of which part were put in force by an act of Parliament of 1854 and part by ordinances of executive commissions provided for by the act. The chief reforms were as follows:

The Hebdomadal Board,[1] the organic embodiment of the college monopoly, gave place to a Council composed of elected representatives, in equal numbers, of the heads of colleges, professors and resident masters of arts. The Convocation, which had come to perform its duties perfunctorily, conducting its transactions in Latin and doing little more than to grant degrees, was superseded by a new body, called the "Congregation" and composed of all resident members of Convocation, and permitted to use English in its deliberations. Existing professorships were reorganized and re-endowed and new ones were founded from contributions levied on the colleges. The colleges were given new constitutions and new codes of statutes and their fellowships were made accessible to all candidates on the basis of merit; new fellowships were required to be created in studies established or recognized by the University. The number of scholarships and their stipends were increased. Private halls were provided for so that the "unattached" or "non-collegiate" element might be restored to the membership of the University. No religious test should be imposed on scholars at the time of their matriculation or of their receiving the degree of Bachelor of Arts, but only on candidates for the degree of Master of Arts and for fellowships in the colleges; in 1871, such religious tests as remained were abolished by act of Parliament, except such as were necessary to maintain the exclusive connection of the faculty of theology with the Church of England.

In 1872, renewed agitation for the reform of the universities resulted in the appointment by the crown of a second commission, purely inquisitorial in character, for the investigation of the revenues and obligations of both the Universities of Oxford and Cambridge and their colleges. After an extended investigation and report, an act of Parliament was passed in 1877 for the appointment

[1] See page 12, *supra*.

of executive commissioners with wide powers to reorganize the interrelations of the two universities and·their colleges; that the pursuit of a conservative course in the readjustment of revenues might be assured, the needs of the several colleges were to be given prior recognition, and representatives elected by them were to sit in conjunction with the commissioners.   The work of the commission, approved by the crown in 1882, provided for the universities and colleges substantially new constitutions and codes of statutes, though some of the old features were retained.   Professorships, readerships and lectureships were newly founded or given an increased endowment.   The appointment and control of the important University examiners were regulated.   The University was provided with more ample funds for the maintenance of its buildings and the satisfaction of its other needs. The courses of study were divided into homogeneous groups under the limited supervision of Boards of Faculties.   The colleges were assessed definite percentages of their revenues to the amount of £20,000 for the payment of the increased expense, and provision was made for the application of surplus revenue to University and college purposes, while a reduction of expenditures was sought in lowering the stipends of fellows.   The fellowships were not to be tenable for life unless connected with an University or college office, though many of them were at the same time given such connection; the remaining fellowships, about one hundred in number, were made terminable at the end of seven years and were freed of obligations of residence and of service in University or college offices; the restrictions on almost all headships and fellowships were removed.   Scholarships were made uniform as to the age and emoluments of the scholars who should hold them.   But the legislative organization of the University remained as it had been left by the act of 1854, while the general form of the colleges was only slightly modified. On its organic side, the University was still, in many respects, only an aggregate of colleges; the autonomy of the colleges had been diminished but not destroyed, while the University's area of activity had been greatly widened. The instruction by University professors and the tuition by college tutors continued to flourish side by side. Scholars were not absolutely required to attend the lectures of the University, though their increased endowments and improved organization made them more attractive to scholars. Though matriculation might be directly in the University by non-collegiate scholars, it might also be indirectly through the colleges by such scholars as should become inmates of them. The extension of the "combined lecture" system, by which, as in a few colleges since the seventeenth century, scholars of one college might attend lectures in others, broke down the barriers between the colleges, while it did not make closer the connection between their inmates and the University; in fact, the tendency was in quite the opposite direction, for the system permitted the tutors to specialize their work, in application of the principle of division of labor, and to make their "combined" work more effective in the presence of competition by the University. The most important fact was that equality of status was established in the fellowships and scholarships of the several colleges; the first step in the amalgamation of confederated states in a single state is the eradication of the differences between them; likewise the Oxford scholar became more truly a member of the University when his status in his own college became the same as that of his fellow-scholars in other colleges. The abolition of religious tests tended to destroy similarity of membership in the University while it had the more important effect of bringing scholars as a class into greater harmony with the outside world—the University became more cosmopolitan. The "university extension" movement is a legitimate outcome of the broadening of the basis of university membership.

The comprehension of a wider area by the University of Oxford in the exercise of its public functions appears plainly from a University statute of 1857 providing for the examination by it of middle class schools as a means of establishing organic relations to them. In 1873, a second step in the same direction was taken by the assumption of the work of examining public schools and granting to their pupils certificates of their proficiency; it is interesting to note, too, that the work was to be done by a joint-board of the two Universities of Oxford and Cambridge,—convincing evidence of the diminishing autonomy of the two corporations; the movement is said to have been inspired by an apprehension of impending "state supervision" of the public schools—a confession that the universities were invading a field of activity rightfully belonging to the state.

"Notwithstanding the bold amendments which it has undergone, the constitution and educational system of the University must be regarded as still [in 1894] in a state of transition."[1] The most that may be said of the changes in the English universities since the beginning of the nineteenth century is: They have greatly increased the activity of the universities not only absolutely, but relatively to that of the component colleges. The plain tendency has been towards the restoration of the university as the real unit of higher education from its former status as a federation of colleges. The colleges have themselves tended to become more similar to each other in constitution and membership, though dissimilar (yet co-operative) in their activity, while the relations of their members to the university have become closer and more vital; in other words, the colleges have tended (though not strongly) to become co-operating departments of the

[1] G. C. Brodrick, *History of the University of Oxford*, p. 202.

university. In their relations to society the universities have largely ceased to contain a membership of persons entirely distinct and different in their rights and duties from other members of society and consequently have become more similar to each other; they have come to a realization rather of their affinity to society than of their distinction from it,—attraction has succeeded repulsion; they have accordingly extended their area of social activity and have (to a slight extent) occupied it in common, while they have been treated by the state in legislation and administration rather as divisions of one body than as separate bodies; in fine, they have tended to develop from autonomous corporations into administrative organs of the state.

VIII—Modern English Universities

The University of Cambridge was so similar in development to the University of Oxford that for the purposes of this study a consideration of it may be dispensed with, but the University of Durham and the University of London possess a few features that may be adverted to with profit.

The University of Durham was founded in 1832 largely through the influence of the Bishop of Durham. It was to consist of a warden or principal, other necessary officers, professors and readers, tutors and students, and was to be established according to such regulations as the dean and chapter of Durham Cathedral (in whom was confided the discipline) with the consent of the bishop (who should be visitor) should prescribe; stalls in the cathedral were to be annexed to the office of warden, and to the professorships of divinity and Greek; the professor of mathematics and other officers were to be elected by the dean and chapter. In 1835, by statute of the dean and chapter, the ordinary management of the University, under the bishop as visitor and the dean and chapter as governors, was vested in the warden, a senate and a convocation; the warden was to be the active head of the University and to convoke, dissolve and preside over both senate and convocation, to have both an original and casting vote in each and to have a previous veto in convocation, subject in some cases to appeal to the dean and chapter and bishop; the senate was to consist of the chief officers [1] of the University, to transact the ordinary business of the University and originate resolutions in more important matters for conformation by convocation; the convocation, composed of the warden and such doctors and masters in divinity, law, medicine and arts from Oxford, Cambridge and Dublin as should be members of the University of Durham, to be increased in future by the doctors and masters of Durham, was to confirm or reject without amendment measures presented by the senate. It was incorporated in 1837 as "The Warden, Masters and Scholars of the University of Durham," with the power to confer degrees. [2] In 1841 the office of warden was annexed to that of the dean of Durham. The original six fellows were eventually increased to twenty-four, of whom all should have the degree of Bachelor of Arts, not more than one third should be laymen and each should hold his fellowship for eight years (or if in holy orders, for ten years) but should lose it on marriage, admission to a preferment in the cathedral or to a benefice; all elections to fellowships were to be on the basis of merit, including both learning and morals. Scholars were to be admitted on examination and to submit to annual public examinations. No religious tests were to be imposed at matricu-

---

[1] More specifically, the senate was to be composed of the warden, the professors of divinity, Greek and mathematics, the two proctors and three members of convocation, one nominated by the dean and chapter, one by the convocation and one by the fellows with the approval of convocation.

[2] Degrees were to be conferred by the warden in convocation after the allowance of grace by the dean and chapter.

lation, but only on application for a degree or other academical privileges, though all scholars were required to attend church services daily. Peculiarly enough, a college was established within the University, and other colleges or halls were contemplated, with tutors and censors to regulate the studies and conduct of scholars, of whom all had to be inmates of some such college, house or hall. An interesting amalgamation of university, college and cathedral chapter! The University of Durham represents very faithfully the structure of the university as modified to suit the purpose of a liberal Church. The control of the Church was assured by vesting the government in the dean and chapter, and by the union of the offices of dean and warden as well as those of the canons and chief instructors. Though the instruction was to redound chiefly to the interest of the Church, not all the fellowships were reserved for fellows in holy orders; not only were some of the fellowships open to those not in holy orders, but religious tests were dispensed with to such extent as the Church, from its own standpoint, could safely permit. If colleges and halls were provided for, they were clearly intended rather as departments for the organization of the domestic life of the scholars than as autonomous units of instruction, and were not allowed to threaten the disintegration of the University itself.

If the organization of the University of Durham was what might reasonably have been expected from a liberal bishop and cathedral dean and chapter after England's six centuries of university history, that of the University of London was what might likewise have been expected from the exercise by the state of the power of establishing a great university on its own initiative after an equal experience. In 1836, William IV. granted to a number of noblemen and gentlemen a charter for a new university, to be called "The University of London," of which

they should constitute the senate,[1] "for the advancement
of religion and morality, and the promotion of useful
knowledge [and] to hold forth to all classes and denominations . . . without any distinction whatever, an
encouragement for pursuing a regular and liberal course
of education." The senate, appointed "for the purpose
of ascertaining by means of examinations the persons who
[had] acquired proficiency in literature, science and art
by the pursuit of [a] course of education and of rewarding
them by academical degrees, as evidence of their respective attainments, and marks of honor proportionate
thereto," was to be composed of a chancellor, vice-
chancellor and thirty-six fellows, of whom all should
be qualified by the possession of doctors', masters' or
bachelors' degrees, besides such persons as the crown
might see fit to add at a subsequent time. In addition
to the senate there was to be a convocation, consisting
of all Doctors of Law, Doctors of Medicine, Masters of
Arts, Bachelors of Law and Bachelors of Medicine of
two years' standing and Bachelors of Arts of three years'
standing, electing its own chairman for terms of three
years, and empowered to discuss and declare its opinion
on any matter relating to the University. The chancellor was to be appointed by the crown and to serve for
life; the vice-chancellor was to be elected annually by the
senate from among the fellows; vacancies among the fellows were to be filled by the remaining fellows or by the
crown from a list of three nominees presented by convocation for each vacancy. The crown was to be visitor.
The power to appoint examiners and other officers and
servants was to be exercised by the senate. The admin-

[1] The charter was found to have technically lapsed by the death of William
IV.; an identical charter was accordingly granted by Victoria in 1837; a
third charter was granted in 1858; for the purpose at hand, the provisions
of the several charters may be considered together without doing injustice
to the subject.

istration of the University and the making of rules relating to degrees were to be vested in the senate, subject to the approval of one of the secretaries of state. The degrees of Bachelor of Arts, Master of Arts, Bachelor of Laws and Doctor of Laws were to be granted only to graduates of University College (London), King's College (London) and such other institutions, whether in London or outside, as the crown should authorize; the degrees of Bachelor of Medicine and Doctor of Medicine were to be granted to graduates of such institutions as should be approved by the secretary of state at the suggestion of the senate.[1] Examinations for degrees were to be held annually and such fees were to be charged for them as should be approved by the Commissioners of the Treasury. The University has been without endowment, has been required to submit annually to the Commissioners of the Treasury an account of its receipts and expenditures, and has been supported by parliamentary grants, its fees from examinations having been expended in rewards and scholarships; the duties of the members of the senate have been gratuitously performed.

The University of London is merely a university superstructure for the colleges connected with it. When considered together, the University and the several colleges connected with it are not unlike either of the older Universities of Oxford or Cambridge except that the new institution touches the state at more points, does not pretend to be a "teaching university" and is far more distinct from its colleges in its administration than are the older universities. In the University of Durham one extreme was attained by the amalgamation of the University and its colleges, while in the University of London the other extreme was attained by making the University

---

[1] It appears that the list of approved colleges for all degrees might later be enlarged, altered, varied or amended with the consent of one of the secretaries of state.

more distinct from its colleges than is any other similar
institution.   It is interesting in the extreme that though
the University of London was merely an institution initi-
ated by the state to confer degrees indicative of work
accomplished by separate colleges, it should be given the
form evolved in the history of the Universities of Oxford
and Cambridge; ·the weak element in its constitution was
its only new feature — the body of fellows; the corresponding bodies in the constitutions of Oxford, Cambridge and Durham were composed of persons having a
vital connection as instructors or administrators with the
colleges, but in the University of London, the distinct
interests and geographical separation of the colleges made
such a body impossible and compelled reliance on a body
composed of prominent educated persons to be gradually
replaced by graduates of its colleges.

IX—Schools and Eleemosynary Corporations

In the grades of schools below the universities and their
colleges a considerable diversity of organization prevailed
until the nineteenth century, during which, however,
comparative uniformity has been attained through the interference of the state.   The reason for the diversity was,
doubtless, that the scholars themselves did not participate
in the control of their own organization.   The scholars of
grammar schools were readily recognized, both by their
age and by the inferior rank of their studies, as a dependent class.   Most of the schools, moreover, originated in
the period of the Renaissance and Reformation, the last
half of the fifteenth and the first half of the sixteenth
centuries; by that time the movement in all mediæval
corporations towards the restriction of the governing
powers of their members to a close administrative class
within them was well-nigh complete; burgesses were no
longer mere citizens but members of close governing
bodies in the towns; the fellowship of a gild was not the

entire body of gildsmen but merely the governing body of wardens and assistants or other higher rank of gildsmen; so, too, in the colleges of the universities, the fellows, who had earlier been merely scholars governing themselves, had become the collegiate body in which was reposed the government of scholars and the administration of college affairs; it might be expected, then, that the grammar schools founded in the fifteenth and sixteenth centuries would be only bodies of scholars subjected to a "governing body" of some kind. As far as the scholars themselves were concerned, their organization for the purpose of instruction was simple and uniform; they were merely grouped in classes according to their work or their social status and subjected to rules made by the governing body and executed by head-masters and their under-masters, ushers or other assistants; a rudimentary element of autonomy existed in the monitorial system, and the status of scholars in some schools was preliminary to the enjoyment of a similar or more exalted status in university or other colleges, or even in the governing body of their own school, but in itself it was purely dependent. In the governing bodies, the real corporations, much variety of form appeared. The corporate bodies to which the grammar schools were subjected were purely ecclesiastical and secular corporations, formed either for their own peculiar purposes or for the express purpose of governing the schools,—municipal corporations, corporations formed for general charitable purposes of which one was the maintenance of a school, and corporations formed expressly for the administration of schools. They may broadly be divided into two classes; in the first, ecclesiastical elements were prominent, and the force of the Reformation was not seriously felt;—in the second, ecclesiastical elements were excluded and the influence of the Reformation appeared in the substitution of secular elements.

Westminster College, or St. Peter's College at Westminster, was an appendage of the dean and chapter of
Westminster, which had been a monastery before the
Reformation, had been suppressed as such and made a
collegiate church and later a cathedral church by Henry
VIII. and even later restored to the condition of a collegiate church by Edward VI.; as a monastery it had
supported a school, though far less important than the
one maintained after its suppression; associated with the
dean and chapter in the appointment of its head-master
and in its government were the dean of Christchurch,
Oxford, and the master of Trinity College, Cambridge.
Winchester College, however, founded by Wykeham in
1379 as a preparatory school for New College, Oxford,
was not subjected to a purely ecclesiastical corporation.
Its governing body consisted of a warden, sub-warden
and ten fellows, elected by the warden and fellows of
New College, while the school itself, superintended by a
head-master and usher, contained seventy scholars; the
members of the governing body, however, were all
priests, and were assisted by a body of chaplains and
choristers in the execution of the religious part of the
bishop-founder's plans; the governing body did not constitute a church, but was exactly modelled on the predominant type of Oxford college; the fellows were
expected and intended to devote themselves primarily to
learning. Eton College was modelled on Winchester
College by its founder, Henry VI., and consisted of a
provost, ten fellows, a schoolmaster and twenty-five poor
scholars, with the necessary chaplains, clerks and choristers; but the provost and fellows constituted a collegiate
church into which a parochial church had been converted
for the purpose of founding the college; its endowment
was derived almost entirely from suppressed alien priories;
it was intended as a preparatory school for King's College, Cambridge, just as Winchester for New College.

But after the end of the fifteenth century, founders of endowed schools appear to have had less confidence in the permanence of ecclesiastical institutions and to have preferred to entrust their benefactions to secular corporations. John Colet, though dean of the cathedral chapter of St. Paul's, conveyed the endowment of St. Paul's School to the Company of Mercers of London with the direction that they should "have all the care and governance of the school [and should] every year choose of their company two honest and substantial men called the surveyors of the school, which in the name of the whole fellowship [should] take all the charge and business about the school for that one year"; he assigned as the reason for his preference of the London company "that there was no certainty in human affairs, but that, in his opinion, there was less probability of corruption in such a body of citizens than in any other order or degree of mankind." The Merchant Taylors' school, however, was founded directly by the Merchant Taylors Company, with the assistance of some of its members, about 1560, and has been maintained by it ever since; the master and wardens and all past-masters were to be the "surveyors" of the school. Shrewsbury School was founded by Edward VI. about 1554 on an endowment consisting of church property appropriated by him; he conveyed the property to the town corporation of Shrewsbury, in which he also vested the government of the school under the Bishop of Lincoln as visitor; in 1798, after a long quarrel between the town corporation and the headmaster over the question of his independence of it, Parliament interfered and vested the government of the school in twelve trustees, together with the mayor, who should preside over them and have both an original and casting vote; vacancies in their body were to be filled by the town corporation from three nominees of the trustees; St. John's College, Cambridge, was to have the power to appoint the head-master. The "free grammar-school of John Lyon, in the village of Harrow upon the Hill" and its endowment were placed in control of six "keepers and governors" of the school, who should, among other things, maintain the school from its endowment and perpetuate their own existence by filling their vacancies by co-optation. In 1611, Thomas Sutton conveyed in trust to a body of sixteen "governors" lands for the establishment of a hospital and free school, who should fill their vacancies by co-optation,[1] make all necessary statutes for the administration of their double charge and appoint the master of the school and other officers; such was the organization of the Charterhouse School. Somewhat similarly, Lawrence Sheriff conveyed lands to two trustees who were to maintain from their revenue a school and almshouses at Rugby, and so reconvey the lands to other trustees that the latter would perpetuate their maintenance.[2] By decree of the court of chancery in 1653, however, the succession of trusts was replaced by a self-renewing board of twelve trustees.

The periods of the Renaissance and Reformation were prolific of endowed grammar schools, and elementary schools, most of which were placed under the government of town corporations, some of them more or less modified for the purpose by the addition of outside members, of distinct self-renewing bodies of trustees or governors,

---

[1] The king and queen were to be governors *ex officio*; if vacancies should not be filled within two months, the crown was to fill them by appointment.

[2] " The desire, confidence and trust of the said Lawrence Sheriffe is, that [the two trustees] will, of the rent, revenues, and sums of money . . . in all respects substantially, truly and effectually accomplish the same, in such ways as by the laws of this realm may most assuredly be devised, and convey and assure the lands, tenements, hereditaments, and other the premises to that only intent and purpose."—See " Intent " of Lawrence Sheriff, published in Appendix Q of the *Report of the Public Schools Commissioners* (1861).

or of bodies more or less composed of members holding their places by virtue of their offices in Church or State. The grammar schools of Edward VI., endowed from the property of suppressed monasteries and priories, were nearly all given over to municipalities, like Shrewsbury School. In very many of the grammar schools, even of those governed by municipalities, the colleges of Oxford and Cambridge obtained a more or less exclusive control of the appointment of the master, and were closely affiliated with them through the medium of scholarships in the colleges held by the schools.

During the seventeenth and eighteenth centuries the schools remained substantially unchanged in their constitutions, though in many of them the members of the governing body came to view their positions almost solely as sources of revenue, to the detriment of the schools as educational institutions. In fact, during the seventeenth and eighteenth centuries many new endowed schools were founded, though nearly all of them were organized on the same plan as those of the later Reformation. When the time to reform them came in the nineteenth century, they were all dealt with by the same general method. The courts of equity had always exercised jurisdiction over them as trusts, whose execution it could enforce, or modify. In many cases the courts had interfered to enforce schemes involving reorganization of the governing bodies, redistribution of revenues or rearrangement of curricula. But the court of chancery was an inadequate medium of reform, and its work had to be supplemented by parliamentary action. The general method of Parliament in the several classes of schools included two steps, (a) an investigation of the corporations, their revenues and the schools maintained by them, with recommendations for their reform, and (b) an enforcement of the recommendations. The first step was undertaken by an inquisitorial and advisory commission, the second step by an executive commission either temporary or permanent in character.

Of the commissions to inquire into the affairs of the endowed schools there were three: (1) The Popular Education Commission of 1859, (2) the Public Schools Commission of 1861 and (3) the Schools Inquiry Commission of 1864. The first commission investigated the elementary schools; the second, nine particular public schools and colleges, Westminster, Winchester, Eton, St. Paul's, Merchant Taylors', Shrewsbury, Harrow, Charterhouse and Rugby; the third, such schools as had not been investigated by the two earlier commissions. The work of each commission, and the action based on its recommendations, will be briefly considered.

(1) The Commissioners of Popular Education were appointed by the crown in 1859, "to inquire into the state of popular education in England, and to consider and report what measures, if any, [were] required for the extension of sound and cheap elementary instruction to all classes of the people." In their report in 1862, they expressed the opinion that the court of chancery was not a suitable body for the reformation and supervision of the schools for popular education and that the powers of the charity commissioners [1] were ineffectual for the purpose; they therefore recommended that the work be placed under a committee of the Privy Council. No action, however, was taken on the recommendation until after the reports of the two succeeding bodies of commissioners.

(2) In 1861 a royal commission was appointed "for the purpose of enquiring into the nature and application of the endowments, funds and revenues belonging to or received by the . . . colleges, schools and foundations" of Eton, Winchester, Westminster, Charterhouse, St. Paul's, Merchant Taylors', Harrow, Rugby and Shrewsbury, "and also to enquire into [their] administra-

---

[1] *Infra*, page 53.

tion and management . . . and into the system and
course of studies respectively pursued [in them] as well
as into the methods, subjects and extent of the instruction given to [their] students." The recommendations
of the commission were carried into effect through a body
of seven executive commissioners appointed by virtue of
the Public Schools Act of 1868. The governing bodies
were allowed a limited period (about a year) in which to
make the changes themselves subject to the approval of
the commission; after the expiration of the time such
changes as were still not made were to be made by the
commission itself. Westminster College was provided
with an endowment of lands, buildings and funds separate from those of the dean and chapter, and was given
a new governing body composed of the dean of Westminster, dean of Christchurch (Oxford), master of Trinity
College (Cambridge), two members elected by the dean
and chapter of Westminster, one member elected by the
dean and chapter of Christchurch (Oxford), one member
elected by the masters and seniors of Trinity College
(Cambridge), one elected by the Council of the Royal
Society, one appointed by the Lord Chief Justice of
England, one elected by such masters of Westminster as
should be graduates of the English universities and not
less than three nor more than five members elected by
the governing body itself. Winchester College (it was
recommended) should have a governing body consisting
of a warden, four stipendiary and seven honorary fellows, the four stipendiary fellows being distinguished in
literature or science and having served as head-master,
second master or assistant master, the seven honorary
fellows being the warden of New College (Oxford), three
appointees of the crown and three chosen by the governing body. Eton was to be governed by a body of nine,
ten or eleven fellows; the provost was to be appointed by
the crown and to be relieved of the spiritual charge of the

parish of Eton, and though to be a member of the Church
of England, not necessarily to be in holy orders.   The fellows were to consist of the provosts of Eton and King's
College (Cambridge) *ex officio*, five nominees of the University of Oxford, the University of Cambridge, the
Royal Society, the Lord Chief Justice and the masters
of Eton, and the remaining two, three or four elected by
the fellows themselves.

Some of the schools under secular control were reformed in a similar manner.   It was recommended that
the governing body of St. Paul's be amended by adding
to the master, wardens and surveyors one or two other
members elected by the Mercers' Company and an equal
number appointed by the crown, but the recommendation was not executed.   No recommendation was made
as to the Merchant Taylors' School.   Shrewsbury School
should have a governing body of thirteen members, three
elected by the municipality of Shrewsbury, one by the
masters and fellows of St. John's College (Cambridge),
one by the master and fellows of Magdalen College
(Cambridge), one by the dean and chapter of Christchurch
(Oxford), three by the crown and four by the governing
body.   Harrow School was to be strengthened by adding
to the six original "keepers and governors" six others
distinguished by a reputation in literature and science.
The recommendations concerning Charterhouse and
Rugby schools were quite similar.   To the sixteen governors of the former it was proposed that four others
eminent in literature and science be added, and then that
the whole number of twenty be gradually reduced to the
original number of sixteen by refraining from filling the
next four vacancies in the original membership; the recommendation was based on the view that "the task
which these bodies will have to undertake . . . is
that of blending a due proportion of modern studies with
the old classical course without destroying the general

character of the public schools." Of the twelve trustees
of Rugby it was desired that they "be persons qualified
by their position or attainments to fill [their] situation
with advantage to the school" and that four of them be
"of generally acknowledged eminence in literature and
science."

(3) The third commission, to investigate the schools
not comprised in the work of the two former commissions, was appointed in 1864. The first commission had
investigated elementary popular schools; the second nine
particular grammar schools; the third was intended to
investigate in general the rest of the grammar schools.
The commission presented its report in 1867–1868. It
proposed that the head-master of an endowed school appoint and dismiss his own assistants and have entire charge
of the administration of the school; and that the governors, subject to schemes adopted by superior authorities,
"use the funds of the endowment as shall be found expedient for the good of the school," appoint and dismiss
masters, determine the subjects of instruction, fix the fees
of scholars and the salaries of the employees, maintain
halls (in boarding schools) and grant or refuse licenses to
separate boarding houses. Through provincial and central authorities the schools were to be graded in districts
with relation to each other, consolidated, enlarged or suppressed. Schemes for the resettlement of educational
trusts proposed by the provincial and approved by the
central authority were to be presented to Parliament.
The schools should be periodically inspected, have their
accounts audited and their scholars examined by the central authority or its representatives.[1] The report was
followed by the passage of the Endowed Schools Act of
1869, providing for the appointment of three commissioners by the crown. They should have power to prepare

[1] *Report of Schools Inquiry Commission* (1867–1868), vol. i., cap. vii., pp.
571–651.

schemes for the administration of endowments of the schools which should be submitted for approval to the committee of the Privy Council on education. The governing bodies of schools might present to the commissioners schemes for their consideration and might appeal from their decision to the Queen in Council, by whom in turn the scheme in controversy might be referred to Parliament for further consideration or back to the commissioners with a proper order. In general, it was provided that endowments supporting both schools and other charities might be divided, part going under the control of the schools commissioners and part under that of the charities commissioners.

Under the legislation based on the above-described investigations the older corporations have been so changed in character that they have become virtually new corporations. The important features of the reforms were the following: (1) Such of the colleges as had been under the control of the Church were released from it, though a sentiment of conservatism gave the older ecclesiastical corporations representation on the governing body. (2) The colleges dependent on the colleges of Oxford and Cambridge were made independent of them, though they, like the Church, were given a limited representation in the governing bodies. (3) Likewise the extensive influence of municipalities was reduced to a limited representation. (4) A national element was added in representatives named by the crown and high officers of state and elected by the governing bodies themselves. (5) A clear distinction was made between the governing bodies and the schools,—which had not been done at all before the Reformation and had afterwards been incompletely done, and such a composition of the former was provided for that they should be fairly representative of enlightened public opinion. (6) The new governing bodies were so broadened that "though not unduly large, they should be protected by their numbers and by the position and character of their individual members from the domination of personal or professional influences or prejudices and [should] include men conversant with the world, with the requirements of active life, and with the progress of literature and science." (7) Perhaps all the other features of the reform are comprehended in the implied recognition that (at least popular and intermediate) education is intended not so much for the benefit of the scholar himself as for that of the society of which he forms a part, and that the schools, if not governed directly by the state, ought at all events to be governed (with slight reference to the wishes of the original founders) by such a composite body that the maintenance of their due relations to society would be assured; the demand that literary and scientific studies be combined with the older classical studies was based on the new view of education.

X—Inns of Court and Inns of Chancery

The origin of the inns of court and inns of chancery, to which Sir John Fortescue accorded the dignity of "The University of the Laws," [1] is involved in obscurity. The generally accepted explanation is that they grew out of the common life of lawyers, students and officers of the courts. When in the thirteenth century the Court of Common Pleas, by the terms of Magna Charta, as originally granted by John and as subsequently confirmed by Henry III.,[2] came to be held in a definite place, the

[1] *De Laudibus Legum Angliæ*, cap. xlix. The writer adds that in his time, the middle of the fifteenth century, more students were in the inns of court and inns of chancery than in any of the French schools of law, with the exception of the school of the University of Paris. Each of the inns of chancery had at least one hundred students, and some of them had a larger number; in the least frequented inn of court were at least two hundred inmates.

[2] The date of the origin of the inns of court partakes of the indefiniteness of its cause; Dugdale was unable to discover positive historical evidence

king's palace at Westminster, instead of following the king from place to place,[1] the attorneys and officers of the court found places of living as near as convenient to both the palace and the city of London. The buildings taken for the purpose, called houses, hostels or inns, and distinguished from others as those of the "court,"[2] had earlier been used as the houses of the suppressed order of Knights Templars and the palaces of noblemen; the four inns of court were accordingly known as the Inner Temple, the Middle Temple, Lincoln's Inn, and Gray's Inn. The practitioners in the courts had earlier been almost exclusively ecclesiastics, but in the thirteenth century the clergy were forbidden by the Church to practise as advocates in the temporal courts; the lay advocates were thereby undoubtedly increased in number and made more distinct as a class. The inns of chancery[3] appear to have been used more by the officers of the courts and younger students of law than by those who had been admitted to the higher ranks of the profession, but their origin may be reasonably assumed to have been similar to that of the inns of court. Each inn of chancery belonged to or was dependent on one of the inns of court. Clifford's Inn, Clement's Inn and Lyon's Inn (the latter torn down in 1868) were dependent on the Inner Temple; New Inn and Strand Inn (the latter destroyed in 1594), on the Middle Temple; Furnival's Inn

of their existence before the reign of Edward III. (*Origines Juridiciales*, cap. lv., p. 141); the most definite statement that can be based on extant evidence is that they probably arose at the end of the thirteenth or beginning of the fourteenth century (*Encyclopædia Britannica, sub verbis* Inns of Court).

[1] "Communia placita non sequantur Curiam nostram sed teneantur in aliquis loco certo." Great Charter, § 17 (§ 12 in the charter of Henry III.). —Stubbs, *Select Charters*, p. 299.

[2] Dugdale, *Origines Juridiciales*, p. 141.

[3] It is possible that the inns of chancery received their name from their serving as *hospicia* for the clerks of the chancery.—Dugdale, *Origines Juridiciales*, cap. lvi., p. 143.

and Thavie's Inn, on Lincoln's Inn; and Staple Inn and Barnard's Inn, on Gray's Inn. There is fragmentary historical evidence of other inns both of court and of chancery, but the ones mentioned were of most importance. Fortescue wrote of ten inns of chancery but a century later only nine of them could be positively identified. All the inns were supported by the rentals of chambers, charges for commons,[1] contributions of members and fees for admission and advancement to successive ranks; their societies owned no property except the houses and the personal property with which they were furnished. A review of the several classes into which the inmates of the houses were divided will show their relations to one another and to the state.

When a student began the study of the common law, he entered one of the inns of chancery, in which his elementary work was to be done. After two or three years of residence and work in an inn of chancery, he might enter an inn of court and later be called to be an inner barrister; the next step was to become an utter barrister. The distinctions of inner barrister and utter barrister probably had no reference to the courts but only to the exercises in the houses. The chief exercises were in the form of moots or discussion of feigned cases. The cases were stated in the form of pleadings by the inner barristers (younger students) after supper in the common hall presided over by the reader; they were then taken up and discussed by utter barristers (older students). They were next discussed by the "cupboardmen"—two more advanced barristers who appear to have participated

[1] In the reign of Henry VIII. payment of dues was enforced by the following rule: "If any of the fellowship be indebted to the house [either] for his diet, [or] for any other duty of the house, he shall be openly in the house proclaimed; and whoever will pay it for him, shall enjoy and have his lodging and chamber that is so indebted."—Report of commissioners of inquiry appointed by Henry VIII., published in W. Herbert's *Antiquities of the Inns of Court*, p. 221.

separately in the exercises of the meeting and occupied a position in the hall near the cupboard,— with whom the benchers present also discussed the legal questions involved in the cases; the reader finally closed the discussions by delivering a formal opinion on the cases. Moots were distinguished as "grand" and "petit," the former appearing to have been held in the inns of court at the time of the "grand readings," and the latter in the inns of chancery before the readers appointed for them, and were preceded by the less formal and elaborate "bolts," private disputations by students on legal questions with a bencher and two barristers. The student became an inner or utter barrister by being formally "called" by the reader to take part in the mootings; the distinction of "inner" and "utter" is said to have arisen from the fact that the younger students sat at the *inner* end and the older students at the *outer* end of the form occupied during the disputations. The rank of utter barrister was attained only by participation in the required exercises in the inns, of which certificates had to be presented to the pension, parliament or council of the benchers. The readings were given and the exercises held chiefly in the vacations of court, though also during the term-times of court; the word vacation accordingly came to be used in the inns quite synonymously with the word term in other educational institutions.[1] Stowe in his *Survey of London*, states that the year was divided into three parts, (1) the learning vacations, (2) the term-times and (3) the dead or mean vacation; the learning vacations were two in number, the Lent vacation, beginning on the first Monday in Lent, and the summer vacation, beginning on the Monday after Lammas-day, each continuing three weeks

[1] In an order of 1577 it was directed that all the sons of Sir Nicholas Bacon should "be of the Grand Company [of Gray's Inn] and not be bound to any vacations."—*Gray's Inn*, by William Ralph Douthwaite, p. 207.

and three days. The readers that officiated in the Lent vacation were full benchers, had read before, and were known as "double-readers"; those in the summer vacation had just been appointed, were reading for the first time and were called "single readers."

Barristers regularly became ancients by seniority, though sons of judges might attain their "antiquity" by right of inheritance and the rank was conferred *causa honoris* on persons of distinction. From the class of ancients the benchers in their periodical meetings elected the readers, whose function it was to lecture to the students on legal topics and preside over the discussion of the moot cases. The benchers (or "masters of the bench") were the governing bodies of the inns of court and filled their vacancies by co-optation from the numbers of the utter barristers; the preliminary step was the election of a candidate each year to the position of reader, from which after having read (or lectured) publicly he entered into the full status of a bencher. Sometimes candidates were made benchers without reading, a considerable fine taking the place of the actual work of reading; in some cases, also, the person elected reader became a bencher at once and made a deposit of a considerable sum to be repaid to him when he should at a future time have performed his duty of lecturing. They were not limited in number, though after the sixteenth century they arbitrarily restricted the admission of new members. They elected annually from their own membership as their presiding officer a treasurer or pensioner. At meetings called pensions, parliaments or councils and held quarterly or more frequently, they elected treasurers, readers and committees to audit the treasurer's accounts, and transacted the current business of their houses; barristers in the preliminary status of benchers were sometimes admitted to a limited participation in the proceedings. On entering an office the officer had to take an

oath to faithfully perform his duties; likewise a common
member began his membership with an oath to obey the
rules and regulations of the society. By the common
law the judges of the superior courts were the visitors of
the inns and might entertain appeals from the orders of
their governing bodies. All members of the societies
of the inns (except the mere beginners below the rank of
inner barrister) were comprehensively called *apprenticii*,
but those who were permitted to practise in the courts
were particularly known as *apprenticii ad leges;* the
term junior barrister was applied to inner barristers and
utter barristers, while the term senior barrister was substantially equivalent to *apprenticius ad legem.*

When a barrister was called to the rank of serjeant—
and only benchers of inns of court were called to it—he
ceased to be a member of the society and became an
inmate of one of the two Serjeants' Inns, Serjeants' Inn
in Fleetstreet and Serjeants' Inn in Chancery-lane.
From the serjeants-at-law alone all the judges of the
superior courts were chosen, as well as the higher legal
officers of the crown, such as the attorney-general and
solicitor-general.

The inns of court had no organic connection with one
another, and though their governing bodies often de-
liberated in conference on matters of common concern,
the orders issued in consequence were made separately
by each house [1]; no one of them enjoyed precedence over
either of the others. The inns of chancery were governed
directly by a principal and small body of ancients, and

[1] In the thirty-eighth year of the reign of Henry VIII. it was ordered by
the bench of the Inner Temple that the gentlemen of the company should
reform themselves in their apparel, and should not wear long beards, and
that the treasurer of the society should confer with the treasurers of the
other inns of court, in order to secure a uniformity of reformation, and
should to the same end learn the opinions of the justices of the superior
courts. When the justices had expressed themselves, orders were made by
each house to enforce their recommendations.

their readers were appointed by the benchers of the inns
of court to which they were severally subject. Those
who had studied in an inn of chancery dependent on one
inn of court might enter a different inn of court on payment of a somewhat larger fee. For example, it was
ordered in the tenth year of the reign of Elizabeth that
if one had been of an inn of chancery belonging to the
Middle Temple, he might enter that house upon payment
of 40s.; if of any other inn of chancery, upon payment
of £5.; if of no inn of chancery at all, he should pay
£6 13s. 4d.

As in most other mediæval institutions of education,
the attainment of learning was not all that was sought;
in addition to their study of law, the inmates of the inns
of court and of chancery were taught to dance and sing,
and to play on musical instruments; "upon festival days
and after the offices of the church are over, they employ
themselves in the study of sacred and profane history."[1]
Connected with each inn was a church or chapel, in which
religious services were provided for the inmates; the
Inner Temple and Middle Temple, however, made joint
use of the Temple Church, in which the anomalous Master
of the Temple officiated. The society of the inns was also
enlivened by masques and revels, at which high officers of
state were sometimes present, and by the elaborate celebration of festival days of the Church, especially of Christmas.[2] The regulations dealing with the attire, personal
appearance and deportment of the inmates were numerous
and minute. The order that the beard be not allowed to
grow long was often made; it was made more definite in
the Inner Temple, in the reign of Philip and Mary, by
limiting the beard to three weeks' growth on pain of

[1] Fortescue, *De Laudibus Legum Angliæ*, cap. xlix., p. 112.
[2] For the particulars of the extended celebration of Christmas in 1562, see
Dugdale's *Origines Juridiciales*, cap. lvii., pp. 149–157. Special codes of
regulations were made by the several benches for the occasion.

forfeiture of twenty shillings, though in other inns persons of the quality of knights were exempt from the restriction. Guests and strangers might not be admitted to the chambers; laundresses and victual-women under forty years of age and maid-servants of any age were rigorously excluded. The fomenting of quarrels, especially on the occasions of revels and Christmas celebrations, was discouraged by appropriate penalties. In Gray's Inn no gown, doublet, hose or other outer garment of light color might be worn, on pain of expulsion. Playing at dice, cards or otherwise, in the hall, buttery or butler's chamber was forbidden except during the twenty days into which the Christmastide was extended. At the end of the sixteenth century it was ordered in the Inner Temple that wearing a hat or cloak in the Temple Church, in the hall, buttery or kitchen, at the buttery-bar or dresser or in the garden, should be punished by a fine of 6s. 8d.; that fellows should not enter the hall with any weapons except their dagger or knife upon pain of forfeiting £5; and "that they go not in cloaks, hats, boots and spurs into the city, but when they ride out of the town."[1] So great was the success in inculcating gentility of manners by the governors of the houses that many persons of quality sent their sons to attend them not so much to study law as to acquire the habits of good society. Nearly every act of importance was accompanied by a banquet; in fact, that feature of the life of the houses outlasted more substantial functions.[2] Almost the only forms of punishment were "excommunication" (deprivation of the privilege of dining in common with one's associates) and expulsion from the inns, though fines were

[1] Dugdale's *Origines Juridiciales*, cap. lvii., pp. 147, 148.

[2] The "readings being attended with costly entertainments, their original object was forgotten in the splendor of the tables, and it became the duty of the reader rather to feast the nobility and gentry than to give instruction in the principles of the law. From this cause they were eventually suspended."—William Holden Spilsbury, *Lincoln's Inn*, p. 21.

also imposed for a few offences; members expelled from
one inn were not admitted into others.

The brief description of the organization and life of the
inns of court and of chancery that has been given applies
to them in most respects as they existed in the fifteenth
century.   In the sixteenth century many evidences of
decadence made their appearance.   The membership,
always largely restricted to the higher classes, became
even more closely confined to the noble and wealthy.   It
was ordered by James I., in the first year of his reign,
that "none be from henceforth admitted into the society
of any House of Court that is not a gentleman by de-
scent." [1]   Many were allowed to omit the elementary
stages of instruction; in the fifth year of the reign of
Elizabeth it was ordered that admission to the Inner
Temple should be only on payment of 40s., unless the
applicant were the son of one of the bench or utter-bar,
or had been for a year of one of the inns of chancery
belonging to the house.   The readings (or lectures) came
to be perfunctory in character, and the mootings were
neglected.   Henry VIII. issued a commission to "inquire
into the form and order of study and course of living in
the Houses of Court."   In the reign of Elizabeth it was
ordered by the two chief justices, the chief baron and all
the other justices of both benches and the barons of the
exchequer that the readings in the inns of chancery be
not discouraged by excessive charges and that readers
be selected on account of learning and merit and not
of mere seniority.   In the seventeenth century further
efforts were made (especially by Cromwell) to regenerate
the houses, but with ill success; they came to be hardly
more than mere "lodgings."   In the nineteenth century,
lectures and moot-courts have been re-established,[2] but

---

[1] William Holden Spilsbury, *Lincoln's Inn*, p. 18.
[2] In 1833, lectureships were revived in the Inner Temple, but were discontinued after two years; a similar movement took place in the Middle

hardly more than partial success can be expected without more radical reforms. A royal commission was appointed in 1854 "to inquire into the arrangements in the inns of court for promoting the study of the law and jurisprudence, the revenues properly applicable and the means most likely to secure a systematic and sound education for students of law, and provide satisfactory tests of fitness for admission to the bar." In the following year it suggested in its report the constitution of a university composed of a chancellor, barristers-at-law and masters of laws, the chancellor elective for life by all barristers and masters of laws, and aided by a senate of thirty-two members (eight elected by each inn of court), one fourth of whom should retire annually; the government of the university should be vested in the chancellor and senate; a vice-chancellor, treasurer and secretary should be elected by the senate; students should be examined for admission to the inns of court, on application for degrees and for admission to the bar, by examiners appointed by the senate; readers in addition to those already in service were to be appointed by the senate on its own initiative or on the application of the bench of any inn of court. The plan was not adopted, however, and the houses have remained substantially unchanged.

The inns of court, in the actual educational work of preparing lawyers for practice, have been largely superseded by other agencies, such as the universities and societies of lawyers.[1] The little that has been accomplished has been in the direction indicated by the suggestion of the com-

Temple and Gray's Inn in 1847, but lasted only four years.—Spilsbury, *Lincoln's Inn*, pp. 22–24.

[1] Such an organization as "The Legal Education Association," formed in 1870 "for the purpose of obtaining a better organized system of legal education" in England, and of securing "the establishment of a central school of law, open to students for both branches of the profession and to the public, and governed by a public and responsible board."—Spilsbury, *Lincoln's Inn*, pp. 22–24.

mission of 1854. Even before the commission had been appointed the inns of court (in 1851) had aimed to secure concerted action through a Council of Legal Education composed of their representatives. In 1869, they issued "Consolidated Regulations of the Four Inns of Court" and shortly afterwards introduced a system of examinations. The inns of court and inns of chancery were essentially mediæval institutions, so similar to the gilds and early universities that the similarity need hardly be suggested; and like other mediæval organizations that were not modified in form or given new functions in post-Reformation society, they were hardly more than survivals, after the beginning of the seventeenth century, of a past social order, not typical of the society in which they existed, not expressing any distinct force of the new time, and existing by the inertia of tradition rather in conflict with their social environment than in harmony with it.

XI.—Charitable Corporations

If a strictly logical order had been followed in considering educational and eleemosynary corporations, the general subject of endowed charities would have preceded that of colleges and schools and would have followed that of the universities. A consideration of colleges and schools seemed to follow appropriately that of the universities, though organically they differed greatly. The general subject of endowed charities would include that of the colleges and schools, because the latter were only particular kinds of charities. It is suggestive of the new views of education entertained in the nineteenth century that the term charity does not usually suggest to the mind an educational institution, though until the beginning of the century the term was more widely used. The difficulty of classifying the corporations considered in

this chapter also suggests the difference in principle between the universities and the eleemosynary corporations,
including colleges, schools, asylums, almshouses and miscellaneous charities; the former assumed an organization
prompted largely by forces within the group of scholars,
a spontaneous form (if the term "spontaneous" is not
too freely used); upon the latter a form was imposed
by forces external to the acting groups, a form hardly
described as spontaneous. But putting aside the question of classification, the endowed charities, exclusive of
those of an educational character, consisted of asylums
or hospitals, almshouses and miscellaneous institutions,
which may be considered together. Little more can be
said of them than has already been said of colleges and
schools; a few paragraphs, indeed, will serve to fairly
complete the subject and show the similarity of such
institutions to others already described.

Before the Reformation, non-educational charities were
not as a rule separately organized, but were administered
as departments or appendages of organizations intended
for a wider purpose. The churches and monasteries,
though much of their charity was unregulated, frequently
had a fixed part of their organization devoted to its management; among the monasteries, especially, the organization varied from the mere maintenance of an official
almoner who dispensed doles indiscriminately at the
monastery gate to monasteries devoted almost entirely
to the entertainment of travellers (particularly pilgrims),
the care of the sick and demented, the rearing of orphans
and waifs and the maintenance and repair of bridges and
highways,—just as schools varied from those taught by
the official scholasticus to the monastic houses of Oxford
and Cambridge devoted almost entirely to study and instruction. The physical basis of the charities varied
correspondingly; nearly all monasteries set apart certain
rooms for the care of monks in their sickness or other

incapacity; some had separate buildings for the purpose, especially when care was extended to outsiders; others had establishments at a distance supervised by a prior or master and his assistants in direct dependence on the superior abbot; finally, the establishment was in a few cases complete in itself and presided over by an abbot and convent of monks. Likewise the gilds extended aid in charity to their own members and sometimes even to outsiders, and maintained for the purpose separate buildings in charge of a master or governor, after the manner of the still existing London Livery Companies; it will be remembered that the bachelor fellowships found in a few of the gilds were maintained largely for the administration of the gild's charities among its common members or freemen.[1] The municipalities also administered some charities, but not so often, like the gilds, from their own resources as from those placed in their hands by individuals. In very many statutes of university colleges and endowed grammar schools, themselves regarded as organs of charity, it was provided that a number of poor persons (not scholars) should be maintained on the foundation.

In the sixteenth century, however, with the suppression of monasteries and of hospitals and almshouses dependent on them, and with the partial decay of the town corporations, a large part of the stream of charitable benefactions was diverted in the direction of corporations created for the express purpose of administering them. Many of the hospitals, lazar-houses and almshouses formerly maintained by the monasteries were bestowed, with their endowments, on the towns corporations; to ensure the faithful performance of their duties by the towns, the bodies of burgesses were frequently modified by the addition of outside members, or their activity was subjected to the visitation of bishops or officers of state.

[1] *Supra*, vol. i, p. 221.

Similarly a few of the new endowments that would formerly have been placed in charge of ecclesiastical bodies
were intrusted to such of the gilds or companies as
survived the sixteenth century. But for the great mass
of eleemosynary endowments new bodies of trustees or
governors were created. And of such bodies there were,
according to their composition, four classes;—consisting
of (1) the original nominees of the founder and their
successors chosen by co-optation to fill vacancies, (2) the
incumbents of offices in Church and State or in other
corporations, (3) the holders of particular lands, usually
those constituting the endowment and (4) heirs of the
founder or of persons designated by him. More properly
it might be said that the corporations consisted of one or
more of the elements described, for a very small minority
of them would fall in only one of the four classes. Whatever the form of the corporate body, a visitor was usually
(but not always) provided for in the person of an officer
of Church or State.

The charitable purposes to which endowments were
devoted were various. The preamble of the Elizabethan
Statute of Charitable Uses[1] recited that

"lands, tenements, rents, annuities, profits, hereditaments,
goods, chattels, money and stocks of money [had] been . . .
given, limited, appointed and assigned . . . some for the
relief of the aged, impotent and poor people, some for maintenance of sick and maimed soldiers and mariners, schools of
learning, free schools, and scholars in universities, some for
repair of bridges, ports, havens, causeways, churches, sea-
banks and highways, some for education and preferment of
orphans, some for or towards relief, stock or maintenance for
houses of correction, some for marriages of poor maids, some
for supportation, aid and help of young tradesmen, handi-
craftsmen and persons decayed, and others for relief or redemption of prisoners or captives, and for aid or ease of any

[1] 43 Elizabeth, c. iv. (1601).

poor inhabitants concerning payments of fifteens, setting out
of soldiers and other taxes."

Very frequently more than one charitable purpose was
intended to be subserved by one foundation or endowment.   For example, Lawrence Sheriff, when he founded
Rugby School, provided for the construction and maintenance of some almshouses on the same foundation with
it; likewise John Lyon provided that the "keepers and
governors" of his school at Harrow should also administer
an endowment for the maintenance and repair of certain
highways in the vicinity; in the last mentioned case, the
estates of the two foundations were separate, but in many
others a single endowment was intended to support several foundations; in some cases the founders were careful
to provide the several fractions of revenue that should be
devoted to several charities, while in others they were to
be supported by the revenues of the endowment in gross.
The bodies described were characterized by their simpli-
city and fixity of form.   No distinct demarkation of classes
of members, and especially of a governing class, appears
to have been developed in them.   In fact, they were, in
themselves, only the governing organs of institutions and
could hardly, in view of the fact that they were composed
of few members (usually not more than twelve), have
developed further in that direction.   No dominant executive office was developed.

By the Elizabethan Act of Charitable Uses, passed in
1601, the first great statute for the regulation of such
bodies, it was aimed to secure, largely through the instrumentality of the court of chancery, the faithful execution of their trusts by such bodies.   It was provided that
the Lord Chancellor or Lord Keeper of the Great Seal
might award commissions to bishops and "other persons
of good and sound behavior" empowering them to enquire
either in groups of four of their own number or by juries

of twelve men or otherwise, concerning the administration of property devoted to charitable uses as described in the preamble,[1] and upon the results of their enquiry to make such orders, judgments and decrees as would secure the faithful employment of the trust estates. The orders, judgments or decrees were not to be repugnant to the orders or statutes of the founders of the charities and were to be valid and capable of execution until reversed or altered by the Lord Chancellor or Lord Keeper of the Great Seal; they were to be certified by the commission- ers to the court of chancery, which might thereupon make such orders for their execution as it should consider fit; if any one should be aggrieved by them, he might, by making complaint to the Lord Chancellor or Lord Keeper of the Great Seal, secure an examination and hearing, with the possible result that the orders might be annulled, modified, altered or enlarged. The statute was not, however, to extend in its operation to colleges or halls of learning in the universities or to the colleges of Westminster, Eton or Winchester, to cathedrals or collegiate churches, to cities or towns, or to charities in them having special governors, or to colleges, hospitals or free schools for which their founders had provided special visitors, governors or overseers. The chief result of the operation of this statute was to bring into har- mony with the mass of "governing bodies" of charities others, rudimentary and imperfect in form, depending for their perpetuation upon successive re-enfeoffments of estates or the untrustworthy incidents of heirship and ownership of land; many such bodies were replaced by self-renewing bodies of from six to twelve members, modified frequently by the possession of members *ex officio*, subject to visitation by some officer of Church or State. The purpose of this statute, like that of the Statute of Laborers, and of most of the other chief en-

[1] *Supra*, p. 50.

actments of the reign of Elizabeth, was conservative; it was to perpetuate old social relations through new social structure; the desires of founders were to be respected and executed, even if a reorganization of governing bodies should incidentally be necessary; in the present century, the reform of universities, colleges, schools and other eleemosynary corporations has been based on a recognition of the impossibility of executing the desires of the founders of past centuries under present social conditions.

From the sixteenth to the nineteenth century, then, the mass of eleemosynary corporations remained substantially unchanged. In 1818, in accordance with recent parliamentary legislation,[1] commissioners were appointed for the investigation of charities (except the universities and colleges) and continued, with their successors, to make frequent reports until 1830. The investigations were carried forward by similar commissions under later statutes until 1853, when by the Charitable Trusts Act[2] of that year a permanent body of four charity commissioners (with a secretary and two inspectors) was created, with power to enquire into the condition of all charities in England or Wales, and to demand and receive from them annual reports of their income and expenditures. Trustees of charities might receive from them on application instructions as to the execution of their trusts and be indemnified by following them. Suits relating to charities (except when property or relief should be claimed adversely to the charity) might not be prosecuted without the consent of the commissioners before whom they were laid for their consideration; they were also to have control of the form and manner in which they were prosecuted and might require that they be delayed; and

---

[1] The 58th George III., c. 91, provided for the appointment of commissioners to inquire concerning charities in England for the education of the poor; the 59th George III., c. 81, was in amendment of the former statute, and extended the powers of the commissioners to other charities in England and Wales.   [2] 16 and 17 Victoria, 137.

they might certify cases to the attorney-general for the exercise of his discretion in the institution of actions. Proposals of trustees to have timber cut, roads laid out or minerals mined on trust land or to sell it might be sanctioned by the commissioners. Schemes proposed by trustees for the application or management of a charity (if they could not be carried out by the courts) might be approved, either with or without modification or alteration, by them, but all such schemes should be annually reported to Parliament. Exempt from the operation of the act were to be the Universities of Oxford, Cambridge, London and Durham and colleges in them or in any cathedral or collegiate church, any building used *bona fide* for a religious meeting-house, institutions maintained by voluntary contributions and missionary institutions or societies—though the exemption might be waived by a formal application to be admitted to the benefits of the act. Between 1859 and 1869 such educational charities as had been within the jurisdiction of the charities commissioners were either reformed or placed under other commissioners.

By the legislation of the nineteenth century therefore the eleemosynary corporations of England have either been reduced or made readily reducible to a greater harmony with modern society through control by the state. In their composition they have had to submit to a liberal infusion of membership especially fitted for the execution of their duties, and to become rather representatives of society in the control of their institutions than bodies of persons enjoying a proprietary interest in them.

XII—*Comparison of Educational and Eleemosynary Corporations*

The corporations considered in the present chapter, it need hardly be suggested, are most confusing in their variety of form and in the counter-currents of their development. The monasteries, cathedral chapters and collegiate chapters, the gilds and the later mercantile and colonial companies may with moderate ease be distinguished from one another, and may be seen to have an even development, but the educational and eleemosynary corporations have the characteristics of all the others in combination, have hardly a distinct form in themselves and are remarkably uneven in development. To add to the confusion, they occupy the whole period from the time of feudalism to the present, and are not confined as are the gilds or great commercial and colonial companies (broadly speaking) to either of the two great periods preceding and succeeding the middle of the sixteenth century, the dividing line between mediæval and modern history. It may be conducive to clearness if the chief features, their form and growth, be briefly recapitulated.

The universities and inns of court before the sixteenth century followed substantially the type of the early gild. The masters among the scholars corresponded closely to the masters of trades, but below the rank of the masters the analogy of the universities and trade gilds was not so close; the scholars corresponded somewhat to the apprentices of the masters of trades; when the bachelor's degree came to be distinctly recognized, it gave its holder a status similar to that of the journeyman; but in some of the European universities the custom of lecturing on probation for a few years after the master's degree was taken supplied a class more similar to the class of journeymen. The truth is that the universities anticipated the restriction of the powers of control to the masters of trades by early confining the corresponding functions to the doctors and masters. The universities of England were almost from the beginning corporations of masters[1]

[1] Hastings Rashdall, in his recent work on *Universities in Europe in the Middle Ages*, suggests two types of the mediæval university, according as

and did not include scholars in their organization except as a subject class.

The colleges in the universities and some of the public schools followed the ecclesiastical type exhibited in the monastery, cathedral chapter and collegiate church chapter. The head and fellows corresponded almost exactly to the abbot and monks or dean and chapter; the scholars were in nearly the same position as the novices of the ecclesiastical bodies. The relation was even closer than one of mere resemblance; the colleges were truly ecclesiastical bodies established and maintained in the service of the Church.

Such of the non-ecclesiastical grammar schools, elementary schools and charitable institutions as were governed by bodies specially created for them, were subject to the control of corporations very similar to what was left of the gilds and municipalities by the sixteenth century. They fall into the same general class as the close corporations of burgesses, the livery companies of London and the great commercial and colonial companies that flourished from the sixteenth to the nineteenth centuries. The universities were at first recognized by the State and Church merely as classes of individuals and not as organized autonomous groups. The powers necessary in the regulation of the relations of masters and scholars to each other and to the rest of the world were not delegated in a body but one after another until the organized groups had attained the status of corporations. At first they were considered as sustaining no more peculiar relations to the State or Church than any other class of subjects as such sustained. When the State came to view the universities as bodies of learned men, of special importance to it because adding

the community of masters or that of scholars was the predominant element in the organization; the University of Paris is taken as the type of the former, and the University of Bologna as that of the latter.

to the other glories of the realm that of learning, and the Church discovered in them their vital importance to it as training schools of its clergy, the attitude of both passed beyond that sustained to ordinary classes of subjects and justified the crystallization of class interests in a compact organization in the enjoyment of exceptional rights and powers. There was never as high a degree of dependence on the universities as on the municipalities or monastic orders, but the time came when the king found the universities quite indispensable as his supporters in obtaining a divorce, and when the pope found them among his strongest adherents against an independent episcopacy. It is worthy of notice that scholars were separated more distantly from the other classes of society as they approached the king or pope in the enjoyment of an exceptional status. They became the ardent supporters of the aggressions of both on the mass of subjects from whose ranks they had risen.

The rise of the colleges in the universities represented a double movement, that of disintegration within the universities and that of the reassertion by the Church of its control over learning. The disintegration began when the units of the domestic life of the scholars, the bodies of them living in halls, attracted some of the work of instructing and studying to themselves. At that point the Church both directly and indirectly through the Friars assumed control of the movement by giving to the common life of the bodies of scholars such a substantial and independent basis that the universities were eventually merely federations of colleges under the control of the Church. When the universities were throwing off the yoke of the Church, they were doing it as gilds of masters; when the Church reasserted its influence it did it through subordinate colleges modelled on its own corporations.

The corporations of the popular schools, and most of

the grammar schools, as well as the charitable institutions, may hardly be said to have undergone any organic development in their relations to the state from the sixteenth to the nineteenth centuries; they were themselves developed forms of organization and carried forward the work that had previously been done, for the most part, by the Church and the gilds.   There was no important addition to or subtraction from their bodies of rights and duties by the crown except such as was implied in remodelling some of the more formless of them into harmony with the others.   Their work was recognized as public in its character and the state was willing to accept it as such, while it made no serious effort to either supplement their activity with its own or to absorb it.   In the nineteenth century the state reformed them by giving them a broader basis of membership and by causing the application of their revenues to purposes more clearly in response to the demands of present conditions.

The contact of corporations or of corporations and subdivisions of State and Church with one another and the consequent readjustment of their relations are always suggestive, especially when the corporations are organizations of social classes.   The universities came into harshest contact with the municipal bodies of the cities and towns in which they were located.   As the learned bodies were closer to the king and pope than were the bodies of burgesses, the latter had to yield step by step until (at least in the case of Oxford) they became virtually subject bodies; even in as large and influential a city as Paris, the university was steadily upheld by both king and crown in the exercise of privileges derogatory to the strength and dignity of the municipal corporation.   It was not likewise, however, in the cases of colleges, schools and charitable institutions.   Unlike the universities they were rather local than national in character and acted with reference to a local unit if not in actual organic subjection to it. Though sanctioned by either State or Church (and sometimes by both) they were considered to be following the directions of a founder or some local organization, though in so doing they might confer a general social benefit; the point of view was shifted and the special protection of the crown was bestowed in a lesser degree. They were considered as organs of a local unit and generally acted in harmony with it, not in opposition to it.

The chancellor as representative of the bishop originally granted licenses to teach to such scholars as had become qualified to do so; as the mass of scholars became free of the Church, the chancellor became the head of their body as organized in the university and was elected by it; later, when the university was brought into closer relations with the state, the chancellor became rather the representative of the university at court than its active head. The interior government of the university gradually assumed form in three representative bodies, of which one, representing the department of arts, had the power of preliminary rejection of measures, the second, the duty of the ordinary administration, and the third the duty of considering most important business. Masters had been those scholars who had been formally found competent to instruct; degrees later indicated that the scholar had completed the work required of him; they became retrospective rather than prospective in significance—they were evidence of what the scholar had done, not his credentials for what he should do in future; hence the division of graduates into regents and non-regents, those who should be actually engaged in teaching and those who should regard their degrees as evidence of the completion of their studies.

The colleges, in their origin bodies of scholars living in common and aided in the prosecution of their studies by an endowment, became eventually bodies of graduates acting as governors and to some extent as instructors of the real scholars, now a subject class. So close was the organization of the life within and under the colleges that the instruction given directly by the university was at length displaced by that of professors, lecturers and tutors in colleges. The scholars under the masters of the university in its early stages came to be inmates exclusively of colleges and dependent halls, so that membership in the university was virtually derivative through the colleges. The university offices, too, came to be occupied by heads or appointees of colleges in rotation and the work of reducing the university to a federation of colleges was completed by restricting the membership of its chief administrative board to the heads of colleges.

In the non-ecclesiastical corporations for educational and other eleemosynary purposes, the relations that had been the product of the preceding centuries of university and college development were expressed by separating the corporation from the scholars or others subject to it, and by identifying them with the endowment rather than with the work of instruction, as had been the case with the earlier corporations.

II

NATIONAL ENGLAND

THE one word that most adequately describes the England of Elizabeth is the adjective "national." From whatever side it be viewed, the historical development of the English people since the Norman Conquest had been in the direction of a greater participation by every Englishman in the common life of all Englishmen.

On the political side, the overlordship of the Norman kings imposed on a feudal nobility had become the kingship of the Tudors with a national people for its subjects. A Great Council of feudal barons had been succeeded by a Parliament of the representatives of the English people. A system of national taxation, though crude and arbitrary, was year by year teaching every English subject that he and his fellow-subjects were joint participants in the new national life, while the crown was learning from it that it had strength and vigor only as it was truly representative of the common thought and sentiment of its subjects. Feudalism as a system had passed away and in place of the sovereignty of a king filtered through a hierarchy of feudal classes was a sovereignty based on the consent of the people. Elizabeth was the first monarch of national England. She was the first, and the last for two centuries, to understand that the English kingship was real and a thing of substance only as it participated in and absorbed the thoughts and sentiments of the English people.

In religion, the national pride had found in the Catholic

Church and its popes a galling foreign power and had replaced them with a "Church of England" and the English sovereign at its head. And the Reformation had given to the movement of religious freedom in England such a distinctive character that the English people could see in the Church of England something peculiarly their own, something that they would love and defend rather from patriotism than from fanaticism.

The outburst of intellectual and literary energy that glorified the Elizabethan half-century of peaceful and conciliatory rule served more than all else to bring the English people to a consciousness of their nationality. The use of English as a literary language became a stronger bond of union for the English people. The knowledge of foreign lands as something more than the spoil of conquests brought self-consciousness to the English nation. The study of English history and English life and the growth of the universities produced a broader sympathy of class with class.

If Elizabethan England was a nation from the standpoints of government, religion, literature and learning, it was not less a nation from that of economics and industry. Feudalism as an industrial system was dead and its hierarchy of industrial classes had decayed. The commutation of feudal dues had swollen the numbers of a free agricultural class. The class of artisans had grown up outside of and independent of the feudal system. The feudal nobility had accepted the verdict of industrial history and the first great period of enclosure had come to an end in 1530; henceforth they were to be landowners, like their freed tenants, differing from them chiefly in the mere extent of their holdings and the form of their industry, itself largely dependent on the size of the parcel of land controlled. The feudal nobility had become great wool-growers with hired laborers instead of feudal tenants for subjects. The gild system, as a form of industrial

activity, had also sunk into impotence, and its functions
of industrial regulation had passed into the control of institutions of the central government. Markets and fairs
had facilitated intercourse among the people and had laid
a broader basis of economic sympathy. The growth of a
foreign market had introduced the elements of capital and
competition into commerce, to a slight extent, and had
broken down the barriers of feudalism and the gilds.[1]
The care and relief of the poor had been taken from the
Church and gilds and was now put by the Elizabethan
Poor Laws under the control of local organizations of the
national state. Except in a few industries, particularly
the woollen industry, the development of England down
to the middle of the sixteenth century had been internal; the reign of Elizabeth marks the overflowing of the
cup of industrial growth; England was now to develop
externally. The principles of internal control that had
been justly inherited from feudalism and the gilds were
now to be consistently applied externally to the relations
of Englishmen with foreign peoples.

The general religious and intellectual activity of the
sixteenth century had brought to the knowledge of the
English people the existence of a great world of material
wealth outside the restricted boundaries of their island,
and for the Anglo-Saxon to know of its existence was
for him to covet it. The peace and quietude of Elizabeth's long reign permitted a sufficient accumulation of
capital in England to enable her people to follow the lead
of the Spanish, Portuguese and Dutch in the exploitation of new worlds. The distinctive feature of English
corporate life in the seventeenth and eighteenth centuries
was its development in the relations of English subjects to
foreign lands. Internally England had attained forms of

[1] " It was indeed foreign trade which did more than any other force to
break down the mediæval social order."—Ashley, *English Economic History*, vol. ii., p. 392.

industrial life that would suffer little change until near
the end of the eighteenth century; externally English life
was to pass through forms analogous to the earlier forces
of internal industry,—though in a shorter period of time,
—and was then to fall into harmony with the general
internal system.

The development of foreign commerce was regarded
not entirely as a matter of interest and benefit solely to
the individuals engaged in it, but even more as a matter of national interest and benefit. The motives that
prompted it were three in kind, (a) industrial, (b) political and (c) philanthropic. (a) The motives were industrial in so far as the foreign commerce was expected to be
a source of gain directly to the persons engaged in it and
indirectly to the people of England whose economic demands would be more cheaply or fully supplied by it.
(b) As there is necessarily a personal element in governments and institutions and their purposes and aims are
bound up and identified with the personal purposes and
aims of those in whom, for the time, the governmental
powers are reposed, and as the individuals themselves
who compose a state are inclined to personify their governments and institutions and find in the extension of
their powers a source of personal gratification, the English crown directly stimulated and encouraged the growth
of foreign commerce with the ultimate purpose of deriving pecuniary gain or more extended dominion from it;
in so far as these considerations entered into the extension of foreign commerce, it was prompted by political
motives. (c) Again, even the individual or spiritual
welfare of the foreign peoples (in some cases savages)
with whom the foreign commerce was to be engaged in,
was a weighing consideration; or in the case of colonists,
the welfare of depressed classes of the English people
was aimed at; these motives, being hardly based on the
desire of gain or of more extended dominion, ought to be

distinguished as philanthropic. All three kinds of motives were usually blended together in such intricacy that no phenomenon can easily be referred to any of them to the exclusion of any other of them.

Whatever motive or motives might prompt an extension of foreign commerce in any direction, the practical question of means would necessarily arise. In the seventeenth century there was little security on the high seas and the stranger in a strange land was not always hospitably entertained. International law, now so refined and reduced to such nicety of distinctions, was crude and quite insufficient for the protection of merchants. Just as in the thirteenth and fourteenth centuries it was quite impossible for the crown to afford adequate protection to travellers and traders on the highways of England, so in the seventeenth and eighteenth centuries it was quite impossible for the crown to provide protection for English vessels on the highways of the ocean. But protection was necessary and had to be provided, if not by the government of England, then by some other agency. The crown simply delegated its function of protection until it should be able to perform the function itself; in the meantime, it recognized the bodies of foreign merchants as performing functions deserving the encouragement of the state and delegated to them for their exercise such powers as should be necessary for the purposes of the trades according to the circumstances of their business and of the peoples with whom they were to deal. Such were the English corporations of the seventeenth and eighteenth centuries.

They may be divided into four classes, according to the ends they were intended to accomplish and the circumstances under which they were to accomplish them, as follows: (1) Regulated Companies; (2) Regulated (with a tendency to become Exclusive) Companies; (3) Joint Stock Companies; and (4) Colonial Companies.

III

REGULATED COMPANIES

THE Regulated Companies were most nearly connected with the older gilds; in fact, they were the result of the application to the foreign trade of England of the form of organization evolved from the experience of England in its domestic trade and industry. Their control was exercised mainly over trade and industry that had been carried on with foreign countries during the fourteenth and fifteenth centuries. They hardly extended into the field of "new trades," commerce to be "discovered"; when an effort was made to extend them over that field, they underwent such modification, as will be seen,[1] that the name "regulated" was not strictly applicable to them. They were, in general, organizations of the merchants carrying on commerce with Flanders, the Netherlands, Denmark and the Scandinavian and Baltic countries; the English merchants in France, Italy, Spain and Portugal appear never to have had an enduring corporate organization. Down to the fourteenth century, the foreign trade of England had been substantially engrossed by foreigners, of whom the most important organization had been the Hanseatic League, with its headquarters at the Steelyard in London.[2]

---

[1] *Infra*, Chapters iv. and v.

[2] More properly, the London Hanse was the organization as far as England was concerned. The Hanseatic League was virtually a league of continental cities under the control of commercial oligarchies; their merchants trading in foreign countries took the name of the foreign city in which their establishment was located. Accordingly, the merchants of cities in the Hanseatic League trading in England were organized as the London Hanse. For a description of their organization, see Ashley, *English Economic History*, part i., p. 111.

The earliest organization of English merchants that came in direct contact with foreigners was that of the Staplers or Merchants of the Staple. The staple was the town or place, whether at home or abroad, to which the English merchants engaged in foreign trade brought their goods to be exported or sold to foreigners, and the English merchants that came to them were called the Staplers or Merchants of the Staple. During the thirteenth century English merchants began to participate in the foreign trade. It is said that a wool-staple existed in the fifty-first year of Henry III. (1266–1267),[1] but the first evidence of the organization of the merchants engaged in foreign commerce dates from the early part of the fourteenth century. In two letters dated in 1313 and written by Edward II. to the Earl of Flanders, Richard Stury de Salop is described as "*major mercatorum de regus nostro*"; together with Sir William of Dean he appears to have been sent by the king to compose certain differences between their respective subjects.[2] Three charters were also granted in the same year, the first being in the form of an ordinance requiring that "in consequence of the losses accruing to the king by merchants, as well natives as foreigners, buying wool and wool-fells within the realm and exporting the same at their will to Brabant, Flanders and Diartoys [Artois]" they should all thereafter send them to a certain staple (and not elsewhere) to be appointed by "the mayor and commonalty of the merchants."[3] The second charter was addressed to the "mayor and merchants of the staple." The third charter granted that all wool and wool-fells bought in England for exportation, whether by natives or foreigners, should be carried to only one

---

[1] Schauz, *Englische Handelspolitick*, vol. i., p. 329, citing as authority Malynes, *The Centre of the Circle of Commerce* (1623), p. 93.

[2] Rymer, *Fœdera*, vol. iii., p. 386.

[3] Patent Rolls, 6 Edward II., No. 5.

staple abroad, to be designated by the mayor and community of the merchants engaged in the trade, who might also change the location of the staple if they saw fit; merchants carrying their goods to other places than the appointed staple might be punished by the mayor and council of the merchants by fines levied on them and on their goods for the use of the king.[1]

In 1341 Edward III. established the staple of wool and other merchandise at Bruges in Flanders, appointed the first mayor and constables of the staple and conceded that their successors should be elected by the merchants themselves, both English and foreign; the mayor was to maintain a court in which controversies between the merchants should be settled according to the "law merchant" and infractions of rules made by the merchants should be punished by the imposition of fines and forfeitures.[2] During the fourteenth century, however, the staple, though usually at either Bruges or Antwerp, was frequently changed, often for political reasons, the concession or withdrawal of the staple being used as a consideration in adjusting international relations. In the reign of Edward III., the two extremes of having no foreign staple at all, the merchants being unrestricted in their exportation of goods, and of establishing the staples in England, the foreigners being compelled to come to England to make their purchases, were tried for short periods of time. In the reign of Richard II., near the end of the century, the staple was finally established at Calais, there to remain until the city should be retaken by the French in 1558. There were not only foreign staples, but also from five to ten home staples; goods exported had to be shipped exclusively to the former

---

[1] Macpherson, *Annals of Commerce*, vol. i., p. 478.
[2] Rymer, *Fœdera*, vol. iv., p. 273, "De Stapula apud Bruges in Flandria tenenda."

and from the latter, "where the king had his beam, his weights and his collectors of customs."[1]

In 1353, the management of the home staples was comprehensively dealt with in Edward's Statute of the Staple.[2] All goods exported from England were first to be taken to either Newcastle, York, Lincoln, Norwich, Westminster, Canterbury, Winchester, Exeter or Bristol, where the home staples should be; there the sacks of wool and quantities of other goods to be exported should be weighed and sealed under the seal of the mayor of the staple, and the customs on them paid. From York such goods should be taken for export to Hull, from Lincoln to Boston, from Norwich to Yarmouth and from Westminster to London, at which places they should be again weighed by the king's customers. Goods brought to other staple towns should be weighed by the mayor of the staple in the presence of the king's customers and indentures made between them showing the quantities of all goods brought for export. The goods should then be exported by foreigners (not by natives), from whom the mayor of the staple and king's customers should take oaths not to hold a staple abroad. If goods had to be carried by water to reach one of the established staples, an indenture should be made with the bailiffs of the town from which the goods should be carried. The rent of buildings used by the staple merchants should be determined by the mayor and constables of the staple with four men of the town duly sworn by them. That the foreign merchants might not be delayed in the transaction of their business, speedy justice according to the law merchant was to be administered "from day to day and hour to hour." In each staple should be annually elected by the "commonalty" of the merchants, both native and foreign, a mayor learned in the law merchant,

---

[1] Gross, *The Gild Merchant*, vol. i., pp. 141–143.
[2] 27 Edward III., Statutes, i., 268–276.

to govern the staple and dispense justice, and two constables to perform the duties "pertaining to their office
in such manner as was customary in other staples." The
mayor and constables should have power to preserve the
peace, arrest wrongdoers in the staple and punish them
according to the rules of the staple. The mayor, sheriffs
and bailiffs of the towns in which the staples should be
or of adjoining towns were to assist the mayors and constables of the staples in the execution of their offices.[1]
If any one should be aggrieved by a decision or act of the
Mayor or Constables of the Staple, he should be given
speedy redress on appeal to the king's council. A certain number of "correctors," both natives and foreigners,
were to make and record bargains between merchants.
The mayor and constables should be sworn by the chancellor to the due performance of their duties, while the
other officers and merchants of the staple were to be
sworn by the mayor and constables, to be judged by them
according to law and custom and to maintain the staple
and its customs. Foreign merchants should be protected
in the transaction of their business; in matters of litigation touching them, two of their number should be chosen
by the remainder to sit with the mayor and constables in
judgment. A century later, in the statute of Edward
IV., substantially the same provisions for the regulation
of the home staples were enacted, though it was also required that all goods exported should be taken to the
foreign staple at Calais and to no other place.[2]

When the merchants of the staple passed from the
status of a broad class to that of a somewhat restricted
company may not be definitely stated. In the middle
of the fifteenth century the Company of the Staple of

[1] "The mayor and constables of home staples were . . . originally
distinct from the municipal authorities, although in course of time it became customary in some towns for the mayor of the borough to act *ex officio*
as mayor of the staple."—Gross, *Gild Merchant*, vol. i., p. 145.

[2] Statute 4, Edward IV., cap. 2 (1464), Statutes, vol. x., p. 93.

England appears to have assumed the form that it retained until the staple system virtually passed away at the end of the sixteenth or beginning of the seventeenth century. Definite evidence of the interrelations of the members of the company is singularly wanting. It is very plain that the merchants of the staple in the several English cities were separately organized and that the entire body was also organized, but it cannot be stated with certainty what organic relations existed between the local and national bodies. Most of the evidence also shows that not only the English but also the foreign merchants were comprehended in the staple organization, but it is difficult to believe that the English merchants were not separately organized for some purposes, especially in the later stages of the staple trade. In the fifteenth and sixteenth centuries the Company of Merchants of the Staple of England were in charge of the collection of the customs on exported goods, and made a return to the crown of a definitely stipulated sum in lieu of what they should collect; they accordingly complained when the crown granted to the merchants of particular towns the right to export their goods without taking them to the staple at Calais—a method of procedure that deprived the company of part of the revenue expected. In such relations to the crown the foreigners could hardly have participated, and the crown could hardly have held the whole body of merchants responsible; the company must have been a select body of the more influential and responsible merchants who had control of the trade.

The merchants of the staple had been engaged chiefly in the exportation of raw products, such as wool, woolfells, leather, lead and tin; with the growth of manufacturing industries and especially of the cloth industry in England in the fifteenth and sixteenth centuries, the transactions of the staplers declined in volume, they being gradually displaced by the Merchant Adventurers, who had control of the rapidly developing trade in manufactured goods. After the fall of Calais in 1558, the staple organization became obsolete, though it survived in some of its features until the nineteenth century and the Company of Merchants of the Staple of England still holds periodical meetings for convivial purposes. It can hardly be doubted that the loss of Calais had a vital influence on the corporation that had originally been based on the organization of the staplers largely for fiscal purposes. Malynes, writing in 1623 in defence of the rights of the company, claimed that Elizabeth in the third year of her reign (1560–1561) had granted to the Mayor and Constables of the Staple of England a charter in confirmation of "all such privileges and liberties as they did, might or ought to have enjoyed, one year before the loss of Calais, by grant, charter, law, prescription or custom, notwithstanding any non-user, abuser, etc."[1] No other reference to the charter can be found, but the company's advocate could hardly have found occasion to make the statement, if the company's corporate status had not been exposed to attack by the loss of the staple town.

Viewed as corporations, the Company of Merchants of the Staple, or the companies in the several staple towns, were rudimentary. In so far as the organization tended to maintain the quality of goods through the facilities for inspection provided by it, and to lend security to dealings not only by affording them a convenient medium but by enforcing them through special courts, it was of advantage to the merchants themselves. But the principal motive for establishing the staples was to give the king control over the transactions with foreigners and especially to make the payment of customs more certain and convenient. The organization was rather

---

[1] The quotation is found in Anderson's *Origin of Commerce*, vol. ii., p. 117, the reference being to Malynes's *Centre of the Circle of Commerce*, p. 93.

imposed by the state as a public necessity than conceded by it in response to the demands of the private interests of the merchants. The view of Gross[1] that the "mayor and constables of home staples were public functionaries of the king" is hardly justifiable; the merchants of the staple were not organized as a part of the state, but were compelled by the state to organize themselves; the difference always exists between a political administrative body and a corporation. The royal purpose is well shown in the preamble of the proclamation of Edward III. in 1341[2]:

"Whereas, many merchants and others, as well foreign as native, seeking their own gain at the expense of the state, have both by stealth and secrecy and by the connivance of royal officers exported wool and other merchandise from England without paying the customs due on it, and continue from day to day so to do, to the great damage of the crown and in contempt of it, we, in order to prevent so great wrong and to protect our own interests and those of our subjects, as we ought. . . ."[3]

It is plain that the primary consideration was the protection of the royal treasury; the secondary consideration was the advancement of the private interests of the merchants. The general view of the foreign trade, as organized in the staples, was rather restrictive than promotive; the king's aim appears to have been to place the native merchant where the foreign merchant might find him, not to enable the former to seek the latter. Even when the legislation was not so restrictive as that of Edward's Statute of the Staple (1353),[4] by which it was provided that goods sold at the staples should be exported only by foreigners, it generally viewed the trade as in need of restraint and not of encouragement.

[1] *Gild Merchant*, vol. i., p. 146.
[2] Rymer, *Fœdera*, vol. v., p. 273.
[3] *Supra*, p. 68.
[4] *Supra*, p. 69.

The exportation of manufactured products, especially of cloth, which was to supersede to a great extent that of raw products, was during the fifteenth century largely under the control of the merchants who controlled the domestic trade in them. The Mercers' Company, one of the twelve great companies of London, was the most prominent organization in that connection. Many of the merchants engaged in the export trade in manufactured goods, called Merchant Adventurers, belonged to that company; indeed, such trade was apparently unorganized, except so far as it was comprehended in the domestic company mentioned, until the beginning of the fifteenth century.[1]

In 1407, Henry IV. granted a charter "Pro Mercatoribus Halendiæ," by which, observing the hardships that had been suffered for want of a better direction and government of their affairs and were likely to be suffered in future by the English merchants in Holland, Zeeland, Flanders and other lands oversea unless he should aid them by permitting them to maintain a government among themselves, he conceded to them the power of electing governors for the administration of justice and the adjustment of controversies among them. The governors should also have power to cause the reparation of all damage caused by or to the merchants and to seek and receive restitution or compensation for injuries inflicted on the English merchants by the foreign merchants with whom they came in contact. They should also, with the common assent of the merchants, make and establish

---

[1] The Mercers' Company and Company of Merchant Adventurers used the same book for recording the minutes of their meetings until 1526 (Gross, *Gild Merchant*, vol. i., p. 149). The hall of the Mercers' Company in London was also used by the Company of Merchant Adventurers until it was destroyed in the great fire of 1666 (Herbert, *History of London Livery Companies*, vol. i., p. 232). Compare the similar use of identical books of record by the Grocers' Company, the Levant Company and the East India Company, *supra*, vol. i., p. 224.

statutes, ordinances and customs for their better government and visit "contrary, rebellious or disobedient"
merchants with reasonable punishments.[1] Nearly a century later the members of the Mercers' Company together
with other adventures of London, acting under the name
of the Company of Merchants of London, appear to have
long exercised a predominating influence over the Merchant Adventurers; they dictated the elections of governors, and had even made an ordinance that no merchant
should trade in Flanders, Holland, Zeeland and Brabant,
unless he should first pay a fine to them; the fine, originally imposed by color of a right of the ancient fraternity
of St. Thomas of Canterbury, of which the Mercers'
Company claimed to be the successors, had at first been
only nominal but had been gradually increased to twenty
pounds. In 1496, it was enacted that the trade should
henceforth be open and free to all and that no fine, imposition or tax of more than ten marks should be exacted
from them for the liberty to buy and sell.[2]

For several years at the end of the fifteenth and beginning of the sixteenth century a contest was kept up
between the Merchant Adventurers and Merchants of the
Staple in which the former appear to have been the ag-
gressors. The question of the limits of their respective
powers came before the star chamber in 1504, whereupon
it was decided that all Merchants of the Staple when engaging in the trade of Merchant Adventurers should be
subject to all acts, ordinances and regulations to which
Merchant Adventurers should themselves be subject, as
well in Calais (the staple town) as elsewhere; likewise all
Merchant Adventurers should be subject to the obligations
of Merchants of the Staple when engaging in their trade.[3]

---

[1] Rymer, *Fœdera*, vol. viii., p. 464.
[2] Statute 12, Henry VII., cap. vi.
[3] See inspeximus of decree of star chamber by Henry VII., printed in
vol. ii., pp. 547, 548, of Schauz's *Englische Handelspolitik*.

The next step was the seizure by the Merchant Adventurers of the cloths of a stapler, not because he failed to pay a fine for engaging in the cloth trade, but because he engaged in it without first having secured membership in the Company of Merchant Adventurers of England; the king on complaint of the Merchants of the Staple addressed a letter to their opponents in which he interpreted the decree of the star chamber as not justifying more than the imposition of a fine or license fee.[1] What was the end of the contest is not known, but it must have been largely influenced by the decreasing trade of the one and the increasing trade of the other body of contestants.[2] It is of most importance as indicating the crystallization of the two bodies of traders in distinct companies with control over separate kinds of trade. The geographical question involved is not unimportant, in view of the later development of companies limited to exclusive territories; the Merchants of the Staple claimed exclusive jurisdiction in Calais, and apparently over all kinds of trade in it, while the Merchant Adventurers had their headquarters in Antwerp and resented what little interference was offered by their opponents outside of Calais.

Henry VII., in 1505, made the organization of the Merchant Adventurers more definite by adding to their power to elect a governor or governors that of electing "twenty-four of the most sad, discreet and honest persons of divers fellowships" of them to be assistants to the governors. Officers were to be appointed by the governor and assistants "to take, receive, levy and gather all manner of fines, forfeitures, penalties and mulcts of every merchant of English subject convicted [of] violating the statutes" made by the governor and assistants. The officers should have power, if need be, to seize the per-

[1] See Letter of Henry VII. to the Merchant Adventurers, printed in Schauz's *Englische Handelspolitik*, vol. ii., pp. 548, 549.
[2] *Supra*, p. 71.

sons and goods of offenders, even in England and Calais. Assistants were removable for incapacity, but otherwise served for life; refusal to accept their office was punishable by fine, payable half to the king and half to the company. All merchants were to be admitted to the freedom on payment of ten marks, and all persons in the trade were to be subject to their government.[1] Whether the "divers fellowships" referred to were the groups of Merchant Adventurers in the several commercial cities of England, in the several foreign countries or in the several branches of foreign trade, cannot be determined with certainty, but they were probably those named second in order.

The often quoted description by John Wheeler of the Company of Merchant Adventurers in 1601 is so complete, while it is almost the only historical evidence of its condition at the time, that it may be quoted again.

"The Company of Merchant Adventurers consisteth of a great number of wealthy and well experimented merchants, dwelling in divers great cities, maritime towns, and other parts of the realm, to-wit, London, York, Norwich, Exeter, Ipswich, Newcastle, Hull [and others.]. These men of old time linked and bound themselves together in company for the exercise of merchandise and sea-fare, trading in cloth, kersey, and all other, as well English as foreign commodities vendible abroad, by the which they brought unto the places where they traded, much wealth, benefit, and commodity, and for that cause have obtained many very excellent and singular privileges, rights, jurisdictions, exemptions, and immunities, all which those of the aforesaid fellowship equally enjoy after a well ordered manner and form, and according to the ordinances, laws, and customs devised and agreed upon by common consent of all the merchants, free of the said fellowship, dwelling in the above named towns and places of the land; the ports and places which they trade unto, are the towns and

[1] Schauz, *Englische Handelspolitik*, vol. ii., pp. 549-553.

ports lying between the rivers of Somme in France, and the Scawe [in Denmark] in the German sea: not into all at once, or at each man's pleasure, but into one or two towns at the most within the above-said bounds, which they commonly call the mart town or towns; for that there only they stapled the commodities, which they brought out of England, and put the same to sale, and bought such foreign commodities as the land wanted, and were brought from far by merchants of divers nations and countries flocking thither as to a fair, or market, to buy and sell. . . . The said company hath a governor, or in his absence, a deputy, and four and twenty assistants in the mart towns, who have jurisdiction and full authority as well from her Majesty as from the princes, states, and rulers of the Low Countries, and beyond the seas, without appeal, provocation, or declination, to end and determine all civil cases, questions, and controversies arising between or among the brethren, members, and supports of the said company, or between them and others, either English or strangers, who either may or will prorogate the jurisdiction of the said company and their court, or are subject to the same by the privileges and charters thereunto granted." [1]

Malynes's complaint in 1622 that the Company of Merchant Adventurers was under the dominance of a coterie of wealthy merchants in London [2] seems to be borne out by the Parliamentary ordinance of 1643, which provided that none should trade in the territory of the company except such as were free of it on penalty of the forfeiture of their goods, that no person should be excluded from the fellowship who should "desire it by way of redemption, if such person by their custom be capable thereof, and hath been bred a merchant"; moreover, the merchant "shall pay one hundred pounds for the same, if he be free and an inhabitant of the city of London, and trade from that port, or fifty pounds if he be not free and

[1] Quoted by Gross in *Gild Merchant* (vol. i., pp. 149–151), from John Wheeler, *Treatise of Commerce* (19, 24).
[2] See Gross, *Gild Merchant*, vol. i., p. 151.

no inhabitant of the city, and trade not from thence."
The ordinance appears to have been largely in confirmation of existing powers and its passage was probably secured by the company as a protection against interference with them by the Parliamentary party in the civil war. The company were given power to levy contributions on members and their goods for the support and maintenance of their government, and to imprison them and bind them by oaths to secure their conformity to the corporate regulations.[1]

During the sixteenth century the bodies of Merchant Adventurers in several of the important commercial cities of England assumed a separate organization and obtained charters of incorporation from the crown, as in Bristol, Chester and Newcastle. Whether organic relations subsisted between the local companies and the national Company of Merchant Adventurers seems impossible to ascertain, but their members must have been subject to its regulations, at least when engaged in commerce abroad. The form of their government was not peculiar in comparison with that of the companies of domestic merchants or that of the national company; it was vested in a master and wardens, or in a governor and from twelve to eighteen assistants, with minor officers such as clerks, beadles and searchers. In addition to the tendency towards dissolution into the companies of merchants in the several cities of England, the foreign trade had expanded beyond its original limits into other countries on the continent, and the Merchant Adventurers in the new territory sought separate organization in distinct companies according to the countries in which they traded. The trade with the original territory of the Company of Merchant Adventurers gradually became free and open to English merchants regardless of their corporate rights; by the eighteenth century, all vestiges of · corporate

[1] Rymer, *Fœdera*, vol. xx., p. 547.

control had disappeared; in the new territories, however, corporate organizations were longer maintained.

Among the rules of the Company of Merchant Adventurers was one forbidding its freemen to marry women born outside the realm of England.[1] Nor might they (in some of the municipal companies) keep shops or engage in a handicraft or retail business,[2] except that in one case they might engage in a single retail business. One of the most notable features of the Merchant Adventurers, as well as of the Staplers, is the decreased importance assigned to their social-fraternal and religious elements. While they were not entirely wanting, they were assigned a position of much less importance than in the classes of corporations previously considered. The trade of members was minutely regulated, especially with a view to preventing an over-supply of goods in particular markets; a "stint" (or limit of amount) of goods that might be taken for sale to any market was frequently imposed and changed to suit changing conditions.[3] A quite elaborate system of correspondence was the means of correlating the separate ventures of the numerous Merchant Adventurers, so that they might not interfere with one another but rather act in harmony.

"By the . . . governor and assistants are also appointed and chosen a deputy and certain discreet persons, to be associated to the said deputy, in all . . . places convenient, as well within as without the realm of England, who all hold correspondence with the governor of the company and chief in the mart town on the other side the seas, and have subaltern power to exercise merchant law, to rule, and look to the good ordering of the brethren of the company every-

---

[1] Macpherson, *Annals of Commerce*, vol. ii., p. 140.

[2] This rule was probably involved in the usual provision in charters that members should be " mere merchants."

[3] Cunningham, *Growth of English Trade and Industry*, p. 372.

where, as far as may be and their charters will bear them out." [1]

Membership in either the Company of the Staple or Company of Merchant Adventurers was not incompatible with membership in the other, as was also true of all the regulated and joint-stock companies. Moreover, while members of the London companies were restricted to one company,[2] they might be members of any or all of the companies engaged in foreign commerce.

As compared with the Merchants of the Staple, the Company of Merchant Adventurers represented a step forward in the organization of the trade of English with foreign merchants. (a) The staple organization comprehended both native and foreign merchants, who united in electing the officers and enacting the statutes and ordinances by which they were governed; but the Company of Merchant Adventurers was composed of native merchants alone, who might not even marry alien women. (b) The trade of the Staplers was for the most part in raw materials, but that of the Merchant Adventurers was in manufactured goods; in domestic industry the former had been virtually unorganized, except as it had been early organized in the merchant gilds, while the latter had acquired a structure in the later craft gilds and trade gilds and in their successors, the companies of the fifteenth and sixteenth centuries. The Merchants of the Staple may be said to have followed the model of the old gild merchant, while the Merchant Adventurers followed that of the companies evolved from the trade gilds and craft gilds, though the distinction is not plain in all details. The staple was an international fair while the market of the Merchant Adventurers was more nearly like the markets of English towns after the differentiation of their traders into separate gilds had taken place. (c) The

[1] John Wheeler, *Treatise of Commerce* (25), quoted by Gross, *Gild Merchant*, vol. i., p. 153.   [2] *Supra*, vol. i., p. 215.

government of the staple was imposed by the state primarily for public purposes, while the interests of the merchants were consulted only secondarily; on the contrary,
the organization of the Company of Merchant Adventurers
was sought by the merchants primarily in protection of
their own interests, while the benefit of the state was
expected to be only secondary.   To secure the payment
of customs was the royal purpose in organizing the staple,
the legislation of Parliament in 1643 was

" for the better encouragement and supportation of the fellowship of Merchant Adventurers of England, which hath been
found very serviceable and profitable unto this state, and for
the better government and regulation of trade, especially that
ancient and great trade of clothing, whereby the same shall be
much advanced to the common good and benefit of the
people." [1]

The aim in the one case was to control what trade existed; in the other, to foster the trade and promote its
increase.   The one organization aimed to place the English market where the foreign trader might find it; the
other, to enable the English trader to find the foreign
market.   (d) The governmental organs of the staplers
were never so fully developed as those of the Merchant
Adventurers, for the reason, probably, that the motive of
private interest was so much weaker in one than in the
other.   The judicial element was more prominent in the
first, the legislative element in the second; consequently
the advisory body of assistants hardened in the second
into a permanent part of its constitution, while in the
first it remained rudimentary and unimportant.   A comparison of the two organizations is a sufficient preparation
for the complaint of Malynes in 1622 that

"all the trade of the Merchants of the Staple, of the merchant
strangers, and of all other English merchants, concerning the

[1] Ordinance of 1643, Rymer, *Fœdera*, vol. xx., p. 547.

exportation of all the commodities of wool into those countries
where the same are especially to be vended, is in the power of
the Merchants Adventurers only; and it is come to be managed by forty or fifty persons of that company, consisting of
three or four thousand." [1]

In the sixteenth century, several new regulated companies were organized on the same general system as the
Company of Merchant Adventurers. In 1564 a perpetual
charter was granted to the Hamburgh Company, which
appears to have been merely an organization of such
members of the Company of Merchant Adventurers as had
acquired an interest in trade within the Empire beyond
their original territory. In 1579 a charter was granted
by Elizabeth (and in 1629 confirmed by Charles I.) to the
"Fellowship of Eastland Merchants." They were to
have the exclusive right of trading through the sound
to Norway, Sweden, Finland, Poland, Lithuania (except
Narva, which was in the exclusive territory of the Russia
Company), Prussia (the province) and Pomerania (the
western limit being the Oder River), the islands of See-
land, Bornholm, Oeland and Gothland; their principal
mart-towns would be Copenhagen, Elsinore, Dantzig,
Elbing and Königsberg. The government of the company was to be in the familiar form of a governor, deputy,
or deputies, and twenty-four assistants, who should enact
laws for the control of the merchants and the trade conducted by them. Only freemen of the company should
participate in the trade, and non-freemen so doing might
be punished by the company through fines and imprisonment. The purpose of granting the charter is said to
have been to give an organization to English merchants
that were opposed by the Hanseatic merchants. After
the Revolution of 1688, the company was unwilling or

[1] Malynes, *Maintenance of Free Trade* (50, 51), quoted by Gross in *Gild
Merchant*, vol. i., p. 151.

unable to secure from Parliament a confirmation of its powers based on royal charters and thereby to conform to the new principle that monopolies of trade should have validity only in Parliamentary statute; they accordingly lost their control over trade but are said to have kept up their periodical meetings for social purposes until the nineteenth century. Complaint had been made of them, moreover, that notwithstanding they were a regulated company, their fees were excessive and consequently restrictive. In 1690 it was enacted that all persons, whether native or foreign, after the first of May, 1693, might trade freely into Norway, Sweden and Denmark without regard to any powers claimed by the company under its charters; and that for the rest of its territory, admission to the company should be granted to any person on payment of forty shillings.[1] In 1560, a partial organization of the trade to France appears to have been given by Elizabeth in a charter to the merchants of Exeter under the name of the "Governor, Consuls and Society of Merchants Adventurers of Exeter"; they were to enjoy an exclusive trade to France and secured the confirmation of their privileges by Parliament in the succeeding reign,[2] but no traces of their activity can be found. A rudimentary organization of the English merchants in Italy was attempted as early as 1485 by the appointment of a consul for them; in that year Richard III., at the request of the English merchants in Italy, appointed Lorenzo Stozzi, a merchant of Florence, to be their consul for Pisa and adjacent territory, with authority to hear and decide suits and controversies among them and to do all other things *in judicio quam extra* which by law or the custom of other nations should appertain to his office; as compensation for his services he should receive one fourth of one per cent. of the amount of all

[1] Statute 2, William and Mary, cap. 4.
[2] 4 James I., 9.

purchases and sales by English merchants at Pisa.[1] Later, however, the trade came largely under the control of the Levant Company.[2]

The purely regulated companies developed as fully as the conditions of the international trade organized within them demanded. The key to an understanding of their rise and growth is in a due appreciation of the extent to which the political organization of England had been perfected. The lack of closer political relations with foreign nations as well as of those between the government of England and its subjects made it necessary to leave for the exercise of groups of subjects prompted by the motive of self-interest many powers that were later to be resumed by the state. When the state became able to extend its functions over the field of activity occupied by the companies, they became obsolete, though, like most English institutions, they were maintained in form long after their efficiency as organs of government had departed. By the middle of the eighteenth century they had all ceased to have an appreciable influence on English foreign commerce. The fact that the merchants of England trading in France were never organized in a corporation is adequately explained by the close relations that had existed between England and France since the Norman conquest. The English government, in that field of activity, had maintained the international machinery necessary for the performance of its functions; the organization of corporations for their exercise was consequently uncalled for. That the regulated companies, where they flourished, were not more highly concentrated in power and management was due to the existence of such partially developed international rela-

---

[1] Rymer, *Fœdera*, vol. xii., pp. 270, 271. Neither Lorenzo Stozzi nor his two successors appear to have been elected by the merchants themselves; the existence of the office apparently implied no extended organization of the trade.　　　　　　　　　　　　[2] *Infra*, Chapter xi.

tions as were possible. Their trade was with European countries west of Russia and Turkey and had previously to a large extent been in existence, but under the control of merchants of the foreign countries. What England accomplished through regulated companies was to substitute English for Hanseatic, Italian and other foreign merchants in a foreign trade that already existed; if the trade increased in volume, it was due not so much to the activity of the companies as to more general causes. It will be seen later[1] that where the trade had to be "discovered," as in Russia and Turkey, or created, as in India and America, the companies incorporated were either originally more compact in form and concentrated in activity, or if originally regulated companies, were soon so greatly modified that they were justly contrasted with purely regulated companies as belonging to a different class.

[1] *Infra*, Chapters iv., v., and vi.

IV

REGULATED COMPANIES TENDING TO EXCLUSIVENESS

ONE class of regulated companies, owing to the peculiar environment with which they came in contact and to the equipment with which they were provided in conducting their operations, exhibited a tendency to exclusiveness of membership and concentration of powers that made them virtually a separate class, midway in development between the purely regulated companies and the joint-stock companies. The tendency was not in complete harmony with the form of organization used by the regulated companies, but, with fidelity to the principle usually followed in the development of institutions, the effort was made to use an established form in the expression of a new social force before a form more appropriate for the purpose should be evolved from experience. Full and unimpeded expression was given to the elements of exclusiveness and concentration in the joint-stock companies, but in the class of companies considered in this chapter the form of the regulated company seemed to be perverted and distorted to the extent that the characteristic elements manifested themselves.

The best example of the class of companies under consideration is the Levant or Turkey Company. The English trade with the countries on the eastern Mediterranean, with Greece and Turkey and with the Asiatic countries to the southeast as far as India had long been carried on wholly overland, or partly overland and by the Mediterranean as far westward as Italy or France; as far as

England was concerned, it had participated in the trade
only mediately, through the merchants of Venice and
other Italian cities or of France.   In the fifteenth century, however, the routes by water came to be used, and
merchants of Portugal served partly as media for the supply of England with Eastern merchandise.   In the same
century English merchants began to meet this branch of
foreign trade as it had met that of the Netherlands and
Holland.   In 1485 there appears to have been a sufficient
body of English merchants in Italy to justify the appointment by Richard III. of a consul for them at Pisa.[1]   Soon
afterwards, in the reign of Henry VII., a few efforts were
made by English adventurers to establish a trade in the
Barbary states, from which were doubtless derived later
accounts of a so-called Barbary Company said to have
developed into the Levant Company.   But commerce by
sea was hampered with many restrictions; it was rendered
especially dangerous and uncertain in the western Mediterranean by the depredations of pirates and the lack of
adequate protection from them.   In consequence, no
substantial progress was made in the extension of English commerce in the Mediterranean until after the middle
of the sixteenth century.

In 1581, Elizabeth granted to Sir Edward Osborn,
Thomas Smith, Richard Staper and William Garrett,
their executors and administrators, and to such other
English subjects, not exceeding twelve in number, as
Osborn and Staper should appoint to be joined to the
four named, together with two others to be appointed by
the queen if she should desire, a charter to trade to
Turkey exclusively of all other persons, in such manner
as they should see fit, under the name of "The Company
of Merchants of the Levant."   They should have power
to enact by-laws (not repugnant to the laws of England)
for their good government, though no business should

[1] *Supra*, p. 84.

be transacted without the consent of the governor, Sir Edward Osborn being named the first governor by the queen in the charter, and his successors being probably chosen annually by the company. Any other English subjects trading thither, either by ocean or land, without the company's license, should forfeit their ships and goods, half to the company and half to the crown. The exclusive powers granted were to be valid for a term of seven years, unless the crown, if they should appear to be "inconvenient," should see fit to revoke them on one year's notice; if, however, they should not "appear to be unprofitable to the kingdom," the crown would renew them at their expiration, on application of the company, for a second term of seven years. The justification of the grant was found by the crown in the fact that Osborn and Staper "had, at their own great costs and charges, found out and opened a trade to Turkey, not heretofore, in the memory of any man now living, known to be commonly used and frequented by way of merchandise, by any of the merchants, or any subjects of us or of our progenitors: whereby many good offices may be done for the peace of Christendom," such as the relief of Christian slaves, and "good vent for the commodities of the realm" might be found, "to the advancement of the honor and dignity" of the crown, "the increase of royal revenue and the general wealth of the realm." It was significantly provided by the charter that the company, during the last six of the seven years of their grant, "shall export so much goods to Turkey as shall annually pay at least five hundred pounds custom to the crown," exclusive of repayments on account of loss of goods by shipwreck and otherwise.[1]

Before the first charter had been granted, William Harbum, Edward Ellis and Richard Staper (one of the incorporators) had been sent by the queen to Turkey to

[1] Anderson, *Origin of Commerce*, vol. ii., pp. 152, 153.

negotiate for privileges of trading for English merchants, and had obtained from the sultan for them the "right to as freely trade and resort to Turkey as the French, Venetians and others."[1] Harbum went out as ambassador on the company's first voyage in 1582, and on his arrival appointed consuls in the several ports and established rules and regulations for the government of the trade, especially as it should come in contact with the sultan's subjects. Though appointed formally by the Queen or her representative, the ambassador, consuls and other officers were named at the request of the company, who also paid their salaries or other compensation and their expenses. Such further privileges of trade, called "capitulations," as were obtained from the sultan appear to have been conceded directly to the company, in contrast with similar privileges of the Merchant Adventurers and other regulated companies, which were usually secured through the negotiations of the crown with the foreign states. The charter must have been renewed on the expiration of the first term of seven years, though no documentary evidence of it has been found. In 1593, however, a charter was granted by Elizabeth that indicates a considerable development in the organization and work of the company. The members named in the charter now numbered fifty-three, "consisting of knights, aldermen and merchants," while the company might admit as new members any who should have served them as factors or in other capacities; leave was given eighteen others (three of whom were to be certain aldermen of London named in the charter) to become members of the company upon the payment by each of them of one hundred and thirty pounds to the company "towards their past charges in establishing the said trades"; members who should fail to conform to the rules and regulations of the company and to make the payments required of

---

[1] Anderson, *Origin of Commerce*, vol. ii., pp. 152, 153.

them should forfeit their right to membership, "where-upon the company may elect others in their stead." The name was extended to "The Governor and Company of Merchants of the Levant,"—an indication of the greater prominence in the company of its governing body. An advisory body appears to have been created, for it was provided that in addition to the governor twelve assistants should be elected annually by the company. The trading territory was extended and made more definite; it should include "(a) the Venetian terri-tories, (b) the dominions of the Grand Seignior, by land and sea, and (c) trade through his countries overland to the East Indies, a way lately discovered by John New-berry and others." The exclusive right to trade in the described territory, the power to enact by-laws and the right to demand repayment of customs paid on goods lost at sea were continued, while duties levied on im-ported goods should be refunded if the goods should be exported within thirteen months by English subjects in English bottoms. "Four good ships, with ordnance and munitions for their defence and with two hundred English mariners, shall be permitted to go, at all times," unless the queen in time of war should notify the com-pany that they could not be spared from the defence of the realm until the return of the royal navy. The com-pany might have a common seal and "may place in the tops of their ships the arms of England, with a red cross in white over the same, as heretofore they have used." The members described in the charter and "their sons, apprentices, agents, factors and servants" should use the powers granted for a term of twelve years, unless they should be revoked, on eighteen months' notice, as "not profitable to the Queen or to the realm "[1]; they

---

[1] *Ibid.*, vol. ii., pp. 181, 182. A peculiar provision of the charter, show-ing the use of the company by the crown as a means of bringing pressure to bear on a foreign state, was as follows : " And whereas the state of Venice

might be renewed for a second period of twelve years, on request of the company, if the "trade shall appear to be advantageous."

With the liberality to corporations characteristic of the Stuarts, James I., in 1605, made the incorporation of the Levant Company perpetual, though he aimed to make it an "open" regulated company by extending admission to its freedom to all sons of members, all merchants on payment of £25, if under twenty-six years of age, and of £50, if older, and to all the apprentices of members on payment of twenty shillings. The machinery of government was more elaborate; all freemen were to elect annually a governor, deputy governor and eighteen assistants, who should have the entire management of the company's affairs; the times of lading vessels and shipping cargoes were to be determined at "general courts," as the annual meetings of all freemen were called.[1] During the civil war, the Levant Company, like that of the Merchant Adventurers,[2] found it advisable to secure a confirmation of its powers by Parliament. In addition to a formal continuance of its incorporation, it was conceded "the free choice and removal of all officers" to be maintained by it either in England or abroad, whether ambassadors, governors, consuls, deputies or other; it should also have power

---

has of late increased the duties on English merchandise carried thither, and on Venetian merchandise exported from thence in English ships; for redress thereof, the Queen forbids the subjects of Venice, and all others but of this company . . . to import into England any manner of small fruits called currants, being the raisins of Corinth, or wines of Candia, unless by this company's license . . . upon pain of forfeiture of ships and goods, half to the Queen and half to the company, and also of imprisonment; provided, always, that if the Venetian state shall take off the said two new imposts, then this restraint touching currants and wines of Candia shall be void."—*Ibid.*

[1] *Ibid.*, vol. ii., p. 225. The provisions of the charter of James I. are also recited in the preamble of the act of 26 George II., cap. 18.

[2] *Supra*, p. 77.

"to levy money on its members and on strangers, upon all goods shipped in English bottoms, or in strangers' bottoms, going to or coming from Levant, for the supply of its own necessary expense, as well as for such sums of money as shall be advanced for the use and benefit of the state, by the approbation of Parliament"[1];

thus three distinct steps were gained by the company. The facts that the trade of the company was approaching the condition of a monopoly and that the company was suffering from the interference of independent merchants may justly be inferred from the strict provisions against so-called "interlopers":

"no person shall bring from or send goods or ships into the limits of their charter, but such as are free brothers, or otherwise licensed by the corporation, on pain of forfeiture of the whole, or other lesser penalty to be imposed by this corporation on their goods or ships; . . . They may also impose fines on persons wittingly contemning or disobeying their orders, but not to exceed twenty pounds for any one offence, and in default, to distrain the goods of persons so fined; and if no sufficient distress can be found, to imprison their persons till they pay their fines, or otherwise give satisfaction."

Yet the provision for admission was substantially what it had been in the charter of James:

"None shall be excluded from the freedom . . . who shall desire it by way of redemption, if such person be a mere merchant, and otherwise capable thereof, and shall pay fifty pounds for the same, if above twenty-seven years of age or twenty-five pounds, if under that age, or so much less as their fellowship shall think fitting."

[1] Possibly some significance is given to the last provision by the fact that in the same year the Company of Merchant Adventurers advanced £30,000 to the government, presumably for the concession by Parliament of similar powers.

The reason assigned for the grant is interesting, being merely "for the better government and regulating of trade"; while the purpose of previous grants had been to establish or increase the trade, the purpose of the present grant was to govern it; the former had in view the activity of merchants, the latter, the form in which their activity should be exercised.[1] The restrictive tendency in the membership was recognized and promoted at the Restoration by the provision in the charter granted by Charles II. that it should be confined to persons who were merchants of London or within twenty miles of it, except noblemen and gentlemen of quality, unless others should first become free of the city of London. As freedom of the city involved freedom of the city mercantile companies, the path to membership in the Levant Company was obstructed by a considerable additional expense.[2]

The tendency towards the restriction of membership and concentration of power was no less plain in the relations of the company to the crown and Parliament than in the interrelations of the members of the company and the other merchants engaged in the trade. During the seventeenth century after the concession of James's charter, the security of the Levant trade was gradually more fully established, communication between European countries became closer, new sources of trade similar to the Levant trade were discovered, and new routes of reaching the same trade were developed, as the water route to India; in consequence the necessity of the corporate organization of the Levant merchants became less apparent. Interlopers increased in number and boldness, and in some cases, as in that of the merchants of Southampton, obtained from the crown an exemption

[1] Anderson, *Origin of Commerce*, vol. ii., pp. 399, 400.

[2] Anderson, vol. ii., p. 461. The provisions of the charter of Charles II. are also recited in the preamble of the act 26 George II., cap. 18.

from the requirement of membership in the Levant Company. Yet the company, designed by James to be open to all merchants, did not expand to comprehend them. A coterie of influential London merchants, by manipulating the management of the company, made it a means of excluding merchants of other cities from the trade. They had sufficient power to secure the amendment of 1661, which partially sanctioned the control of the company by their oligarchy. In most of the regulated companies trade had been carried on in private ships or in ships owned by groups of members; such had been the manner of carrying on the Levant trade, but the company inaugurated the plan of using ships owned or controlled by it in its corporate capacity in addition to the private ships of its members, and made the new system a means of excluding from the trade members outside of London. It appears that in 1718 the company's vessels had not been used for a few years and the company had in consequence lost its control over the trade; in order to regain control a regulation was made that for the future all trading should be carried on by the company's vessels to the exclusion of others, and that they should set out on their voyages at such times and from such places as the company should determine. The dates of sailing were arbitrarily postponed for the purpose of preventing the exportation of goods until prices in the foreign market should rise. London was designated as the port from which vessels should be laden, a measure manifestly prejudicial to the interests of merchants outside of London. Appeals to the ministry were unavailing and a threat of remedy by Parliamentary legislation was necessary to make the company (or the interior group in control of it) recede from their position.

The most prosperous period of the company's career was probably the first three decades of the eighteenth century but they confessed to a committee of the House of Commons in 1744 that their trade was at that time greatly decayed by reason, as they alleged, of the competition of French merchants and the interruption of their supply of silk by wars in the East; a pending bill to lay the trade open to all English merchants was defeated, Parliament considering, whether justly or not, that the trade could be better restored by maintaining than by abolishing the privileges of the company. But nine years later, in 1753, it was enacted that after the 24th of June, 1754, "every subject of Great Britain, desiring admission into the Turkey Company, shall be admitted within thirty days after . . . request" upon payment of twenty pounds to the company;

"all persons free of the company may, separately or jointly, export any goods . . . from any place in Great Britain to any place within the limits of the [company's] charter . . . at any time and to any persons . . . free of the company, or to the sons or apprentices of freemen . . . so long as they shall remain under and submit to the protection and direction of the British ambassador and consuls . . . ; and may import . . . commodities purchased within the limits of the [charter] upon paying the king's duties and customs and such impositions as shall be assessed upon all merchandise exported or imported, or upon ships laden therewith, for defraying the necessary expenses of the company."

The governor or deputy governor and company were to make, at a general court, such rules for the good government of the company as should seem necessary to the majority of members present, but they should not be valid unless comfirmed at a subsequent general court, held at least one month later on twenty days' notice by publication. If any seven or more of the freemen should think themselves aggrieved by any rule, they might appeal within one year after its enactment to the Commissioners for Trade and Plantations, who should, after an early hearing of the appeal, either approve or disapprove the rule in such manner as they saw fit.[1] The enactment of the law marked a revolution in the affairs of the company. The exclusive element in it was virtually destroyed. Admission into it and the commerce of its members were so conditioned that its purely corporate functions were hardly more than would have been reposed in an administrative branch of the English government. For many years in the latter part of the century the revenue of the company was insufficient for the payment of its expenses; Parliament accordingly granted to it from £5000 to £10,000 per annum to relieve its successive deficits. In 1803, the British government resumed the power of appointing ambassadors, which had long been reposed in the company. In 1825, in response to a suggestion from Canning, the company expressed their willingness to execute a deed by which they should surrender all the powers granted to them by their charters. Parliament, by an act[1] in the same year, provided that as soon as the deed should be delivered, the company should be dissolved and all its rights, powers and privileges should determine; all the company's property should vest in the crown, and all powers of government possessed by the company's consuls or other officers should in future be exercised by royal officers. The reason assigned for the enactment of the law was simply that "it would be beneficial to the trade of the United Kingdom, and especially to the trade carried on in the Levant Seas, that the exclusive rights and privileges of the governor and company . . . should cease and determine."

Very similar to the Levant Company in its organization and course of development was the Russia or Mus-

[1] "An Act for Enlarging and Regulating the Trade into the Levant Seas," 26 George II., cap. 18.

[2] 6 George IV., cap. 33.

kovy Company. Certain nobles and others named having "already fitted out ships for discoveries northward, northwestward and northeastward [to lands] not as yet frequented by subjects of any other Christian monarch" in amity with England, they were in 1554 granted a charter by Philip and Mary for further voyages and adventures as "The Merchants Adventurers for the Discovery of Lands, Territories, Isles and Seigniories unknown, and not by the Seas and Navigations, before this said late Adventure or Enterprise by Sea or Navigation, commonly frequented."[1] Sebastian Cabot, during his life, was to be governor; four others, of the most "sad, discreet and honest of the fellowship," should be consuls; twenty-four other such members should be assistants. They had the usual power to admit new members, to make laws for the government of their members and trade and to punish offenders against their privileges by mulcts and forfeitures. As one of their ships had wintered in Russia and the adventurers had obtained the concession of important trading privileges from the Czar, they were given by the charter full permission to trade thither; other parts to which the company might trade should be only such as were not known to English subjects. They might make conquest of the lands of infidels discovered by them. As in similar companies, their right to trade in the territories described was exclusive, and non-members trading in them without their license were subject to forfeiture of their ships and goods.[2] Among the many privileges conceded to them by the Czar, their chief factor was to have full power to govern all the English in Russia and administer justice among them according to such laws as he, with his assistants, should

[1] The name (or description) is at least so recited in the statute 10 and 11 William III., cap. 6. It was fortunately shortened in 1566 to the "Fellowship of English Merchants for Discovery of New Trades."

[2] Anderson, *Origin of Commerce*, vol. ii., pp. 98, 99.

make and enforce by means of fines and imprisonment;
the Czar's officers were to assist the English in making
and enforcing their laws even to the extent of affording
them the use of prisons and instruments of torture; in
general the Czar assured them justice in their relations
with his subjects. A few years later (in 1566) he granted
the company immunity from tolls and customs in his
dominions. Four years after their charter was granted
they began the trade to Persia by way of Moscow and
the Caspian.

In 1566 their charter is said to have been confirmed by
Parliament.[1] The chief additional provisions were intended to restrict the trade of merchants outside the
company and plainly indicate a strong tendency to exclusiveness. The company's territory was now defined
as any part of the continent lying north, northwest, or
northeast of London and not known or frequented by
subjects before the company's first voyage, together with
the Czar's dominions, Armenia, Media, Hyrcania, Persia,
and the lands tributary to the Caspian Sea. No English
subject should trade to them without the "order, agreement, consent, or ratification " of the company, on pain
of the usual forfeiture; the reason given for the prohibition was

" that sundry subjects of the realm, perceiving that divers
Russian wares and merchandise are now imported by the said
fellowship, after all their great charge and travel, some of
which be within this realm of good estimation, minding, for
their peculiar gain, utterly to decay the trade of the said fellowship, have, contrary to [their charter], in great disorder,
traded into the dominions of Russia . . . to the great
detriment of this commonwealth."

An exception was made, however, of such inhabitants of
York, Newcastle, Hull and Boston as had been merchants

---

[1] It is not published in the Statutes, but is compiled by Anderson (*Origin
of Commerce*, vol. ii.,) on the authority of Hakluyt.

for the past ten years, which shows some features of the company's management; they were permitted, by December 25, 1567, to

" contribute, join, and put in stock to, with and amongst the company, such sums of money as any of the said company, which hath thoroughly continued and contributed to the said new trade from the year 1552, hath done, and before the said 25th of December, 1567, shall do, for the furniture of one ordinary, full and entire portion or share ";

every such merchant who should "in all things behave himself as others of the society are bound to do, shall, from said date, be accounted free, as one of the said society and company in all respects." It is very evident that the activity of the company was not that of a purely regulated company; such merchants as those of "fair estimation" described in the preamble of the statute would otherwise hardly have been trading outside its membership. Even the merchants of the four eastern ports were not admitted so much because they were merchants as because they were so situated as to be able to engage in the independent trade most advantageously; even when they were admitted to share in the privileges of the company, they were limited in number by the requirement of ten years of mercantile life; moreover, they were limited in the amount of capital they should invest according to the amount invested by the original members of the company. Finally, the trading of the company was plainly carried on not by individual traders separately but by many in combination, though probably not all members were participants to the same extent in successive voyages or adventures.

Considerable difficulty was experienced in getting confirmations from the Czar of the exclusive privileges of the company and of additional privileges for the company as distinguished from other English subjects. As early as

1571, the Czar deprived the company of the exemptions and other privileges granted so readily less than twenty years before, but soon regranted them. Later in the century the condition of their rights in Russia was unstable; every year efforts were made to regain lost powers, to gain new ones or to secure better protection of those nominally possessed. In the treaty of 1623 made by James I. and the Czar, the company considered themselves as having made a distinct gain in the provision that the subjects of either monarch trading without his permission in the dominions of the other should be surrendered for punishment; the company expected that thereby they would secure the exclusion of English merchants trading in Russia without their license. On the execution of Charles I. in England, however, the power of the company, as far as it was derived from the Czar, was greatly weakened. The facts that account for the hostile attitude of the Czar are not fully known. He is said to have claimed that a messenger from Charles II. requested him to abrogate the privileges of the company. He was certainly disposed to resent the execution of the king by depriving his subjects, especially merchants closely identified with the rebellious classes, of the exclusive privileges he had granted to them. A more potent factor was doubtless the rivalry of Dutch merchants, who sought to improve their commercial relations with the Czar, as compared with those of the English company, by inflaming his mind against them. At all events, after 1649, the best status that the Russia company could obtain in Russia was one of equality with the Dutch merchants. In 1654, the trade from Archangel into the interior of Russia was not open to the company. They might remain at that port until they had disposed of their merchandise; unsold goods they might leave there or take back to England, as they saw fit, but they might take them no farther inland; in the same year the

English are said to have been expelled entirely from Archangel on the request of an emissary of Charles II.

The change in the attitude of the Czar must have seriously affected the ability of the company to maintain its monopoly even against other English merchants. When the first charter was granted, the company had consisted of 207 members; in 1600 there were only 160 members; in 1654 the number had decreased to only 55 members; the numbers may be variously interpreted; they can hardly be construed as evidence of a decline in the trade between 1555 and 1600, while they may be so considered of the trade between 1600 and 1654; they probably indicate that during the whole time the trade was being concentrated in a few hands. In 1604, when the Free Trade bill was under consideration in the House of Commons, it was stated by the committee in its report on the bill that the directors of the company had limited the amount that might be adventured by individual members, they made "one purse and common stock," they placed all their exported merchandise for sale in Russia in the hands of one agent or factor at Moscow, they likewise placed all their imported merchandise for sale in England in the hands of one agent in London; after the business was entirely transacted it was charged that they rendered to common adventurers such an account as they pleased.

The Revolution of 1688 had its effect on the organization of the company. It had become plain that under its management as a monopoly it was of slight public service. Accordingly, in 1698, it was enacted by Parliament that after Ladyday in the following year admission to the fellowship should be freely permitted to any subject upon payment of five pounds.[1] During the eighteenth century the company remained intact but exercised no control over commerce; in 1741 and 1750, the trade with

[1] 10 and 11 William III., cap. 6.

Russia (especially in silk) was still restricted to its free-men; in 1854 customs were still levied by it though "every individual admitted into the company conducted his business entirely as a private adventurer, or as he would do were the company abolished."[1] In 1882 it was said of it that "in truth, for business purposes [it had] ceased to exist, its only meeting now being an annual social gathering."[2]

In this class of corporations ought also to be included the Morocco Company created by charter of Elizabeth in 1588 to the Earls of Warwick and Leicester and forty other persons for the development of a trade in Morocco, which proved not to be important or permanent. In 1604, James I. incorporated the "President Assistants and Fellowship of Merchants of England Trading into Spain and Portugal,"[3] usually called the Spanish Company, which aspired to have France included in its grant. In the following year great Parliamentary opposition to its monopoly of the trade resulted in the Free Trade Act, providing that all the king's subjects should in future as freely trade into and from the dominions of Spain, Portugal and France as they had since the beginning of his reign or before the grant of the company's charter.[4] The charter was thereupon revoked by the king. In 1665, Charles II. chartered the Canary Company, to consist of all subjects who had traded to the Canary Islands within seven years past to the extent of £1000 annually and of all others who should be admitted to membership by them; they were to enjoy the trade exclusively, and were to be governed by a governor, deputy governor and twelve assistants. The preamble of the charter is

---

[1] J. R. McCulloch, *Dictionary of Commerce* (edition of 1854), *sub verbis* Russia Company. In the edition of 1882, no mention is made of duties or customs payable to the company.

[2] *Ibid.* (edition of 1882), *sub verbis* Russia Company.

[3] *Calendar of State Papers*, Domestic Series, 1605.

[4] 3 James I., cap. vi.

the most instructive part of it; it is alleged in justification of the grant of powers

"that the trade to the Canary Isles was formerly of greater advantage to the king's subjects than at this time, that by reason of the too much access and trading of subjects thither, . . . merchandise was decreased in its value, and the Canary wines, on the other hand, were increased to double their former value, so that the king's subjects were forced to carry silver and bullion thither to get wines: and that all this was owing to want of regulation in trade."

The charter was vigorously assailed in Parliament, as in violation of the Free Trade Act of 1605, the Canary Islands being part of the dominions of the King of Spain. The House of Commons passed a resolution "that the patent of the Canary Company is an illegal patent, a monopoly and a grievance of the subject,"[1] and moved the king to revoke the charter. In the next year the king yielded to the opposition by revoking the charter, for which he was thanked by both Houses. When Lord Clarendon was impeached by the House of Commons one of the charges against him was that he had "received great sums of money for passing the Canary patent, and other illegal patents, and granted illegal injunctions to stop proceedings at law against them and other illegal patents formerly granted."[2]

Several other corporations organized for the prosecution of discoveries of new lands or ocean passages, and for engaging in commerce and in the fisheries would also have to be included in the class under consideration. Most of them were of little importance and none of them were permanent. A few may be mentioned as examples. In 1583, the "Colleagues of the Fellowship for the Discovery of the Northwest Passage," consisting of Adrian

[1] *Commons Journals*, October 29, 1666; vol. viii., p. 643.
[2] *Commons Journals*, November 6, 1667; vol. ix., p. 16.

Gilbert and others, were chartered by Elizabeth for a term of five years.[1] Likewise in 1607 the "Colleagues of the Fellowship for the Discovery of the North Passage," consisting of Penkevell of Cornwall and others, were chartered by James I. for a term of seven years for the "sole discovery of a passage to China, Cathay, the Moluccos, and other parts of the East Indies by the north, northwest, or northeast."[2] The Russia Company and East India Company formed together a joint stock to engage in the Spitzbergen whale fishery in 1618 and maintained it for two years.[3] In 1636, Charles I. prohibited the importation of whale fins or whale oil except by the Russia Company, which might form a joint stock for that purpose.[4] The "Royal Fishery Company of Great Britain and Ireland," of which the Duke of York, Lord Clarendon and others were the members, received a charter from Charles II. in 1661. The "Company of the Royal Fishery of England," which may have been the successor of the preceding company, consisted of the Duke of York and others and was chartered by Charles II. in 1677. By act of Parliament in 1693[5] Sir William Scawen and forty-one others were incorporated for a term of fourteen years as the "Company of Merchants of London Trading to Greenland."

The staple organization had comprehended the foreign trade as it existed, no change in the relations of native and foreign merchants had been contemplated; the most that had been sought was the regulation of established relations. The general purpose of the purely regulated companies was to displace the foreign merchants and to substitute the native merchants for them, with an

[1] Macpherson, *Annals of Commerce*, vol. ii., p. 174.
[2] Rymer, *Fœdera*, vol. xvi., p. 660.
[3] Anderson, *Origin of Commerce*, vol. ii., p. 271.
[4] Rymer, *Fœdera*, vol. xx., p. 16.
[5] 4 and 5 William and Mary, cap. 17.

incidental enlargement of the trade. The aim of the former was harmony, even at the expense of perpetuating the control of the trade by foreigners; on the contrary, the aim of the latter was to satisfy the ambitions of English merchants in their competition with foreigners. In both cases the trade was already established, and its further development was to be along lines already defined. The object of the regulated companies that have been distinguished as exclusive and concentrated (both terms being inexact) was the organization of newly "discovered" trade with lands like Turkey and Russia previously not "frequented" in trade by Englishmen or subjects of other Christian nations. It was the third stage in the growth of the English foreign trade as far as it was organized in corporations. In the first stage all the merchants, both English and foreign, were comprehended in one organization; in the second, all the English merchants to the exclusion of foreigners alone; in the third, only a part of the English merchants, to the exclusion not only of all foreigners but also of many English merchants.

The exclusion of the foreign merchants may be easily explained by the different national purpose that has been suggested as distinguishing the regulated companies from the earlier staple organizations. The normal purpose of social organization is to promote harmony between the social elements organized, not to enable one element to make a conquest of a field occupied by another. It was hardly in the nature of things' that the merchants of the Eastland Company and Hamburgh Company should be expected to oust the Hanseatic merchants from international trade by being merged in one organization with them. But the second step in exclusiveness of corporate membership is not so easily explained. Some considerations bearing on the question may be profitably presented in detail.

1. The regulated and regulated-exclusive forms may be distinguished, from the standpoint of their application to the social activity contained in them, as subsequent and antecedent. The former was a structure that trade had acquired in the course of its evolution; the latter was applied to trade is its establishment and was intended as a structure within which its evolution should be at least begun. It is the difference that is frequently expressed by the terms "spontaneous" or "natural," as applied to the former, and "arbitrary" or "compulsory," as applied to the latter. The importance of the distinction is that fitness of form for content is usually assured by the test of experience in the former and subject to be determined by future experience in the latter, as is well exemplified in the Levant Company and East India Company, of which one became finally a purely regulated company and the other a joint-stock company. To express the distinction implied in the somewhat exceptional use of the terms "subsequent" and "antecedent" in a different and perhaps better way, the regulated companies were formed *after* and the regulated-exclusive companies *before* the trade was *established*. The effort involved in the *establishment* was capitalized, so to speak, in the form of an exclusive right to enjoy the trade established. The granting of a charter to the Russia Company had been preceded by a voyage in which the adventurers had demonstrated on their own initiative, and at their own expense, the possibility of developing a trade to Russia; likewise the granting of corporate powers to the Levant Company had rewarded the enterprise of a group of English adventurers who "had, at their own great costs and charges, found out and opened a trade to Turkey." The fishery companies had their origin in the express purpose of establishing a new or reviving a decayed industry. With the merchants of the staple, the "merchants of Holland" and Merchant Adventurers, it had been otherwise. They

had established no new trade; the trade had existed before they were organized, though it had been carried on by foreign merchants.   There was no effort of discovery or establishment to encourage or reward in their cases.

2. England enjoyed no settled international relations with the nations whose trade had been "discovered." The international relations that in the trade of the regulated companies had been maintained through the political machinery of the state were formed and maintained by the regulated-exclusive companies themselves in their commercial territory.   Even the formal appointment by the crown of ambassadors and consuls in Turkey recommended by the Levant Company was soon discontinued, and the company was expressly allowed by charter to do directly what it had previously done indirectly,—to appoint the political representatives of the English nation in Turkey.   When Elizabeth sent costly presents to the Czar, they were paid for by the Russia Company; it was virtually the corporation that was propitiating him, and the royal name was being used merely as a matter of form.   From the side of England, then, a large part of the political sovereignty of the nation, or more properly, of the powers through which it was expressed, was reposed in the company—a far larger part than, in the state of political development in Europe, had been necessary in the commerce of the regulated companies in Western Europe.   Perhaps it is not necessary to add that from the side of the nations in whose territories the companies traded, a very similar grant of powers was made.   If England presented itself to the foreign nation in the personality of a trading company, the foreign nation acted reciprocally through the same medium.   If trading privileges were granted, they were granted not at first through the normal political means of treaties between the sovereigns, but by "capitulations" directly conceded to the companies.   From both sides the companies derived a

considerable body of purely political powers. If the effort of discovering or establishing a new trade in foreign countries seemed to justify its restriction as a reward or compensation to the adventurers who had put forth the effort, the success in securing concessions from the rulers of foreign countries was even more deserving of reward; the concessions were usually either in derogation of exclusive privileges granted to traders of other countries or themselves exclusive of such other traders; in Turkey the English merchants were granted the same rights to trade that had previously been enjoyed by the French and Venetians to the exclusion of others; in Russia they were granted an exclusive trade and suffered a loss when the Dutch were afterwards admitted to an equality with them. The English and foreign rulers had the same object in view, the increase of commerce by encouraging merchants through grants of exceptional powers. If the foreign ruler happened to be passive, and not desirous of the new trade, a less commendable motive had to be supplied through the bestowal of gifts or some other less disguised form of payment; in either case, the result represented an outlay of time, effort and goods, and formed a substantial basis for grants of powers to the groups of adventurers exclusively of their fellow-countrymen. Any interloper that tried to engage in a new trade established by English adventurers must have profited to a greater or less extent by their labors in founding the trade and in providing the political machinery necessary for its prosecution; if he were required to pay membership fees in just proportion to the advantages enjoyed by him as a result of the company's work, he might not hesitate, from a selfish point of view, to risk the forfeiture of his ship and cargo in preference to paying the large fees demanded. The prevalence of interlopers was not always convincing evidence of their unjust exclusion from the corporations. On the other hand, the companies, who

perhaps regarded their privileges as property, had no inclination to undervalue them and accordingly demanded
exorbitant payments for their acquisition by others; even
further, they certainly placed arbitrary and unreasonable
restrictions on the trade to perpetuate their exclusive enjoyment of it.　What is important is not that they denied
to others opportunities to participate in their trade—that
was to be expected—but the conditions that made it
possible for them to do so.

3. Corporations are, in a broad view, institutions of
government.　The regulated companies made rules for
the government of their members in their individual
activity, and exercised judicial and other functions readily
recognized as governmental.　For most purposes their
activity may be said to have fallen into two classes, political and commercial, though the analysis is certainly
superficial.　The difference between the regulated and
regulated-exclusive companies was, in general, from this
point of view, that in the former the commercial activity
predominated, while in the latter the political activity
was greater in volume and more important in substance.
The coercive power behind the political activity was
stronger than the purely voluntary motive behind the
commercial activity of the merchants.　In consequence
of their greater ratio of political to commercial powers
and of the normal difference in the effectiveness of the
two powers, the regulated-exclusive companies developed
to a higher degree in the direction of government; they
did not stop at the regulation of the individual, but proceeded to absorb him and to merge his activity in the
organic activity of the group to which he belonged; they
built "company" ships and enacted that private ships
should not be used in their trade; they passed beyond
the imposition of a "stint" of trading by the individual
and enacted that all trading should be by the group as
such, or at least through the companies' factors; in fine,

their governmental machinery was made to do not only the work of government, but also that of trading.

4. It may be contrary to some accepted theories of the state to suggest that, before an individual may safely be left to conduct his own business without regulation, he must be an efficient unit of activity. It is certain, however, that in the trade conducted by the regulated-exclusive companies the individual merchant was unable to act separately. It is not too much to say that if he had been permitted to do so, he would have acted contrary to his ultimate best interests; as it was sometimes expressed, he would probably have "spoiled" or "decayed" the trade. The companies were exercising the functions that were later to be exercised by the English nation through its government in providing the political framework within which the trade had to be carried on; the individual merchants, acting separately, could undoubtedly not have exercised them; the trade could only become "open" when the English government should have assumed the exercise of the companies' political powers, or should have separated the political from the commercial powers. The trade to Russia and Turkey in the sixteenth and seventeenth centuries was based on such an accumulation of capital as individual merchants had not attained. Trade by sea could not be in smaller units than single vessels, and the ownership of a whole cargo was undoubtedly beyond the capacity of the individual merchants of the time. But such was the insecurity of the sea from pirates and hostile peoples that the unit of trade to Russia and Turkey could hardly with prudence be less than a small fleet, provided with marines and armament as well as with sailors. The power of the governing bodies of the companies to designate the places and times of lading vessels for voyages was not wholly unwarranted; on the contrary it was quite necessary that it be exercised, though it was arbitrarily made an instrument of

oppression. The concentration of management was due, for the most part, to the conditions of the commerce of the time; increased exclusiveness of membership was derived from it through the undue advantage given by it to the interior body of members in whom the management was concentrated.

The history of the companies under consideration may be divided into periods and, though it has not been done before, it may add clearness to suggest such a division now. (1) They first appeared as groups of adventurers actuated by their personal interests in seeking new fields of commerce. (2) When the "new trade" had been discovered and foundations had been laid for its prosecution, the founders, with others taken into their groups, received grants of powers both from the English crown and from foreign rulers, by which their numbers were determined, and their relations to each other, to other subjects and to foreigners were settled. In this stage of development the terms during which the corporate relations should continue were limited, and the membership restricted. (3) The first charters were followed by others by which the powers already granted were supplemented by others wider in scope. This and the preceding period were the ones in which the characteristic exclusiveness and concentration of the companies made themselves manifest. This period was particularly the one in which interference from interlopers and private traders called for attention. (4) After the influence of private traders acquired sufficient strength, the trades were opened to all merchants by Parliamentary intervention and the companies became purely regulated companies. (5) As regulated companies they eventually became obsolete, exercising only a nominal influence over trade but in some cases exercising political powers such as would belong to an administrative department of the government. (6) Finally the nominal control over trade that had been permitted them was taken away and their political powers assumed by the state even if their technical corporate existence was not also terminated by a revocation of their charters. Such at least would be the periods into which the history of the developed corporations of the class might properly be divided. Such corporations as the Spanish Company and Canary Company were so manifestly out of harmony with the conditions under which they were created that they were very properly short-lived.

VOL. II.—8 .

V

JOINT-STOCK COMPANIES

IN the purely regulated companies the joint-stock principle was not theoretically applied, and in such of them as it prevailed was permitted to be introduced only covertly and in response to the demands of peculiar circumstances; it was at no time regarded as a legitimate part of their organization. In the joint-stock companies, however, the principle was fully applied and was the distinctive feature of their organization and growth. By far the most important of the joint-stock companies were the old, new and united East India Companies, which may fairly and by writers usually are regarded as different stages or phases of one great organization—the East India Company.[1]

The Levant Company, it will be remembered, was a regulated company, typical of the class that tended to become exclusive and in which the principle of the joint stock was introduced to only a limited extent by the coterie of merchants in control of them. The East India Company appears to have been an offshoot of the Levant Company or at least to have been closely connected with it at the time of its formation.[2]

[1] It was provided by the Act of 3 and 4 William IV., cap. 85, that the last organization should in future be known as the "East India Company."

[2] See preface of *Court Records of East India Company* (printed from the original by Henry Stevens). "The letters printed on pages 265 to 283, are probably draft letters of the 'Company of Levant Merchants,' and they commence at the opposite end of the manuscript volume to the minutes of the East India Company. From the first letter being dated March, 1599,

On the 31st day of December, 1600, Elizabeth, "greatly tendering the honor of [the nation], the wealth of [the] people, and the encouragement of [her] subjects in their good enterprises, for the increase of . . . navigation, and the advancement of lawful traffic, to the benefit of [the nation's] common wealth," granted to George, Earl of Sunderland, and two hundred and fifteen others, that they "from henceforth be one body corporate and politic . . . by the name of the 'Governor and Company of Merchants of London, trading into the East Indies,' " have corporate succession with power to admit and expel members, be capable of receiving, holding and granting property, sue and be sued in the corporate name and use a common seal. "The direction of the voyages, . . . the provisions of the shipping and merchandise thereto belonging, . . . the sale of all merchandise returned in the voyages, . . . and the managing and handling of all other things belonging to the company" were reposed in a governor, deputy governor and twenty-four committees (directors) elected annually by the members of the company at a general court but removable by them at any time; the first governor (Sir Thomas Smith) and committees were named in the charter. The governor and deputy governor were required to take an oath to well and truly execute their offices, and the members such an oath as should be

while the first entry of the East India Company is September, 1599, it would appear that the book originally belonged to the Levant Company, but was afterwards used by both companies in common. This tends to show that the East India Company was partially an outgrowth of the Levant Company, as several persons mentioned appear to have been prominent members of both companies, notably Sir Thomas Smith, who held the office of Governor of each." The two companies appear also to have been jointly interested in the Spitzbergen fisheries from 1600 to 1613 (Hewins, *English Trade and Finance*, p. 37). The East India Company and Russia Company were also jointly interested in the Spitzbergen fisheries in 1618 (Anderson, *Origin of Commerce*, vol. ii., p. 271).

prescribed for them by the company.[1] The courts (or
meetings) should be held from time to time at any place
in England or elsewhere. For a term of fifteen years
the members of the company (and such others as should
afterwards be admitted to membership) and their sons
(more than twenty-one years old) were exclusively empowered to

"freely traffic and use the trade of merchandise, by seas, in
and by such ways and passages already found out and discovered, or which hereafter shall be found out and discovered,
as they shall esteem and take to be fittest, into and from the
. . . East Indies, . . . and into and from all the
. . . places of Asia and Africa and America . . . beyond the Cape of Good Hope to the Straits of Magellan
. . . so always the . . . trade be not undertaken or
addressed to any . . . place already in the lawful and
actual possession of any . . . Christian prince or state
. . . in league or amity with [England] and who doth not
or will not accept of such trade, but doth overtly declare and
publish [it] to be utterly against his . . . good will."

They might

"make such . . . reasonable laws, constitutions, orders
and ordinances as to them . . . shall seem necessary and
convenient for the good government of [the company] and of
all factors, masters, mariners and other officers employed
. . . in any of their voyages, and for the better advancement and continuance of [their] trade,"

if only they should be "reasonable and not contrary or
repugnant to the laws, statutes or customs" of England;
and in order to enforce them they might "impose . . .
such punishment and penalties by imprisonment of body,
or by fines and amercements . . . upon all offenders
[against] such laws . . . as to [them] shall seem

---

[1] For the oath administered to freemen of the company under the charter
of 1609, see Bruce's *Annals of the East India Company*, vol. i., p. 157, note.

necessary, requisite and convenient for [their] observation," all fines levied to be for the use of the company. For the first four voyages, the company should be exempt from the payment of export duties, and thereafter, if exported goods were lost, the export duties paid on them should be refunded; import duties should be paid, half in six months and half in twelve months, and if imported goods should be exported in English bottoms within thirteen months after importation, no export duties should be levied on them. They might take out of England each year silver in foreign coin or in bullion of a value not in excess of £30,000, provided £6000 be first coined at the royal mint; within six months after the end of any voyage except the first the company was to bring into England at least as great value of gold or silver in bullion or foreign coin as had been taken out at the beginning of the voyage. "In any time of restraint, six good ships and six good pinnaces, well furnished with ordinance and other munitions for their defence, and five hundred [English] mariners, to guide and sail in [them] shall be . . . suffered to depart," unless they should be needed by the government for the prosecution of a war. The East Indies and other places described in the charter should not be "visited, frequented or haunted" by English subjects during the term of fifteen years except by license of the company,

"upon pain that every such person . . . that shall trade or traffic into or from [the described territory] other than [the company] shall incur . . . the forfeiture and loss of the goods . . . which so shall be brought into [England] as also the . . . ships, with [their] furniture . . ., wherein [they] shall be brought,"

half to the company and half to the crown, should suffer imprisonment during the royal pleasure "and such other punishment as . . . for so high a contempt shall seem meet," and should not be released until he had executed to the company a bond in the sum of at least £1000 not in future to trade or traffic in their exclusive territory. Though the company might grant licenses to non-members to engage in the East India trade, the crown promised not to grant them without the company's consent. If not earlier terminated by the crown on two years' warning, the grant was to become void at the expiration of fifteen years, when it might be renewed on application of the company with or without amendment, if its continuance should be found "profitable" and not "prejudicial or hurtful" to the realm.[1]

The first voyage was in 1601 and proved extremely profitable. Eight voyages undertaken from 1603 to 1613 also terminated, on the whole, successfully, though the vessels fitted out in 1607 were lost at sea. All of the voyages had been undertaken by groups of members of the company on joint stocks, and not by the company in its corporate capacity; in the seventh voyage, in 1610, several classes of "adventurers" had united and were called joint adventurers, each captain of the four vessels sailing under separate orders, but all the vessels forming one fleet.[2] The authority exercised by the corporation over the activity of its members was that of a regulated company. In 1612 it was resolved that thereafter the trading should be only by the corporation with a joint stock, but even under the new plan there was not what is now known as a joint stock. Each member subscribed or "adventured" as much as he desired, or even declined to subscribe any amount at all, to a common fund to be placed in the hands of the governor and committees (directors) for management in behalf of such of the members as had participated in the subscription. After the

[1] Volume of Letters Patent granted to the East India Company, pp. 3–26.
[2] Bruce, *Annals*, vol. i., p. 160. Anderson, *History of Commerce*, vol. ii., p. 241.

change of organization in 1612 a stock of £429,000, known as the "Company's First Joint Stock," was subscribed and devoted by the governor and directors to four separate voyages or adventures in the years 1613, 1614, 1615 and 1616, the profits being distributed *pro rata* among the subscribers according to the amounts of their subscriptions. In 1617–1618 the "Company's Second Joint Stock" was raised in the amount of £1,600,000, the company now having thirty-six vessels and 954 proprietors of stock.[2]

"But as the accounts of the company have never been remarkable for clearness, or their historians for precision, we are not informed whether these ships belonged to the owners of the first joint stock, or to the owners of the second; or if to both, in what proportion; whether the 954 proprietors of stock were the subscribers to both funds, or to the last only; whether any part of the first joint stock had been paid back to the owners, as the proceeds came in; or whether both funds were now in the hands of the directors at once, employed for the respective benefit of the respective lists of subscribers: two trading capitals in the same hands, employed separately, for the separate account of different associations. That such was the case, to a certain extent, may be concluded from this, that of the last of the voyages, upon the first of the funds, the returns were not yet made. Afterwards, the directors had in their hands, at one and the same time, the funds of several bodies of subscribers, which they were bound to employ separately, for the separate benefit of each; . . . they, as well as their agents abroad, experienced great inconvenience in preserving the accounts and concerns separate and distinct; and . . . the interests and pretensions of the several bodies were prone to interfere." [1]

A "Third Joint Stock" followed, when a "Fourth Joint Stock" was projected in 1640 as the condition of

[1] Bruce, *Annals*, vol. i., p. 193.
[2] James Mill, *History of British India*, vol. i., p. 27.

the withdrawal by Charles I. of the privileges of Courten and his associates.[1] The confusion of the several joint stocks and the fact that they did not belong to identical sets of subscribers became most apparent.

"The proprietors of the third joint stock had made frequent but unavailing calls upon the directors to close that concern, and bring home what belonged to it in India; . . . payment was demanded of the capital of those separate funds, called the joint stocks of the company. . . . To encourage subscription to the new joint stock, it was laid down as a condition, 'that to prevent inconvenience and confusion, the old company or adventurers in the third joint stock should have sufficient time allowed for bringing home their property, and should send no more stock to India, after the month of May [1640].' The subscribers to the new stock were themselves, in a general court, to elect the directors to whom the management of the fund should be committed, and to renew that election annually.[2] As this was a new court of directors, entirely belonging to the fourth joint stock, it seems to follow that the directors in whose hands the third joint stock had been placed, must still have remained in office, for the winding up of that concern. And in that case there existed, to all intents and purposes, two separate bodies of proprietors, and two separate courts of directors, under one charter."[3]

[1] Bruce, *Annals*, vol. i., pp. 362–365.

[2] For the conditions of the subscriptions of the "Fourth Joint Stock," see Bruce, *Annals*, vol. i., p. 364.

[3] James Mill, *History of British India*, vol. i., pp. 49, 50. The writer raises in the connection a question as interesting as it is impossible to answer. "Upon this occasion a difficult question might have presented itself. It might have been disputed to whom the immovable property of the company, in houses and in lands both in England and in India, acquired by parts indiscriminately of all the joint stocks, belonged." As a partial answer it is suggested, "It would . . . appear that the proprietors of the third joint stock, and by the same rule the proprietors of all preceding stocks, were, without any scruple, to be deprived of their share in what is technically called the 'dead stock' of the company, though it had been wholly purchased with their money."—*Ibid.*, pp. 49, 50.

In 1609 the company had obtained from James I. a confirmation of their charter with an amendment making it perpetual, but revocable on three years' warning. Their monopoly had been maintained intact during the life of Elizabeth, but James, in 1604, had granted to Sir Edward Michelborne and his associates a license to discover "the countries and dominions of Cathaia, China, Japan, Corea and Cambaia and the islands and countries thereunto adjoining, and to . . . trade with the . . . people inhabiting [them] not as yet frequented and traded unto by British subjects or people." [1] Interlopers less prominent interfered continually with the trade, eliciting repeated protests from the company that they were ruining it. In 1635, Charles I. granted to William Courten and others a license to trade in the territory of the East India Company, on the ground that the latter had not made settlements and established trade as promised and expected.[2] In 1637 he confirmed the privileges of Sir William Courten (son of the earlier man of the same name) and his associates (later known as the "Assada Merchants") "as to all places in India where the old company had not settled any factories or trade before the twelfth of December, 1635"; but without prejudice to the old company in other respects.[3] When the Council of State was asked by the company in 1649 to recommend to the House of Commons the passage of an act favorable to their exclusive privileges, it was suggested to the company that they enter into a conference with the Assada Merchants for a termination of their long contest with them.[4] Accordingly the contending parties

---

[1] Rymer, *Fœdera*, vol. xvi., p. 582. Bruce, *Annals*, vol. i., pp. 153, 154. Anderson, *History of Commerce*, vol. ii., p. 223.

[2] Anderson, *History of Commerce*, vol. ii., p. 372.

[3] Bruce, *Annals*, vol. i., p. 329 *et seq.* Anderson, *History of Commerce*, vol. ii., pp. 372, 373. Rymer, *Fœdera*, vol. xx., p. 146 *et seq.*

[4] Bruce, *Annals*, vol. i., pp. 435, 436.

agreed on a union in 1649–1650, and a joint stock was subscribed by them for future trade. But the union did not long prove harmonious, and in 1654 a large group of the subscribers to the joint-stock, including the Assada Merchants, but known collectively as the "Merchant Adventurers Trading to the Indies" filed two petitions with the Council of State, in which they prayed

" that the East India Company should no longer proceed exclusively on the principle of a joint stock trade, but that the owners of the separate funds should have authority to employ their own capital, servants, and shipping, in the way in which they themselves should deem most to their own advantage." [1]

The East India Company and Merchant Adventurers were engaged in fitting out separate fleets for voyages. The select committee of the Council of State to whom the petitions of the Merchant Adventurers and counter petitions of the East India Company had been referred, could reach no conclusion after holding hearings of interested parties, and returned them to the Protector and the Council; finally the Council of State advised Cromwell to continue the exclusive trade and joint stock, and a new committee of the council was appointed to consider the terms of a charter.[2] The outcome of Cromwell's settlement was a nearer approach to the modern status of a joint-stock company. The interests of all the other adventurers in previous funds or joint stocks and "dead stock" were bought up by the members of the East India Company and Merchant Adventurers, and the new joint stock subscribed was the only one left in charge of the directors.[3]

[1] Mill, *History of British India*, vol. i., p. 57.

[2] Bruce, *Annals*, vol. i., pp. 512–517. Mill, *History of British India*, vol. i., p. 61.

[3] No new charter appears to have been actually granted by the Protector; if there was, it is remarkable that no trace of it has been found. The com-

On the accession of Charles II., a new charter was obtained, which increased substantially the body of powers already possessed by the company. The privileges granted in earlier charters were recited and confirmed. In addition, it was granted, "for the preventing of secret and clandestine trading," that no merchandise of the growth, production or manufacture of the territory in Asia, Africa and America exclusively limited to the company should be brought into England without their consent. All plantations, forts, factories or colonies in the territory should be under the power and command of the company, who should have power to appoint governors and all other officers to govern them. The governor and council of the several places in which the company had factories or places of trade, "may have power to judge all persons . . . that shall live under them, in all causes, whether civil or criminal, according to the laws of [England] and to execute judgment accordingly." If a crime should be committed in a place in which there were no governor and council, the offender might be sent for trial to some other place in India or to England, as the head authority of the place should deem the more convenient. The company were permitted to send ships of war, men and munitions into their factories or other places of trade

"for the security and defence of the same, . . . and to choose commanders and officers over them, and to give them power and authority . . . to continue or make peace or war with any prince or people that are not Christians, . . . as shall be most for the advantage and benefit of the [company] and of their trade, and also to right and recompense themselves upon the goods, estate or people of those parts, by whom [they] shall sustain any injury, loss, or damage, or upon pany and others interested proceeded on the theory that the privileges granted by James I. had been confirmed in a new charter granted by Cromwell.—Bruce, *Annals*, vol. i., p. 529.

any other people whatsoever, that shall anyways intercept, wrong or injure them in their trade. . . . It shall be lawful to erect and build such castles, fortifications, forts, garrisons, colonies or plantations . . . within the bounds of [their trade] as they in their discretion shall think fit and requisite,"

to send to them

" all kinds of clothing, provision of victuals, ammunition and implements necessary for such purposes, without paying of any custom, subsidy or other duty, . . . to transport such number of men . . . and govern them in such legal and reasonable manner as [they] shall think fit, and to inflict punishment for misdemeanors, or impose fines upon them for breach of their orders."

They might "seize upon the persons of all [English subjects that] shall sail . . . or inhabit in those parts without [their] leave and license . . . or that shall contemn or disobey their orders, and send them to England." All employees of the company should be liable to such punishment for any offences committed by them as the company should think fit and the degree of the offences should require. If a person convicted and sentenced by the president and council in India should appeal, he should be seized by them and sent a prisoner to England, there to receive from the governor and company "such condign punishment as the merits of his case shall require and the laws of the nation allow of." "For the better discovery of abuses and injuries to be done unto the [company] by their servants," they should have power to examine them on oath "touching or concerning any matter or thing [concerning] which by law and usage an oath may be administered, so as the oath and the matter therein contained be not repugnant to the laws of [the] realm." [1]

[1] Letters Patent granted to the East India Company, pp. 54-79.

In 1669, the island and port of Bombay, which had been ceded to Charles by Portugal in accordance with his marriage contract, was conveyed by him to the East India Company with power to govern it, to defend it by war and arms, to repel any hostile force from it, to pass laws for the government of its inhabitants and enforce them by punishment, fines, imprisonment and "taking away life or member," to appoint and dismiss officers and servants bound by oath to perform their duties, to maintain courts, sessions, forms of judicature and manners of procedure, "like unto those established and used " in England and presided over by judges appointed by the company, and even to declare and enforce martial law when occasion demanded. The laws enacted by the company, however, were to "be reasonable and not repugnant or contrary, but as near as may be agreeable to the laws, statutes, government and policy " of England. The powers granted with relation to Bombay were moreover to extend to territory afterwards acquired by the company elsewhere.[1] The island of St. Helena was granted to the company, in 1674, with substantially the same powers. The justification urged for the last grant is instructive:

" For as much as we have found, by much experience, that the . . . trade with the East Indies hath been managed by the [East India Company] to the honor and profit of this our realm, and to that end and out of our earnest desire that the [company] may, by all good and lawful means, be encouraged in their difficult and hazardous trade and traffic in those remote parts of the world." [2]

In a subsequent charter in 1677, amendatory of that of 1669, was granted the power to coin money in India in such denominations as the company wished, except those

[1] Letters Patent granted to the East India Company, pp. 80-95.
[2] *Ibid.*, pp. 96-107.

of English money.[1] It had been originally provided that
the vessels and cargoes of unlicensed traders should be
forfeited[2] and later that they should not be brought into
England.[3] It was finally granted, in a charter conceded
by Charles II. in 1683, that the East India Company
might "seize all ships, vessels, goods and wares going to
or coming from the East Indies," one half to be retained
by the company and one half to be turned over to the
crown. A special court was also to be established, to
consist of "one person learned in the civil laws" and two
merchants, all appointed by the company, with jurisdiction to pass on cases of seizures of vessels and cargoes,
and all other mercantile and maritime cases, "all which
cases shall be adjudged and determined . . . upon
due examination and proof, according to the rules of
equity and good conscience, and according to the laws
and customs of merchants."[4] Notwithstanding the com-
prehensiveness of their powers, they not infrequently ex-
ceeded their limits, while sometimes they were unable
to use them fully; indemnifying provisions became
common in later charters and appear to have been readily granted by the crown. In the charter of Charles
II. granted in 1677,[5] the exculpatory provision was as
follows:

"Whereas divers transactions have happened, wherein the
proceedings of the [company] may be liable to some question
how far they are warranted by the strict letter of [their

[1] Letters Patent granted to the East India Company, pp. 108–115. The
phraseology of the charter granted by James II. in 1686 was somewhat more
precise : " To coin . . . any species of money usually coined by the
princes of those countries only, . . . so as the monies . . . be
agreeable to the standards of the same princes' mints both in weight
and fineness, and . . . they do not make or coin any European money
or coin whatever ; . . . all money or coins, so to be coined . . .
shall be current in any city, town, port or place within the limits" of the
company's trade.—*Ibid.*, pp. 125–140.   [3] *Supra*, p. 117.

[3] *Supra*, p. 123.   [4] *Ibid.*, pp. 116–124.   [5] *Supra*, p. 125.

charters] and the charters themselves may be in danger to be impeached, as forfeited for some misuser or non-user of [their] rights, liberties and franchises . . . we, for the removal and prevention of all questions and doubts of that nature, . . . ratify and confirm . . . all the rights, liberties and franchises to them formerly granted . . . notwithstanding any former misuser, non-user or abuser whatsoever." [1]

Even at the Restoration "the joint stock was not yet a definite and invariable sum, placed beyond the power of redemption, at the disposal of the company, the shares only transferable by purchase and sale in the market. The capital was variable and fluctuating, formed by the sums which, on the occasion of each voyage" or series of voyages "the individuals who were free of the company chose to pay into the hands of the Directors, receiving credit for the amount on the company's books, and proportional dividends on the profits of the voyage." [2] The final stage of development was hardly reached until after the Revolution of 1688. The greater powers given to the company in the charters of Charles II. for the suppression of the traffic of those who engaged in "a loose and general trade" prepared the ground for such an organization as was attained under the charters of William and Mary. [3] For twenty years after the grant of the first

[1] See also a similar provision in the charter of William and Mary (1693), cited *infra* p. 129, which was granted on condition of the payment of £9300 in satisfaction of the last of four quarterly payments of a tax levied by Parliament on joint stocks, and for the non-payment of which the opponents of the company declared that they had rendered themselves liable to forfeiture of their charters.

[2] Mill, *History of British India*, vol. i., pp. 64, 65.

[3] The language of the charter granted by Charles II. in 1683 shows plainly the view of the trade to the East Indies entertained at that time. "Considering of what import it is to the honor and welfare of the nation, and of our good subjects thereof, to endeavor the utmost improving of the said trade; and being satisfied that the same can by no means be maintained, and carried on with such advantage as by a joint stock, and that a

charter of Charles II., in 1661, the company enjoyed its monopoly of the East Indian trade with comparatively little interruption.[1] Of course the rivalry of the Portuguese, French and Dutch (and especially of the latter), the competition of a few interlopers and the drain of the "private trade" of its officers and servants had a hurtful influence on dividends, but such trade as was conducted was under the control of the company and subject to such limitations as they saw fit to impose. By 1682, however, the opposition to the company, which had been increasing, manifested itself in a project for a competing joint-stock company, which for the present was not attained. The opposition is said to have been prompted largely by the old Levant Company, whose traffic in Indian goods by way of the Gulfs of Persia and Arabia and the Mediterranean had been almost superseded by that of the East India Company by sea.[2] Though the opposition held an "open trade" in no more favor than the existing company, they were ready to accept the assistance of the interlopers, private traders and "pirates" (as the company were inclined to class those who traded without their license); in consequence, the number of interlopers increased rapidly. In 1685, the court (body of directors) of the company appear to have resolved to prosecute forty-eight of the principal interlopers in the Court of King's Bench.[3] What was evidently intended as a test case had been brought against one Sandys, wherein it had been decided in January, 1685, "that the Crown had a right to grant exclusive charters, and that

loose and general trade will be the ruin of the whole; to the end, therefore, that all due encouragement may be given to an undertaking which is so conducing to the general good, and that the undertakers may have all lawful assistance from us to promote the same, . . . we grant" more ample powers for the suppression of traders acting without the company's license.—*Ibid.*, pp. 116–124.   [1] Bruce, *Annals*, vol. ii., pp. 351, 434.

[2] *Ibid.*, vol. ii., pp. 475, 476.   [3] *Ibid.*, vol. ii., p. 551.

such right had been repeatedly acquiesced in by Parliament "; the defendant had sought justification of his independent trade in the plea "that his attempt to trade to India was not contrary to the laws of the realm."[1] After the Revolution of 1688, the political theory that monopolies of trade could be granted only by act of Parliament acquired new force, and the Commons began an active interference in the affairs of the East India Company. A committee of investigation appointed in 1689, having extended hearings to both the company and interlopers or traders desirous of forming rival associations, reported in the following year a resolution

"that the best way to manage the East India trade is to have it in a new company and a new joint stock and this to be established by act of Parliament, but the present company to continue the trade, exclusive of all others, either interlopers or permission ships, till it be established."[2]

On the failure of legislation by Parliament, the affairs of the company were left to the king, by whom their chartered rights were confirmed without diminution in 1693.[3] In the same year, however, a new charter was granted, which recognized to some extent the rights of traders outside the old company by allowing them to participate in its business without affording them the opportunity of separate trading, and made the membership of the company more nearly co-terminous with the membership of the groups interested in the adventures. The "general joint stock" was to be increased by £744,-000; subscription books were to be opened to the public; no subscription was to be in excess of £10,000, and if the aggregate subscriptions were in excess of £744,000, the separate subscriptions were to be decreased *pro rata*.

---

[1] Bruce, *Annals*, vol. ii., p. 530.   [2] *Ibid.*, vol. iii., pp. 81, 82.
[3] Letters Patent granted to the East India Company, pp. 141–151.

Each subscriber should have a vote in general court for each £1000 (but no vote for less) up to £10,000 subscribed.[1] Formerly sons (more than twenty-one years old) of members and their apprentices, factors and servants might engage in the trade; now persons formerly eligible to membership were to be admitted *gratis* to the freedom of the company, if they should subscribe for stock; other subscribers should pay £5 each for admission; the organic difference between a company whose members had the privilege of engaging in a particular business and one whose members were jointly engaged in the business seemed difficult to recognize. The governor and deputy governor were to be qualified for their offices by ownership of £4000 of stock; committees (directors), of £1000 of stock. The charter was to be forfeited if licenses were granted to private traders. All goods imported by the company were to be sold publicly "by inch of candle" in lots of less than £500 in value, except jewels. At least £100,000 worth of goods "of the product and manufacture" of England was to be exported annually. If demanded, the company should sell annually to the government five hundred tons of saltpetre (for gunpowder). The joint stock was to be continued for twenty-one years, during the last year of which books "for the continuance of the joint stock" were to be kept open.[2] In the next year, however, the

---

[1] By the charter granted in 1698, the qualifications of proprietors to vote in general court were amended so that holders of less than £500 should have no vote; of £500, one vote; of £1000, two votes; of £2000, three votes; of £3000, four votes; of £4000 or more, five votes.—Letters Patent granted to the East India Company, pp. 183–187. The charter very significantly contains several provisions limiting the powers of the company's officers and servants, and providing the stock-holders with protection against abuse of power by them; which indicates that the participation of new holders of stock in the company's business had probably been interfered with by the original members of the company.

[2] *Ibid.*, pp. 152–168.

House of Commons resolved that "it is the right of all Englishmen to trade to the East Indies, or any part of the world, unless prohibited by act of Parliament." It was plain to the East India Company that they must have their powers sanctioned by Parliament or eventually lose them; until it could obtain such sanction it must protect itself by insistence on the validity of its royal charters, by more vigorous prosecution of interlopers and by profuse and extravagant bribery of public officials and members of Parliament.

The struggle of the company for a Parliamentary confirmation of its powers against its opponents, whether favoring the right of private trade or the establishment of a new company, came to a head in 1698. The government being in need of funds to carry on the European war then in progress, the East India Company offered it a loan of £700,000 at interest of four per cent. in return for a confirmation of their charter by Parliament, but their rivals met the offer with one for a loan of £2,000,000 at interest of eight per cent. for a charter granting a monopoly of the trade but allowing the traders to determine for themselves whether it should be by joint stock or otherwise. The result was an act favorable (on its face) to the opponents of the old company. The subscribers to the loan of £2,000,000 were to be incorporated under the name of the "General Society Trading to the East Indies," and each of them was to trade for himself if he desired; if any number of them should wish to trade on a joint stock, they should have a charter permitting them to do so; the capital of all traders was to be equal to their subscriptions to the loan. The great majority were incorporated under the name of the "English Company Trading to the East Indies," with a constitution and powers almost identical with those of the existing company. The old East India Company, however, was not to be undone. By the terms of the statute it still had three years (until 1701) of corporate life, and had pro- . vided for its future by subscribing £315,000 of the loan of £2,000,000. It obtained an act of Parliament (which could hardly be refused) granting it in 1699 a charter to trade by a joint stock (like the English Company) on its subscription of £315,000. When they presented the new charter to King William, he wisely recommended to them a union with the English Company.

The next (and in many respects the last) step was the union of the old or London Company and the new or English Company, or more properly, the absorption of the former by the latter. By an "Indenture Tripartite" between Queen Anne and the two companies, in 1702,[1] it was agreed that the English Company should transfer to the London Company at par enough of its stock of £1,662,000 to make the holdings of the two companies equal, the original stock of £315,000 of the London Company becoming part of that of the English Company. The "dead stock" (forts, buildings, etc.) of the old company was transferred to the new company. The two companies were to maintain separate organizations for seven years, during which period each was to distribute its "quick stock" (trading stock) among its members and do no business on its separate account. During the same time the business on the joint account of the two companies was to be transacted by the English Company under a board of twenty-four managers, twelve elected by and acting under the orders of the governing body of each company; each company was to furnish one half the stock for the new trade. At the end of seven years the London Company was to distribute its stock among its members, thus making them stockholders in the English Company, and surrender its charters to the crown. The name of the English Company was then to be changed to the "United Company of Merchants of England

[1] Letters Patent granted to the East India Company.

Trading to the East Indies." By act of Parliament in 1707 it was provided that the subscription to the government loan should be increased from £2,000,000 at eight per cent. to £3,200,000 at five per cent.,[1] that £1,500,000 might be borrowed or raised by assessment of proprietors (shareholders), and that the amount of stock held by private traders[2] might be redeemed by the company on three years' notice after September, 1711; finally, the terms of the union of 1702 were confirmed.[3]

The constitution of the company during the eighteenth century was fairly simple. The Court of Proprietors (or stockholders) was composed of all holders of at least £500 of stock and elected annually at a General Court, a Governor and Deputy Governor, and a Court of Directors (early called Committees) twenty-four in number and qualified by the ownership of at least £2000 of stock.[4] The Directors elected two of their number Chairman and Deputy Chairman, and distributed the bulk of their business among ten committees. In India the business of the company was managed under the three presidencies of Bengal, Bombay and Madras, each independent of the other and acting directly under instructions from the Court of Directors in England. Each presidency was under the supervision of a Governor (or President) and a Council appointed by the Court of Directors. Under the

---

[1] Note that the annual interest on the two amounts was the same, £160,000. The annuities based on the loan remained unchanged in amount.

[2] The subscriptions to the government loan had amounted to £2,000,000, of which £1,662,000 had been subscribed by those who afterwards formed the English Company, and £315,000 by the London Company, leaving £23,000 in the hands of private subscribers, who of course had the privilege of carrying on a "private trade" with India.

[3] 6 Anne, cap. 17.

[4] It was provided by act of Parliament in 1773 (13 George III., cap. 63) that only one fourth of the directors should in future retire each year; the earlier term of the office had been one year.

powers conferred by their charter and supplementary legislation, a mayor's court and court of quarter sessions were established in each presidency, from which the president and council constituted a court of appeal. The presidents were the commanders-in-chief of the military forces of the company in their several jurisdictions.[1]

The success of the company's commercial activity was always necessarily dependent on political conditions. With its body of privileges owing to Royal or Parliamentary grant and likely at almost any time to be taken away if the king or legislature should be persuaded that the trade was "unprofitable for the realm," it had to protect itself as corporations have usually found it necessary. Again, the relations, whether amicable or hostile, of England to the continental nations of Europe were certain to have an influence on the company's commercial

---

[1] In a letter of the Court to the President of Madras (quoted by Bruce in *Annals*, vol. ii., pp. 591, 592), the Governor and Deputy Governor are reported to have been called before the cabinet council in 1687 in connection with the contemplated incorporation of Madras, and to have expressed themselves in favor of its incorporation by the company rather than by the king. "In conclusion, his Majesty did so apprehend it, as to think it best, that the charter should go under our own seal, because the corporation must be always, in some measure, subject to the control of our President and Council; and so, at length, it was agreed, and the charter is now engrossing." The corporation, it is added by Bruce (*ibid.*, p. 593), was to consist of a mayor and ten aldermen, three servants of the company and seven natives, who were to be justices of the peace; the town clerk and recorder and all other subordinate officers were to be elected by the mayor and aldermen, subject to the approval of the company's president; a record of their proceedings was to be kept and regularly transmitted to the court of directors. The "Mayor and Aldermen" of Madras, Bombay and Calcutta were incorporated by George I. in 1726 (Letters Patent granted to the East India Company, pp. 368–399), but almost entirely for the sake of their judicial services. The nine aldermen in each city constituted a close body serving for life and filling their own vacancies; the mayors served for terms of one year, and became aldermen on the expiration of their terms; they were justices of the peace from whom an appeal lay to the President or Governor and Council; the aldermen were subject to removal from office on complaint made to the President or Governor and Council.

activity in India and the other parts of its territory. Historians of the East India Company have all found it unavoidable to devote many pages to the foreign relations of England in order to make plain the course of events in the company's career in India. The Dutch, Portuguese and French were all interested in the Indian trade, and shared in it in the same general way as the English, through the medium of great commercial corporations. When the relations of England with any of them happened to be unfriendly, as was too often the case in the seventeenth and eighteenth centuries, the trade of the East India Company was exposed to all the dangers of war; even when the European countries were at peace, it was difficult for them to keep their companies in the East from coming into conflict. In India the commerce of the company was more completely dependent on the understandings that might be secured with the native powers. Until near the end of the seventeenth century the political privileges that the company obtained by treaty or otherwise from native princes were held subordinate to the commercial aims of the company; if they were profitable, they were rather indirectly so, because they enabled the company to prosecute their trade more successfully, than directly as a source of revenue. When the power of the Mogul went to pieces just before the end of the century, the company began, largely as a matter of necessity, because the great central power in India had been destroyed, to build itself up as a political power in India. After the beginning of the eighteenth century, when the union of the two companies had been accomplished, it might be assumed that a great increase in Indian trade took place, but such was not the case. During the whole of the eighteenth century the trade was much smaller than would be believed.[1] The truth is that the activity of the company was more largely political,

[1] McCulloch, *Commercial Dictionary*, *sub verbis* East India Company.

instead of being almost wholly commercial. Alliances with native potentates or rival claimants to Indian thrones were paid for by grants of taxes or customs (which the company always called its revenue, as distinguished from its profits derived from trade) and territorial rights; and these were so closely connected with the administration of the courts that they also passed under the control of the company. The field of peaceful acquisition of political powers was left between 1740 and 1750 for the greater field of war and military conquest.

"A new scene is now to open in the history of the East India Company. Before this period they had maintained the character of mere traders, and, by humility and submission, endeavored to preserve a footing in that distant country, under the protection or oppression of the native powers. We shall now behold them entering the lists of war, and mixing with eagerness in the contests of the princes." [1]

The servants of the company engaged in private trade at the expense of their master; the internal trade of India had been, theoretically, left largely to the natives, the company concerning itself rather with the import and export trade; the officers and servants now acquired enormous private fortunes from the internal or inland trade and were given great advantages over the native traders by exemptions from customs, duties and taxes obtained by them nominally for the benefit of the company, but really for their own benefit. From the native rulers and rival claimants they exacted immense bribes (commonly called presents) for affording them the aid of the company's military and commercial power. The treatment of the natives by the English was oppressive and tyrannical and occasioned loud and frequent complaints in England. It became constantly clearer that the mission of the East India Company written between

[1] Mill, *History of British India*, vol. iii., p. 60.

the lines of its commercial charters was to build up in India a political dependency of England; the time must have come when such relations could not longer be sustained through the medium of a corporation designed primarily for the field of commerce.

The Crown and Parliament began to assert more vigorously the doctrine that political and territorial rights acquired by Englishmen were the property of the state and not of the company. The double government of Clive did not conceal the fact that the activity of the company in India was a political and military conquest. The English nation became conscious that the sovereign functions and powers delegated by it to the East India Company, if the time was not ripe for their reabsorption into the English state, ought at least to be regulated and controlled by the English government—and more truly so because their exercise had been perverted and prostituted to the enrichment of tyrannical and oppressive subjects. But it was no easy matter for the English government, in the second half of the eighteenth century, to assume effective control over the East India Company, so powerful and ubiquitous was its influence in Parliament and among the controlling classes of English society. The liquidation of the great expense incurred by the government in assisting the company in its military enterprises in the middle of the century demanded attention so urgently that a committee was appointed by the House of Commons in 1767 to investigate the matter; as the result, the company agreed to pay £400,000 each year for two years, and two years later renewed the agreement for five years. In 1773, however, such were the straits to which the company had been reduced both by the maintenance of its immense political establishment in India and by the peculations and private trade of its officers and servants, that instead of its making the stipulated payments, it had to secure from the government a loan of

£1,400,000, and submit to a reduction of dividends to six per cent. until it should be repaid; as an apparently necessary improvement of its administrative machinery in India, the presidencies of Madras and Bombay were subordinated to that of Bengal and Warren Hastings appointed Governor-General, while the mayor's court at Calcutta was replaced by one consisting of a chief justice and three associates to be appointed by the crown. Ten years later, when the company had to apply to the government for another loan of £900,000, the ministry of Fox and North proposed the replacement of the Court of Directors and Court of Proprietors of the company by a body of seven commissioners; but their proposal failed of acceptance and the ministry fell from power largely because it was considered, whether justly or not, that the vesting of the appointment of the commissioners in Parliament (as was proposed) would unduly exalt the ministry above the crown.

The bill of the Pitt ministry, which became law in 1784, was not so radical in the reforms for which it provided. While the constitution of the East India Company was left nominally intact, a Board of Control consisting of six members of the Privy Council was to be appointed by the crown; the chancellor of the exchequer and one of the principal secretaries of state were always to be two of the six members, and in their absence the senior of the others should preside under the title of the President of the Board of Control. The duty of the Board was "from time to time, to check, superintend and control, all acts, operations and concerns, which in any wise relate to the civil or military government, or revenues, of the territories and possessions of the . . . United Company in the East Indies." The Court of Directors were to appoint a Secret Committee of not more than three members to transmit secret orders of the Board of Control without the knowledge of the other directors. Any act of the

Court of Directors that had been approved by the Board of Control might be in no way affected by the Court of Proprietors. The servants of the company, on their return from India, were required to present an inventory of the fortunes that they had brought with them. A new legal tribunal to sit in England was created "for the prosecuting and bringing to speedy and condign punishment British subjects guilty of extortion, and other misdemeanors, while holding offices in the service of the king or company in India." [1]

The passage of the Pitt bill was the beginning of the end. The history of the East India Company during the remainder of the period of its existence was a succession of changes by which the great institution was deprived of the sovereign functions and powers, one after another, that had formerly been delegated to it. When the charter rights of the company were confirmed in 1813, it was provided that after April 10, 1814, the trade between the Cape of Good Hope and the Straits of Magellan, except the tea trade and all trade in China, should be open to all British subjects, though with many restrictions such as the exclusive use in it of the company's vessels; moreover, the exclusive privileges of the company should terminate on three years' notice after April 10, 1831, and on the payment to it of the amount of government loan held by it,—though the company might continue to engage in the trade on an equal basis with other traders. [2] By act of 1823 the trade was made free, except the trade in tea and the other trade with China. [3] The act of 1833 provided that after April 22, 1834, the company should close its commercial business and dispose of all its property

---

[1] 24 George III., cap. 25, " An Act for the better Regulation and Management of the Affairs of the East India Company and of the British Possessions in India ; and for Establishing a Court of Judicature for the more speedy and effectual Trial of Persons accused of Offences committed in the East Indies."   [2] 53 George III., cap. 155.   [3] 4 George IV., cap. 80.

that should not be necessary for the government of India; that the British territories in India should remain under the government of the company until April 30, 1854; that such debts of the company as should not be discharged from the proceeds of the sale of its property should be assumed by the English government; that annual dividends of ten and one half per cent. on the capital stock of the company should be paid by the English government, with the privilege of redemption at the rate of £200 for each £100 of stock after April, 1874, on one year's notice; that the company should pay to the government £2,000,000 to be made the basis of a sinking fund for the payment and redemption of the dividends; that commissioners for the affairs of India should be appointed by the king,

"to superintend, direct and control all acts, operations and concerns of the . . . company; that the superintendence, direction and control of the whole civil and military government of all the . . . territories and revenues in India . . . be vested in a Governor General and Councillors, to be styled ' The Governor General of India in Council,' "

the council to consist of three servants of the company appointed by the Court of Directors and one member (not a servant) appointed by the Court of Directors with the approval of the king, and all vacancies to be filled by the Court of Directors with the approval of the king.[1] By the act of 1858 the territories under the government of the East India Company and all its other property except its capital stock and future dividends were vested in the crown, together with all the governmental powers that had previously been exercised by it. The company and the Court of Directors and Court of Proprietors were to be replaced in the government of India by a Secretary

[1] 3 and 4 William IV., cap. 85.

of State for India assisted by a "Council of India," the Board of Control being abolished. The Council of India was to consist of fifteen members, eight appointed by the crown and seven by the company, who were not to sit in Parliament, were to serve during good behavior[1] but were removable on address by both Houses of Parliament; a majority of it were to have served ten years in India and not to have left India more than ten years previously; vacancies in the seats of the eight crown members were to be filled by the crown, in the seven other seats, by the Council itself. "The Council shall, under the direction of the Secretary of State . . . conduct the business transacted in the United Kingdom in relation to the government of India." The Secretary of State should preside over it, have authority to appoint and remove a vice-president for it and should divide it into [ten] committees. He might, moreover, send secret orders to India, when occasion required, without consulting the Council. Each year he was required to lay before Parliament an account of receipts and expenditures, indebtedness and other matters relating to India.[2] When the English government had finally been substituted for "John Company" in the administration of India, it retained almost intact the political structure that had been erected by the company. A proclamation by Queen Victoria announced the replacement of the company by the English government.[3] The company, however, was not immediately dissolved, but remained in existence for the purpose of receiving payment of its capital stock and dividends. By a later act of Parliament[4] it was provided that dividends should cease from April 30, 1874, and the company was finally dissolved June 1, 1874. Queen

---

[1] A term of service of ten years has since been substituted for the life service.

[2] "An Act for the better Government of India," 21 and 22 Victoria, cap. 106. [3] *State Papers*, vol. lix., p. 505. [4] 36 and 37 Victoria, cap. 17.

Victoria became Empress of India in 1877 by virtue of an act of Parliament of the preceding year.[1]

The most important of the other joint-stock companies, except such as are included in the class of colonial companies,[2] were the African Company, the Hudson's Bay Company and the South Sea Company.[3] Each of them had an extremely interesting history, but in general they differed only in unimportant particulars from the East India Company. A brief consideration of some of their features may be of advantage.

Some latitude is used in speaking of *the* African Company, for there were four successive companies to which the name was applied, each more distinct from the other in form and composition than the successive East India Companies from one another; the several African Companies superseded their predecessors somewhat arbitrarily; they did not represent a continuous development as did the East India Companies, though it is nevertheless true that they fairly represented the several stages in the same course of development. The Portuguese had been the predecessors of the English in the trade to the west coast of Africa. As early as 1536 a voyage of discovery and trade was made by Englishmen to south Barbary. In 1588 Elizabeth granted a charter for ten years to merchants of Exeter and London for an exclusive trade to

[1] 39 and 40 Victoria, cap. 10.   [2] *Infra*, Chapter VI.

[3] This group of companies, including the East India Company, call to mind the Bank of England, or, more technically, " The Governor and Company of the Bank of England," incorporated in 1694. Important though it was and still is, it is not considered here because it differed vitally from the others in one respect,—it had to do rather with the development of the infra-national relations of the English people than with their extra-national expansion. It was the earliest prominent institution in which the structure of the great commercial and colonial companies was utilized in the relations of Englishmen to one another instead of to foreigners. If such a view of it is correct, it belongs properly to the class of organizations that have been distinctively called Modern Corporations. See p. 12, *supra*.

the territories tributary to the rivers Senegal and Gambia because "the adventuring of a new trade cannot be a matter of small charge and hazard to the adventurers in the beginning." [1] In 1618 Robert Rich and other merchants of London were granted a charter by James I. to trade to the west coast of Africa on a joint stock, but the company suffered so much interference from interlopers that it was soon dissolved. Thirteen years later (in 1631) a similar company, organized by Sir Richard Young and others, and chartered by James I. for thirty-one years to enjoy exclusively the trade from Cape Blanco to the Cape of Good Hope, [2] laid a more substantial basis for future commerce by erecting forts, factories (agencies) and warehouses in the territory. It seems to have accomplished very little else, however, for in 1651 a new company was chartered, not so much to engage in the trade as to control it by licensing others to engage in it, charging therefor ten per cent. of the cargoes or three pounds per ton on the ships in which they were carried. A third company (if the " discovery " company be omitted) was chartered by Charles II. in 1662 with the Duke of York at its head and containing "many others of rank and distinction," chiefly for the purpose of transporting negro slaves to the English West Indies, which it was obligated to do at the rate of three thousand per annum. The fourth and last African Company, appropriately called the Royal African Company, followed in 1672, and contained among its subscribers of stock the king himself, his brother, the Duke of York, and many others of the nobility. The company paid its predecessor for its three forts and conducted considerable trade until the Revolution of 1688, when the trade became virtually open by reason of the hostility of Parliament to exclusive trading privileges; in 1698, however, it was

[1] Macpherson, *Annals of Commerce*, vol. ii., p. 189.
[2] Rymer, *Fœdera*, vol. xix., p. 370.

provided by statute[1] that non-corporate traders should
pay to the company a charge of ten per cent. of their
exports, probably in return for the use of its forts, factories and warehouses. In the early part of the eighteenth century it was continually under discussion in
Parliament and by the pamphleteers outside whether the
trade of the African Company as well as of the East India
Company and others should not be opened freely to all
merchants; in 1713 a resolution was passed by the House
of Commons that the African trade ought to be free and
open on payment by the traders of duties for the support of the forts and settlements. From 1730 to 1746
the company was reduced to such financial straits that
Parliament granted it annually £10,000 (except in 1744,
when the grant was £20,000) for the support of its forts
and factories, while the trade was made free to all. In
1750 a unique settlement of the trade was made by Parliament. It was to be free and open to all English subjects. The Royal African Company was to be abolished
as soon as its debts should be paid, and all merchants
trading between Cape Blanco and the Cape of Good Hope
were to be incorporated as the "Company of Merchants
Trading to Africa," and to be made owners of all the
forts, factories, settlements, coasts, islands, rivers and
other property then claimed by the existing company.
The new company should have no power to trade in its
corporate capacity, to have a joint or transferable stock
or to borrow money. All traders were to be admitted on
payment of forty shillings and were to enjoy the use of all
forts and other property for the storage of goods and
protection of persons. The government was to be reposed in a committee of nine members elected annually,
three each by the traders admitted to membership at
London, Bristol and Liverpool; members of the committee and officers and servants of the company were to

[1] 9 and 10 William and Mary, cap. 26.

be removable for misbehavior by the Board of Trade and Plantations. The committee should pay the salaries of employees and other expenses and retain the balance of the company's revenue for their own compensation, making annual reports to Parliament of all receipts and expenditures.[1] Two years later the old company was paid for its property and the new company was empowered to train soldiers at its forts, to visit offences with punishments not extending to life or limb, and to maintain courts of judicature for mercantile and maritime cases.[2] Early in the reign of George III. the fort of Senegal, with its dependencies, was vested in the crown,[3] and later re-vested in the company.[4] In the latter part of the century annual grants were made to the company for the support of its forts and other establishments; in 1795, £20,000 was allowed to it; as late as 1800, £20,000 was granted "for the forts on the coast of Africa." Finally, in 1821, it was enacted by Parliament that after the third of July of that year the company should cease and determine and should be divested of all the forts, castles, buildings, possessions and rights previously owned or acquired. All the forts between 20° north latitude and 20° south latitude were made dependent on the colony of Sierra Leone.[5]

Of the Hudson's Bay Companies, the "Governor and Company of Adventurers of England Trading into Hudson's Bay," less is to be said. As Prince Rupert and seventeen others, "persons of quality and distinction," had "at their own great cost, undertaken an expedition for Hudson's Bay, in order for the discovery of a new passage into the South Sea and for the finding of some trade for furs [etc.]," Charles II. granted to them in 1670 a charter of incorporation conceding to them the exclusive

---

[1] Statute 23 George II., cap. 31.   [2] Statute 5 George III., cap. 44.
[3] Statute 25 George II., cap. 40.   [4] Statute 23 George III., cap. 65.
[5] 1 and 2 George IV., cap. 28.

commerce of all the bodies and streams of water within
Hudson Strait, with all the land tributary to them and
not already possessed by other English subjects or those
of any other Christian prince or state.   The company, as
formally organized, might fall into the class of regulated-
exclusive companies, but it was always virtually a joint-
stock company.   A governor and "committee" of seven
members (directors) were to be elected annually by the
proprietors (stockholders); a deputy governor was also to
be elected from among the committee.   The governor
and any three committeemen

" shall have the direction of the voyages, and the provision of
the merchandise and shipping, and of the sales of the returns,
as likewise of all other business of the company; and they shall
take the usual oath of fidelity, as shall also all persons admitted to trade as a freeman of the company."

They were given power, of course, to make by-laws for
the government of their forts, plantations and for the
regulation of their factors and other servants and to impose fines for their violation; to send out ships of war
and erect forts and towns, to make peace and war with
princes or peoples not Christians, to make reprisals on
others who should interrupt them in the pursuit of their
trade or otherwise wrong them, and to seize and send to
England for trial all English subjects who should sail into
Hudson's Bay without their license.   It was a somewhat
unusual provision that their land should be reckoned and
reputed as one of the plantations or colonies of England
in America and " be called 'Rupert's Land.' " [1]   Prince

---

[1] The original charter is printed as Appendix II. of the Report of the
Select Committee of the House of Commons " to consider the state of those
British Possessions in North America which are under the Administration
of the Hudson's Bay Company, or over which they possess a license to
trade."—*Reports from Committees*, 1857, Session 2, vol. ii.   The charter is
found on pages 408–414.

Rupert was the first governor of the company. In 1690 it obtained from Parliament a confirmation of its charter, but for the limited period of eight years. In 1821 it was given, in conjunction with certain private fur-traders, a license for an exclusive trade during twenty-one years in what was called the Indian Territory of the British Possessions in North America; it soon secured an assignment of the interests of the private merchants and accordingly enjoyed the trade exclusively. The additional grant was renewed for a second term of twenty-one years in 1839; in 1848 Vancouver's Island was also added to the company's domain, but with the reservation that bodies of English colonists should be permitted to make settlements in it. In 1857 the affairs of the company were fully investigated by a Special Committee of the House of Commons, chiefly at the suggestion of the Canadian government.[1] But it was not until 1868 that an act was passed by Parliament permitting the crown to accept a surrender of the company's grant of privileges on terms to be agreed on.[2] By 1870 the negotiations were completed: the company was still to trade in its corporate capacity, to be paid £300,000 by the Canadian government for its franchise, to retain the ownership of all its posts and stations with a block of land at each of them, and to have a twentieth section of the "fertile belt"; titles to lands previously conveyed by the company were confirmed.[3]

The South Sea Company, the "Governor and Company of Merchants of Great Britain Trading to the South Seas and other parts of America, and for Encouraging the Fishery," was peculiar in several respects. It was the first of the great stock companies for foreign trade (except colonial companies) that had not had a previous

---

[1] *Supra*, p. 146, note.

[2] Rupert's Land Act, 31 and 32 Victoria, cap. 105.

[3] Winsor's *Narrative and Critical History of America*, vol. viii., chapter i., " Hudson Bay Company," by George E. Ellis; see particularly page 64.

development in the form of a regulated or regulated-exclusive company; it was a complete joint-stock company from the time of its original incorporation in 1711. Certain debts that had accumulated during the European war, amounting to £9,471,325, were unpaid; their holders were incorporated as the South Sea Company by the crown in accordance with an act of Parliament,[1] their debt made to bear interest at the rate of six per cent. (£568,279. 10s. annually) and made redeemable on one year's notice after Christmas, 1716; for the payment of the interest (the surplus to be applied on the principal) certain duties, originally imposed temporarily, were made permanent until the debt should be repaid. Its government was vested in a governor and court of directors, but none of them during their terms of service might occupy a corresponding office in the Bank of England or East India Company. Their exclusive territory extended on the eastern side of South America from the Orinoco River on the north to Terra del Fuego on the south, and on the west side of the continent from Terra del Fuego to the "northernmost part of America," including all the territory within the limits described which should be reputed to belong to the crown of Spain, or which should be afterwards discovered within the limits or not more than three hundred leagues distant from the west side of the continent; the exclusive trade was not to extend to the territories of Holland, or to Brazil or other territories of Portugal; to the Portuguese territories all English subjects might trade freely. Trade, moreover, was not to be carried on by the company within the limits of the East India Company's grant; even sailing more than three hundred leagues west of the continent should be punished by forfeiture of goods, one third to the crown and two thirds to the East India Company. All the company's trading to the South Sea (Pacific Ocean)

[1] 9 Anne, cap. 21.

should be by way of the Straits of Magellan or Terra del Fuego and by no other route. One per cent. of their capital stock might be employed in the fisheries, but not to the exclusion of other subjects. The penalty imposed on interlopers was unusually severe—forfeiture of ships and merchandise and double their value, one fourth to the crown, one fourth to the informer and one half to the company. As usually, the power was given to establish courts of judicature in their forts, factories and settlements, to determine mercantile and maritime causes subject to an appeal to the queen in council and to raise and maintain a military force. In the following year the commercial privileges of the company were made perpetual and not subject to termination by the repayment of its public debt.[1] By the treaty of 1713 with Spain, the so-called "assients contract" for the transportation of negro slaves to the Spanish colonies, at the rate of 4800 annually for thirty years, was granted to England "or to the company of [English] subjects appointed for the purpose, as well the subjects of Spain as all others being excluded"; the privilege of sending annually one ship of five hundred tons burden to the Spanish West Indies, laden with European goods, was also granted.[2] The contract had until that time been held by a French company (and even earlier by the Portuguese), but by the Treaty of Ghent its transfer to English subjects was agreed to. The queen immediately assigned the contract to the South Sea Company. In the first year of the reign of George I. the company's capital (the amount of public debt held by it) was increased to £10,000,000, on which, two years later, the interest was reduced from six to five per cent.; it was later increased to £33,000,000 at

[1] Statute 10 Anne, cap. 30.
[2] See article 12 of Treaty of 1713 in Macpherson's *Annals of Commerce*, vol. iii., pp. 32, 33. See also Postlethwayt's *Dictionary of Trade and Commerce, sub verbis* " Assients Contract."

five per cent. (reduced to four per cent. after 1727). The effort to incorporate the entire funded national debt into its capital resulted in the disastrous "South Sea Bubble" of 1720. The foreign commerce of the company was of minor importance; the assients contract was rather a burden than a source of profit, and the sending of the annual ship was hedged about with so many conditions and restrictions that it proved a disappointment; the fishery voyages, to the slight extent that they were engaged in, brought only losses to the company. In 1750,[1] when, by the Treaty of Madrid, England released to Spain the "assients of negroes and annual ship," on consideration of the payment of £100,000, the commerce of the company practically ceased; the consideration paid by Spain was passed over to the company. The trade to no part of its exclusive territory was legally opened to English subjects, however, until 1807,[2] though an extensive commerce was carried on clandestinely. In 1815 it was deprived of the remainder of its exclusive privileges, though it was still permitted to trade on an equality with others; as compensation it was provided that the

[1] There is some confusion in the dates of the assients contract. Macpherson assumes (*Annals of Commerce*) that it was to run for forty years, but that statement lacks proof. The following may be an adequate explanation: By its terms the contract was to be in force for thirty years from 1713, but it was interrupted by the outbreak of war in 1739, leaving four years of its term. By the treaty of Aix-la-Chapelle it was provided that the contract should be revived for the remaining four years, but that, "at a proper time and place," negotiations should be entered into to determine what equivalent Spain should render for a cancellation of it. Two years later it was agreed by the Treaty of Madrid that Spain should pay £100,000; the contract was accordingly terminated at that time.

[2] Statute 47 George III., cap. 23: "An act for repealing so much of an act made in the ninth year of the reign of Her late Majesty Queen Anne as vests in the South Sea Company . . . the sole and exclusive privilege of carrying on Trade and Traffic to and from any part whatsoever of South America, or in the South Seas, which now are or may . . . hereafter be in the Possession of his Majesty. . . ."

proceeds from certain customs and tonnage duties imposed on the trade from what had previously been the exclusive territory of the company, and known as "the South Sea duties," should be put into a guarantee fund until it amounted to £610,464, and should then be paid over to the company, while in the meantime the government should guarantee an annual dividend of one half of one per cent. on the company's trading stock.[1]

The most important feature of the development of the East India Company was its contribution to the extra-national expansion of England. Remarkable as the extreme powers given to the company may appear, it is difficult to understand how they could have been less under the circumstances by which its activity was conditioned. The English state was not sufficiently developed to provide the conditions under which the trade in India might be carried on; it had in consequence to give the traders themselves the power to modify their conditions or create new ones. If even in times of peace among European nations, amicable relations could not be maintained between their bodies of traders, how could security of property and trade be provided among peoples with whom the Europeans enjoyed no settled international relations? The East India Company is the best illustration of the part performed by a corporation in national expansion, because its development was so evenly graduated. Great political powers were bestowed on it originally for the purpose of promoting the economic welfare of the English people and of swelling the revenues of the crown. It can hardly be said that any other purpose was entertained at the end of the sixteenth century. The building up of a political power in India by the company was only indirectly involved at first. The tendency to the increased restriction of corporate activity to the work of government observed in other kinds of corporations

[1] Statute 55 George III., cap. 57.

manifested itself in the history of the East India Company in the gradual encroachment on the field of the political government in India, while its commerce either failed to increase or fell into the hands of officers and servants. The accumulation of political powers, at first a secondary aim, became eventually a primary aim, while the commerce for the protection of which it had originally been sought was subordinated to it in importance. So true was it and so clearly did the English government see the truth that for the last twenty years of the corporation's existence its commercial functions had been taken from it and it had been left as the government of India. The inevitable expansion of nationality enabled the English state to extend itself over the political field occupied by the corporation, first indirectly through an intermediate supervisory body and then directly by supplanting it. From being the commercial territory of the corporation, India became a province of England. Even the forms of the corporate political machinery were preserved; the only essential difference was that the national hand replaced the corporate hand at the lever.

Without entering into a discussion of the theoretical justice of the monopoly granted to the East India Company, or of the extent to which it was the result of an artificial element in the cupidity either of the sovereign or the East India traders, it is significant that it existed and continued to exist even in the face of vigorous and aggressive opposition. Until the end of the eighteenth century it was hardly a question whether individual traders might engage in the trade; the real question was whether the company should be a regulated company under which the activity of individual and associated traders should be correlated, or a joint-stock company under which their activity should be unified. It must be remembered that at the beginning the East India Company was (with some qualifications) "regulated" and that it became a purely joint-stock company only after a century's development. The change was so slow and yet so persistently in the same direction that it cannot be safely ascribed entirely to arbitrary personal influences. The corporations of the Middle Ages did not express the idea of combined but of correlated activity, not of association of effort but of harmony of individual effort. The former in each case is the idea expressed by the state in action; the latter, the result of the activity of the state on the subject. It was the growth of the political side of the East India Company that gradually caused the elimination of the regulated feature and made its restoration impossible until the English government itself stepped into the place formerly occupied by the company. The question might possibly be approached from the opposite direction. The individual trader was confessedly unable to engage in the trade, unless he might stealthily profit by the system of protection set up at great labor and expense by the company to whose support he did not contribute. The single vessel could not serve as the unit of transportation; the trade had to be carried on by fleets of merchant vessels—vessels larger than had ever before been known in England—accompanied by the necessary war vessels; moreover, the voyages were long and the risk great. The larger the unit of activity, whether imposed by physical conditions or by others, the greater the need of association. It was not correlation of activity that traders needed; it was association of activity. From both points of view, then, from that of the corporate group exercising political power and from that of the individual acting under the limitations of his environment, the evolution of a joint-stock company with a monopoly of trade from a regulated company open to all who wished to be admitted was quite in harmony with the conditions under which the East India Company flourished. It might be contended that the monopoly was maintained longer than accorded with necessity or justice. Corporations, like all forms of social organization, acquire a momentum; if more force is required to set them in motion, more force is also required to stop them. In the presence of the traditional conservatism of English society, it is perhaps more remarkable that the East India Company was subjected to governmental control so early than that its monopoly was maintained so long.

Likewise the African Company and Hudson's Bay Company, though they did not positively lay a foundation for colonial governments, at least accumulated a body of political and territorial powers that were afterwards incorporated in colonial governments independently established. In preventing the subjects of other nations from gaining a foothold in their territories they performed a service for the mother country that may, with little exaggeration of its importance, serve as a justification for the extravagantly generous treatment that they enjoyed. The South Sea Company, however, performed no such service; substantially the only parts of their commercial powers that they exercised were those secured to them under the treaties with Spain, which did not involve the exploitation of new and unsettled territory; the powers that they did not use, though granted to them, might have resulted in a later extension of English dominion.

The African, Hudson's Bay and South Sea Companies were all representative of what has already been described as a secondary stage in the development of corporations. The East India Company filled a nearly legitimate field; the organization seemed to be demanded by the conditions under which the company had to act. But the three other companies do not appear so clearly to have grown out of the conditions of their activity; they were rather imposed on their fields of commerce than evolved from contact with their conditions. The circumstances

of the foreign trade on the west coast of Africa and in the
territory tributary to Hudson's Bay did not contain so
much of the political element as to fully justify the presence of a concentrated organization like that of the East
India Company. The career of the African Company
clearly showed that it was not in harmony with its environment, and its supervision by a modified regulated
company was hardly avoidable. The South Sea Company was clearly anomalous, from the standpoint of its
commercial life. In a less formal classification it is doubt-
ful whether it ought not to be classed rather with the
Bank of England than with the East India Company. It
was primarily a body of holders of the national debt and
the grant of its commercial privileges was in the nature of
a premium on the debt held by it. Its character as a
trading company was always insignificant when compared with the other companies or with itself as a lender
of funds to the state. Though none of the great companies used the powers granted to them to their limit,
the South Sea Company fell much farther short of the
limit than any of the others. The corporate organization was hardly called for; the truth seems to be that
the success of other great commercial companies had
given a fictitious value to corporate privileges and had
made it possible to "strengthen the credit" of the state
by offering to its creditors the imposing structure of a
great corporation with exclusive control of a trade that
had outgrown the stage in which exclusiveness was either
appropriate or possible. The South Sea Company was
peculiar among the corporations of its class in having as a
large part of its commercial territory the dominions of
another Christian state; other things equal, that alone
would indicate an abnormal development of structure;
companies in such trade, where indeed they had existed
in it at all, had developed but little above the grade of
purely regulated companies.

The lands in which the joint-stock companies traded were not occupied by peoples recognized by the English or other western Europeans as being on the same level of civilization with them. The natives of India, and in a greater degree the negroes of Africa and the savage Indians of North and South America, were viewed by the Europeans as inferiors, to be subjected to control rather than to be dealt with. In general, no system of international relations existed between them and England; such political relations as were required had to be created by the English traders themselves. The facilities of commerce were wanting in the strange lands; their peoples had not engaged in international commerce, and even their internal trade had been rudimentary and unsystematic; such property as wharves and commercial settlements, which in commerce between European nations were provided by the state or by subjects of the state in which the commerce was carried on, was wanting and had to be supplied by the companies. Again the lands were far from England, and trading voyages to and from them were attended with the greatest risk of attack by pirates, shipwreck and destruction by savages; larger investments of capital were necessary, and the danger of losing it was greater. If the establishment of trade in Russia and Turkey by adventurers involved effort which, when expressed in property in the trade, tended to exclude others from it and to concentrate its management in the hands of a few, how much stronger must the twofold tendency have been in the trade of India, Africa and North and South America, which had to be absolutely created; the former trade had been known to exist in other hands or to be accessible; the latter did not exist and was not known to be possible until the trading companies demonstrated the truth by creating the commerce.

VI

COLONIAL COMPANIES

THE expansion of England and of other nations of western Europe after the middle of the sixteenth century was promoted not only by establishing commercial relations with peoples of settled foreign lands, but also even more effectually by the colonization of new lands, previously unsettled or peopled only by savages, which the several nations claimed by virtue of prior discovery. Colonization was merely one of the agencies through which the general movement sought expression. There was one important element in colonization, however, that was not present in the establishment of mere commercial relations with foreign peoples. Wherever an English colony was planted, there was a body of English subjects to be governed. The English trade with other nations of western Europe and even with Russia and the Levant involved most prominently the establishment of international relations, whether directly through the national governments or indirectly through the medium of commercial corporations; the trade with India and Africa was to involve rather the absorption of the governments of the foreign peoples; but the colonial trade involved an extension of the national government of England over bodies of its own subjects. The colonial commerce did not consist merely in exchanging English products for the goods produced by foreigners through their development of the natural resources of their land, but much more largely in the primary production of goods by direct development of natural resources; the purpose had to be accomplished by actually settling the land with English colonists. Moreover, the tracts of land colonized were manifestly part of the domain of England and not of foreigners. The presence of bodies of English subjects on English domain as an essential factor in colonization is suggested at the outset because it had great influence on the social structure through which the colonies were planted and fostered. The government of England, largely because of its actual impotence, did not plant the English colonies directly, at least not those that were afterwards a part of the United States, but made use of the corporate system for the purpose,—it aimed to secure the development of colonies, a public purpose, through the stimulation of private interest by grants of political and commercial privileges. The necessity of providing governments for bodies of English subjects on geographical areas of English domain, and concurrently of establishing and regulating their economic relations with one another and with the merchants of England, caused a resort to two classes of institutions, as the one purpose or the other was magnified in importance; the two classes of agencies were accordingly the colonial proprietary, whose rights and duties were based on those of the older English nobility, and the colonial corporations, derived from the institutions in which the powers of regulation over English trade and industry were reposed; in a single colony, Georgia, the corporation was formed on the model of the English charitable corporation of the eighteenth century. Neither class of institutions conformed strictly to their model, and as both were engaged side by side in the same work, each was affected by the other in form and development.

By a charter of James I. in 1606, the territory of "Virginia" between the parallels of 34° and 45° north latitude was divided for purposes of trade and colonization be-

tween two companies, the London Company and the
Plymouth Company, the former to plant a colony at any
place between the parallels of 34° and 41°, and the latter
at any place between those of 38° and 45°, neither, however, to make a plantation within one hundred miles of
one already made by the other.   The colony of the London Company was to be called the "First Colony" and
that of the Plymouth Company the "Second Colony."[1]
Each company was to consist of certain "knights, gentlemen, merchants and other adventurers" named in the
charter, together with such others as they should elect to
be joined with them.   Each colony should be governed
by a resident council of thirteen members "in all matters
and causes which shall arise, grow, or happen to or within
the same . . . according to such laws, ordinances and
instructions as shall be in that behalf " given by the king.
Moreover, the members of the council should be "ordained, made and removed . . . according as shall
be directed and comprised in the same instructions."
In addition to the resident councils there was to be a
"Council of Virginia" in England, consisting of thirteen[2]
members appointed by the king, for "the superior managing and direction, . . . of and for all matters that
shall or may concern the government, as well of the said
several colonies as of and for any other part or place,
within the . . . precincts of 34° and 45°."

The king was to grant land to any person recommended by the council of the colony on its petition.
Wherever a plantation should be made by either company
it should have all the land extending directly inland one

[1] In the strict language of the charters of 1606 and 1609 the companies
themselves appear to have been called the " First Colony" and " Second
Colony," but in some places the terms were applied to the settlements or
groups of settlements established by them ; no violence is done by the use
of the terms as in the text.

[2] It is said that fourteen members were actually appointed, and that the
number was later increased to twenty-five.

hundred miles from a coast-line fifty miles on each side of the plantation or settlement, and all the islands within one hundred miles of the coast and directly opposite the one hundred miles of coast-line. Each company might fortify its settlements in the discretion of its resident council, and resist or repel by military power, both on land and by sea, all who without its license should attempt to live in them or molest them in any way, and to seize all who should essay to traffic with them without having paid a duty of two and one half per cent. upon the goods "trafficked, bought or sold," if English subjects, or of five per cent. if foreigners; for twenty-one years such customs duties should be for the use of the companies, afterwards, of the king. They had license to take out English subjects as colonists, and all such persons and their children born in the colonies should "have all liberties, franchises, and immunities, within any of [the king's] other dominions, to all intents and purposes, as if they had been abiding and born" in them. They might also transport goods and munitions from England to their colonies without paying customs on them for a term of seven years, "for the better relief of the several colonies and plantations." The companies and their servants and colonists should not "rob or spoil" the subjects of other nations. They were permitted "to dig, mine and search for all manner of mines of gold, silver and copper . . . and to have and enjoy" them upon yielding to the king one fifth of the gold and silver and one fifteenth of the copper. "For the more ease of traffic and bargaining," they might establish and put into circulation among the colonists a coin "of such metal, and in such manner and form," as their councils should determine.[1]

By virtue of the powers granted by the first charter, a substantial beginning was made in the colonization of

[1] Poore, *Federal and State Constitutions*, vol. ii., pp. 1888–1893.

Virginia. In 1607 Jamestown was founded and governed by a council as contemplated by the provisions of the charter. But it must soon have become plain to the adventurers of the London Company that the organization of the two companies under the Council of Virginia, with its members, as well as those of the resident councils, appointed by the king, was lacking in the concentration of powers necessary to success. The intention of the king, in settling the terms of the charter, must have been to separate the political and commercial powers, reserving the former for himself and bestowing the latter on the companies. The royal purpose appears from the character of the seals provided for the councils of the companies; each should have the king's arms on one side and his image on the other; on one side of each of them should be the words, "Sigillum Regis Magnæ Britanniæ, Franciæ, et Hiberniæ"; on the other side of that of the "Council of Virginia," the words, "Pro Concilio suo Virginiæ"; of those of the resident councils the words, "Pro Concilio primæ (secundæ) Coloniæ Virginiæ." An amendatory charter was accordingly asked for and granted.

By the charter of 1609 the request of the London Company was recited

"that such councillors and other officers may be appointed amongst them, to manage and direct their affairs, as are willing and ready to adventure with them, as also whose dwellings are not so far remote from the City of London, but they may, at convenient times, be ready at hand to give their advice and assistance upon all occasions requisite."

The "Council of Virginia" had evidently been intended to represent rather the interests of the king than those of the company. It was accordingly remodelled to a council of about fifty members elected by the company annually from their own number, though the first members were named in the charter. The company should now be called the "Treasurer and Company of Adventurers and Planters of London for the First Colony of Virginia," and consist of all who should "adventure any sum . . . of money in or towards the . . . plantation of the . . . colony in Virginia and shall be admitted by the council and company, as adventurers of the . . . colony [and so] enrolled in the books or records"; the treasurer and any three of the council should have power to admit new members; any member might be discharged and disfranchised by a majority vote of the company in a general assembly. The treasurer should "give order for the warning of the council and summoning of the company" to their courts or meetings, and should appoint a deputy treasurer from the members of the council. The council should appoint all officers, and make all laws for the government of the colonies and the regulation of the voyages to and from it. The president and council in the colony, previously appointed by the king, were abolished. The treasurer and all other officers were to govern according to the laws enacted by the council; in the colony, in cases of necessity and lack of legislation by the council, the governor and his officers should exercise their own discretion. In the company's colonial courts justice should be administered as well "in cases capital and criminal, as civil, both marine and other; so always as the . . . statutes, ordinances and proceedings as near as conveniently may be, be agreeable to the laws, statutes, government and policy of . . . England." In cases of mutiny or rebellion martial law might be enforced.[1]

The territory of the company was to be limited to a coast-line two hundred miles north and an equal distance south of Cape Comfort, to extend "up into the land throughout from sea to sea, west and northwest," and to include all the islands in each ocean within one hundred

[1] Poore, vol. ii., pp. 1893-1902.

miles of the coast. Goods were still to be exported to
and imported from the colonies upon the payment of
merely nominal duties for seven years, and to be re-
exported from England without additional duties, if
within thirteen months of importation.

A third charter, granted by James I. in 1612, conceded
chiefly more particular powers for the government of the
company. The treasurer and company might hold a
court once a week or oftener, at their pleasure, "for the
better order and government of the said plantation, and
such things as shall concern the same"; any five members of the council, including the treasurer or his deputy,
with fifteen of the "generality" of the company, should
constitute a sufficient court for the disposition of all
"casual and particular occurrences and accidental matters,
of less consequence and weight . . . concerning the
said plantation"; for

"matters and affairs of greater weight and importance, and
such as shall . . . concern the weal public and general
good of the said company and plantation, as namely, the manner of government . . . to be used, the ordering and
disposing of the lands and possessions, and the settling and
establishing of a trade there, or such like,"

four "great and general courts" should be held each year.
In the quarterly courts members of the council and officers
should be chosen, laws and ordinances should be passed,
new members should be admitted and members who refused to "adventure" in furtherance of the plantation
should be expelled. The territory of the company was
made to include all islands within three hundred leagues
of its coast-line.[1] Incidentally, "for the more effectual
advancing of the said plantation," the company was
empowered to "set forth, erect and publish" lotteries.[2]

[1] This provision was important chiefly because it brought the Bermudas,
or Somers Islands, within the company's limit.

[2] Poore, vol. ii., pp. 1902–1908.

In its relations to the crown the company had established its substantial independence. The importance of
its history after its third charter was granted lies in its
political relations to the colonists, but before considering
them it will be best to consider the economic relations
that had been developed. By the "Articles, Instructions
and Orders" composed by James I. it was provided that
for five years the companies (the London and Plymouth
or "first" and "second" colonies) should

"trade together in one stock, or in two or three stocks at
most, and should bring all the fruits of their labors there, with
all their goods and commodities from England or elsewhere,
into several magazines or storehouses, for that purpose to be
erected [and] there should be annually chosen by the [resi-
dent] President and Council of each colony . . . one
person of their colony, to be Treasurer or Cape-Merchant of
the same, to take charge of, and to manage, all goods and
wares, brought into or delivered out of, the said magazines";

two clerks should also be appointed, one to enter all the
goods coming into the magazine and the other to enter
all going out of it.

"Every person of each of the colonies should be furnished
with necessaries out of the said magazines for the space of five
years, by the appointment, direction and order of the President and Council of their respective colonies, or of the Cape-
Merchant and two clerks, or the major part of them."

Similarly, in England, each company should appoint subordinate bodies of at least three members each, to remain
in London and Plymouth respectively, and to

"take care and charge of the trade, and an account of all the
goods, wares and merchandise that should be sent from England to their respective colonies and brought from the colonies
into England, and of all other things relating to the affairs
and profits of their several companies." [1]

[1] Quoted in Stith, *History of Virginia.*

After the second charter was granted in 1609, the plan contemplated in 1606 was modified somewhat. For seven years a joint stock was to be maintained of which each share should be £12 12s. The investors were of two classes, the adventurers, who paid their subscriptions in money, and the planters, who went to the colonies and paid no money. One share was given to each adult and child over ten years of age who should go to Virginia; "everie extraordinarie man," such as a knight, gentleman or physician, should be given additional shares, in the discretion of the company. At the end of the term of seven years all the profits as well as the land should be distributed among the shareholders according to their holdings.[1] In 1619 it appeared that land had been distributed among many of the colonists in severalty, and that a tract had been appropriated by the company in its corporate capacity. A fund subscribed in England for the founding of a college in Virginia in which "infidels' children" might be educated was administered by the company; a tract of ten thousand acres at Henrico was granted in aid of the project and tenants placed on it by the company to cultivate it "on halves," the profits to be applied in furtherance of the college project. Some lands were leased by the company to tenants who should pay a definite rent in produce. All persons who should settle in Virginia at their own expense should have a grant of fifty acres and fifty acres in addition for each person taken with them. Boys and girls were sent out to serve an apprenticeship of seven years in the colony; at the end of the apprenticeship they were each to have from the company a year's provision of grain and other supplies, a cow, forty shillings "for apparel," weapons, household utensils and agricultural implements. "Maids" were sent at the company's expense to become wives of the planters, who should reimburse the company for the

[1] *Nova Britannia*, Force's Tracts, vol. i.

expense incurred. A body of sixteen committees (directors), presided over by the deputy governor and known as the court of committees, was "to perform the orders of courts, for setting out ships and buying provisions for Virginia," and to manage the sale of goods brought to England in return. After the termination of the joint stock subsisting in 1619 the trade was to be free and open to all British subjects, on payment of the small duties prescribed by the charters. In future joint stocks for magazines the company should "bear part as an adventurer; they shall ratably partake like profit, and undergo like loss, with other adventurers."[1] Only two features of the industrial development of the colony of Virginia under the London Company seem to be worthy of mention, but both of them serve to differentiate the company from others. (1) The economic as distinguished from the political affairs of the company passed under the control of a separate administrative body, the court of committees; that did not happen in any other of the great corporations (except colonial companies) because their work of government was not so much more important than their commerce. (2) The membership of the London Company expanded to include not only the purely investing element in England, but also the producing element in the colony, apparently for two reasons: (a) The colonists were British subjects and consequently in closer sympathy with the English investors, while the producers with whom other companies dealt were foreigners and many of them on a lower social level, and (b) the company did not trade with the colonists so much as it shared with them in production; its profits depended not

[1] *Virginia Colonial Records, London Company*, vols. i. and ii. "Orders and Constitutions collected out of his Majesty's Letters Patents, and partly ordained upon mature deliberation, by the Treasurer, Council and Company of Virginia, for the better governing of the Actions and Affairs of the said company here in England residing" (1619 and 1620).—Force's Tracts, vol. iii., No. 6.

on buying and selling what the colonists produced, but
in enabling them to produce and then sharing the resulting gains; there was consequently an identity of interest
between the producer and investor that did not exist in
the purely commercial companies.   In the nature of
things the shareholders in the colonies could not participate in the deliberations of the company in England,
though by the company's charter they had the right to
do it.   The expansion of membership laid a basis for de-
manding participation in the deliberations of the governor
and council resident in Virginia.

The economic relations of the company and colonists
could have hardly failed to be reflected in the wider and
inclusive political relations, but they are hardly sufficient
to account for the political institutions that were created
by the company in Virginia.   It can hardly be doubted
that an enlightened desire on the part of the company to
make an application of the political theories cherished by
its members united with the demands of economic conditions prevailing in Virginia to influence them in the
concession of modified popular government.   More or
less harshness characterized the contact of the colonists
with the company's governor in Virginia, perhaps not so
much because they were not represented in his government as because they were actually ill-governed.   The
appointment of a resident council for him, however,
seemed to afford no relief.   Samuel Argall, sent out by
the company as governor in 1617, was so tyrannical in
his government that he had to be recalled on account of
the opposition aroused in the colonists.   His successor,
George Yeardly, came in 1619 with "commissions and
instructions from the company for the better establishing
of a commonwealth," by virtue of which it was ordered
that an annual assembly should be held in the colony, to
be attended by the governor and his council and two burgesses elected from each plantation by its inhabitants; in

such an assembly such laws should be made as to the entire body should seem best for the common good of the colony. The first assembly—the first representative legislature in America—was held in 1619 in the church at Jamestown, and was attended by Governor Yeardly and his council, and twenty-two burgesses representing eleven localities; all took part in the proceedings in the same room.

In 1621 the company at a general court took more formal action by an "Ordinance and Constitution" for the government of Virginia.

"The intent is ' by the divine assistance to settle such a form of government as may be to the greatest benefit and comfort of the people, and whereby all injustice, grievances and oppression may be prevented and kept off as much as possible from the said colony.' The governor is to have a council to assist him in the administration. He and the council, together with the burgesses chosen, two from each town, hundred and plantation, by the inhabitants, are to constitute a general assembly, who are to meet yearly, and decide all matters coming before them by the greatest number of voices; but the governor is to have a negative voice. No law of the assembly is to be or continue in force unless it is ratified by a general court, and returned to them under the company's seal. But when the government of the colony is once ' well framed and settled accordingly . . . no orders of court afterwards shall bind the said colony unless they be ratified in like manner in the general assemblies.' " [1]

[1] Cooke's *History of Virginia*, p. 119. A copy of "An Ordinance and Constitution of the Treasurer, Council, and Company in England, for a Council of State and General Assembly," dated July 24, 1621, is added to Stith's *History of Virginia* as Appendix IV. It is peculiar that the assembly was at first regarded as merely an additional council. It was provided that there should be two "supreme councils," one the " council of state," to assist the governor, and the other the " general assembly," consisting of the council of state and two burgesses from each " town, hundred and plantation " in annual meeting.

Such grants of free and popular government, conceded by a company under the control of members of the liberal party in England, could not be suffered by a Stuart; James, therefore, consistently secured the dissolution of the corporation by proceedings in *quo warranto* in 1624. He thereupon began the formulation under his own hand of a new code of laws for Virginia, but died before his work could be completed. Though Virginia became a royal colony Charles I. was in too much trouble with his subjects in England to interfere with the rights of self-government formerly conceded to the colonists by the London Company; the only material change in the government of the colony consisted in the substitution of a royal governor and council for the earlier governor and council appointed by the company; in Cromwell's time, even the right of electing the governor and council was transferred to the colonists.

The Plymouth Company, which had been included with the London Company in the charter of 1606,[1] was not so enterprising as its companion company. Its attempt to plant a colony at the mouth of the Kennebec in 1607–1608 ended in failure, and it appears to have later confined its interest in the colonization of North Virginia (called New England after Captain John Smith so named it in 1614) largely to granting to others licenses to trade, or to plant colonies on tracts of land granted to them. In 1620,

"for their better encouragement and satisfaction . . . and that they may avoid all confusion, questions and differences between themselves, and those of the . . . first colony," James I. was "pleased to make certain adventurers, intending to erect and establish fishery, trade and plantation, within the territories, precincts and limits of the said second colony . . . one several, distinct and entire body."

[1] See page 158, *supra*.

The territory was now to extend from sea to sea between the parallels of 40° and 48° north latitude so that it would not overlap that of the London Company. But the Plymouth Company, as reorganized under its new charter, was somewhat different from the London Company in its constitution.

The name should now be "The Council established at Plymouth, in the County of Devon, for the planting, ruling, ordering, and governing of New England, in America"—a name conveniently abbreviated to "The Council for New England" in common usage. The body was limited in number to forty members, who held their membership for life and were succeeded by members chosen by co-optation; the members of the first council were named in the charter. A president should be chosen for a term limited by the council. All the corporate powers, such as the creation of offices and the appointment of officers, and the making of laws and ordinances, were reposed in the council. In other respects the company was very similar to the London Company. Its laws and ordinances were to be enforced by a variety of punishments; in cases of rebellion, insurrection and meeting, its governor might enforce martial law. It might mine the precious metals, yielding one fifth of the gold and silver to the crown. Customs duties should not be levied for seven years and goods might be re-exported from England without payment of duties within thirteen months of importation. Land might be conveyed to planters and colonies might be protected by the use of military power. No other subjects were to engage in trade in the company's territory without its permission, and the crown should not grant trading licenses without its consent. Neither the company nor its officers or colonists should "rob or spoil" aliens or others. The colonists should have all the rights of British subjects. Persons who should neglect to go to the colonies after

having agreed to go, or having gone, should be seditious
or return to England by stealth, or circulate ill reports of
the company, and be impudent and contumacious when
examined by the council as to their conduct,[1] might be
bound with sureties for their good behavior, or sent back
to the colony to be proceeded against and punished by
the governor in his discretion or according to existing
ordinances.[2]

The purpose of the Plymouth Company was not so
much to colonize New England directly as to permit
others to do it through grants of its lands.   In the granting of lands and trading privileges it was more than liberal, often making grants with slight regard to other
grants previously made.   In 1621, it made a grant to the
Puritans and the London adventurers who were interested with them in their colony of the Plymouth settlement; they had previously obtained a license to make
a plantation from the London Company, but by error or
deception had been landed outside of the company's
territory.   Likewise, Robert Gorges tried unsuccessfully
to utilize a grant from the company by founding a colony
in 1623 on Massachusetts Bay; his representatives were
more fortunate in making settlements in the same year
on the sites of modern Boston, Chelsea and Charlestown.
Wallaston made a short-lived settlement on the site of
modern Quincy in 1625.   Sanctioned by the company, a
fishing settlement was established as Gloucester in 1623
by merchants of Dorchester in England, which was soon,
however, removed to Salem, and was later aided in its
development by English Puritans.   The most important
enterprise was inaugurated by a grant of land in 1628 to
a body of adventurers afterwards incorporated as the

---

[1] The London Company had experienced trouble with a similar class of
colonists, and had been given power in its charter of 1612 to deal with them
by the same means conceded to the Plymouth Company in 1620.

[2] Poore, vol. i., pp. 921–931.

Massachusetts Bay Company. In 1635 the Council for
New England surrendered its charter to the king with
the significant stipulation that the land held by it as a
corporation should be distributed among its members.

The London and Plymouth companies appear to have
developed in opposite directions, the former expanding
its commercial and the latter its political side. What
constituted the governing body of the former was what
was incorporated in the latter. Even in matters of government the council of the London Company had been
unable to maintain itself and the charter of 1612 had
made the council merely a part of the real governing
body, all proceedings being participated in by the "generality," but in the Plymouth Company what was virtually the generality was excluded from the corporation
by the charter of 1620. The organic development of
each was quite in harmony with its purposes; the London
Company had as its aim the settlement of a colony and
the establishment of commerce with and through it; it
accordingly included in its membership all who should
actually "adventure," and excluded all who should refuse to do so; on the contrary, the Plymouth Company
aimed rather to let others settle the colonies and establish the commerce by virtue of its grants, while it should
rely on its revenue from the land for its profits and should
undertake the general supervision of the colony, especially
on its political side. Much of the difference must have
been due to the difference in character of membership.
The London Company was composed largely of London
merchants and men of eastern England, who infused into
the work of the corporation the spirit derived from the
commercial life with which they came in close contact; in
political life they were largely liberals and opposed to the
tyrannical methods of the Stuarts; the Plymouth Company, however, was composed more largely of landowners
and gentlemen of the west of England, and contained

much less of the mercantile element; they were more conservative in their ideas, and viewed the work of the colonization of America in the light in which a landlord might have been expected to view an agricultural enter-prise, with the owner of the soil governing the body of tenants and deriving from his ownership a return that he did not primarily aid to produce.

In 1628 Sir Henry Rosewell and others secured from the Plymouth Company (or Council for New England) a grant of the land from sea to sea between a point three miles north of the Merrimac River and another three miles south of the Charles River.   In the year following the grant was confirmed by Charles I., and Rosewell and his associates incorporated as the "Governor and Com-pany of the Massachusetts Bay in New England."   A governor and deputy governor and eighteen assistants (the first ones being named in the charter) were to be periodically elected from the freemen of the company, and were to meet once a month or oftener (at least seven assistants and the governor or deputy governor attend-ing) in court or assembly "for the better ordering and directing of their affairs."   Four "great and general courts," to be attended by the governor or his deputy, at least six assistants and the freemen, were to be held each year for the admission of new freemen, the constitu-tion of offices, the election of officers (by a majority vote of those present) and the enactment of laws and ordinances not repugnant to the laws of England; the general court at which officers were chosen was called (though not in the charter) the "Court of Elections."   The company had most of the powers, exemptions and disabilities characteristic of colonial companies,—to transport colo-nists and goods from England, to retain English citizen-ship for the colonists, to be free of customs duties for seven years, to make and enforce laws on its members and colonists, to expel intruders by force of arms, to refrain from "robbing and spoiling" other subjects and friendly aliens, and to permit other English subjects to fish in the waters adjacent to their land and use the land on the shores as much as should be incidentally necessary.[1]

The economic relations of the company to its colonists were remarkably similar to those of the London Company to its Virginia colonists after 1609 (the date of the second charter). The stage of semi-communal industry passed through by Virginia under the charter of 1606 appears to have been wanting in the experience of Massachusetts Bay. The distinction between adventurers and planters was maintained but not reflected in the organization of the company. Mere adventurers (investors) should be granted two hundred acres of land for each subscription of £50 to the company's enterprise; such as settled in the colony should have fifty acres for themselves and fifty acres for each person that they should take to the colony with them. If the settlers should be of superior social "quality," they should receive such additional allotments of land as should seem to the governor and council to be just. Special grants were made to a few persons by way of reward for services rendered or influence exerted. A tract of land was also set aside by the company for cultivation by it in its corporate capacity through servants and employees. But the system was not so fully developed in Massachusettts as in Virginia; the company soon transferred its land to the separate towns of the colony. Likewise the management of the company's joint stock and "magazine" was delegated to a subsidiary board of "undertakers," but early dwindled to a matter of slight importance, and private trade supplanted trade by the corporation. In fact, the Massachusetts Bay project was so predominantly political in character that its economic organization had almost no influence on its execution. When the election of colonists to the freedom of

[1] Poore, vol. i., pp. 932–942.

the company came to be passed on in 1631, there was no mention of their economic relations to it as a qualification; the test imposed was the broader one of general social fitness, though it was narrowed somewhat by reduction to membership in colonial churches.

The significant development was in the political relations of the company to its colonists. From the beginning the company was more closely identified in interest with its colonists than the London or Plymouth Companies had been. Behind the movement was the same desire of the Puritans to escape religious oppression in England that had justified the foundation of the New Plymouth settlement; it was shared alike by the incorporators and the colonists sent out by them. Moreover, the purely commercial purposes of the company were less prominent than they had been in the preceding companies; while the membership of the London Company had been restricted to "adventurers," that of the present company contained many statesmen, clergymen and scholars. Even before the charter had been granted, a body of colonists had already been sent to join those at Salem[1] who had originally settled at Gloucester. As soon as the charter had been granted, the company removed its "domicile" to New England, many of its members themselves becoming residents of the new colony; whether the removal was technically legal or illegal, it made possible organic changes within the corporation that in preceding colonial companies had taken place outside of them. As early as 1630 the freemen had become so numerous that, divided as they were among several towns, they were unable to make their influence felt in the government of the company; the election of the governor and deputy governor and the enactment of laws consequently fell into the hands of the body of assistants; in the next year it was provided that the assistants should

[1] See page 171, *supra.*

retain their offices until deprived of them by vote of the freemen. The concentration of powers was, up to that point, quite similar to the movement in the English gilds that developed into the London Livery companies; in fact, the constitution of the Massachusetts Bay Company needed but little further modification to attain the model furnished by the London companies. But the activity of the colonial company came too often in contact with that of its colonists for the establishment of an oligarchical court of assistants. Accordingly when the freemen of Watertown were assessed £60 as a contribution to the expense of colonial fortifications at Cambridge, the assessment encountered the objection that the freemen were being "taxed without representation." At a later general court it was provided that the freemen should participate in the proceedings of the company through representatives, two to be chosen by each town to sit with the governor and assistants in deliberation on the affairs of the colony; even the election of the governor and deputy governor was reposed in the representatives after having been for a time exercised by the freemen according to the orginal provisions of the charter. In 1644 a question of jurisdiction in the celebrated "pig case" occasioned a disagreement between the assistants and representatives that caused them thereafter to hold separate sessions. The government of the colony had assumed a form that it maintained until the charter of 1691 was granted.

Within five years after the granting of the corporate charter in 1628 it was a just ground of complaint in England that a separate and independent state and church were being established in Massachusetts. An oath of allegiance was exacted of prospective colonists and a royal commission was sent to New England in 1634 for the general purpose of re-introducing harmony between the colonists and the home government, with the power to use the extreme remedy of revoking colonial charters. In the following year, on writ of *quo warranto*, the charter of the "Governor and Company of the Massachusetts Bay in New England" was annulled, though the home government was unable to execute the decree.

Until after the Restoration, Massachusetts was allowed to go its own way with little interference from England. The framework of the corporation had become the political constitution of a colony. In 1664 four royal commissioners were sent out to restore the colonists of New England to their allegiance to the English crown, and to reduce the independence to which they had attained, whether under corporate charters or under governments originated and fostered by them in the absence of supervision or regulation by the English government,—an independence that had been greatly strengthened by confederation of the several colonies. The commissioners, having accomplished nothing, returned to England. In 1684, another writ of *quo warranto* was followed by a decree in the high court of chancery in England annulling the charter of the company, that had become an English colony. New England was now to be governed by James II., if possible, through a royal governor and council, whose jurisdiction was expanded in 1688 to include the colonies as far southward as Delaware Bay. With the Revolution in England Governor Andros and his council were driven out of office and the colonial charters restored.

The Massachusetts Bay Company had ceased to exist and its direct work in the establishment of the colony had been done. The charter of 1691 must be considered not because it is a part of the history of the company, but because it is evidence of the enduring effects of corporate activity on the constitution of the political communities of New England. By the charter of William and Mary the colonies of Massachusetts Bay and New Plymouth, the province of Maine, the territory of Acadia or Nova Scotia and between it and Maine were united under the name of the "Province of the Massachusetts Bay in New England." A governor, deputy governor and secretary were to be appointed by the crown, and twenty-eight assistants or councillors to "advise and assist" the governor were to "keep a council from time to time" with him when summoned to do so. A general court or assembly was to be held each year, consisting of the governor and his council and two deputies elected by the inhabitants of each town to represent them, the number to which each "county, town and place" should be entitled being left to future regulation by the general court. The governor was given power to adjourn, prorogue and dissolve the general court. The councillors were to be chosen each year by the general court, eighteen being allotted to Massachusetts Bay, four to New Plymouth, three to Maine and one to the territory between Maine and Nova Scotia,[1] and they should be removable by the general court. The governor, with the advice and consent of the council, was to appoint all judges, sheriffs and other officers. Wills were to be probated by the governor and council. Judicial courts for hearing causes of all kinds were to be established by the general court, but an appeal to the king in council should be permitted in all controversies involving an amount in excess of £300. The governor and general court should make all laws and enforce them by fines, mulcts and imprisonments, and should have power to levy taxes. The governor should have a veto on all acts of the general court, and no act should be valid without his approval. All laws enacted should be referred to the king in council,

[1] Only twenty-six councillors seem to be accounted for by the charter as printed in Poore's collection, but none are assigned to Acadia; whether the remaining two councillors were for that province has not been determined; it is, however, of no importance in the connection. The governor and deputy governor were usually considered a part of the council, though they hardly appear to have been so in the present case.

by whom they might be annulled within three years.
Lands should be granted by the governor and general
assembly. The governor, for the protection of the province, should have power to raise, train and instruct the
provincial militia, undertake military expeditions and enforce martial law in time of war. The right of English subjects to fish in provincial waters should not be
abridged.[1] The election of a speaker of the house of
representatives had not been provided for in the charter
of 1691; it was accordingly granted by George I., in
1726, that he should be elected by the general court and
approved by the governor; if a vacancy should occur in
the office or if a candidate elected by the general court
should be disapproved, the vacancy should be filled by
the same procedure. It was also provided that the general court might adjourn from day to day or for two
days, but not for a longer time without the consent of
the governor.[2]

By the charter of 1691, and the charter of 1726 in
amendment of it, the governmental structure of Massachusetts Bay as a colony, rapidly evolved by it from the
structure conceded to the Massachusetts Bay Company
as a corporation, was merely perpetuated. The governorship was somewhat exalted in the provincial government, as is likely to happen when the state essays to
absorb the results of independent corporate activity, but
the other branches of the government suffered little
modification; the council and house of representatives,
by far the more important parts of the provincial constitution, remained substantially what they were after
the colonial company had adjusted its structure to the
colonial environment with which it came in contact, and
had expanded until it was virtually identical with the
colony.

The two charters of Connecticut and Rhode Island

[1] Poore, vol. i., pp. 942-954.   [2] Ibid., vol. i., pp. 954-956.

granted by Charles II., the former in 1662 and the latter in 1663, would in a classification of the charters of colonies, companies and provinces stand midway between the charter of the Massachusetts Bay Company and that of the Province of Massachusetts Bay. They represent with a fair degree of fidelity the colonial constitution of Massachusetts after it had been transformed from a colonial company into a politically organized colony and before it had been restored to organic subordination to the English crown as a province. The earlier constitutions of both colonies had been such as they had independently devised for themselves, though of course they had been affected by the prior experience of their framers in other colonies and by their knowledge of the constitutions concurrently in force in neighboring communities.

The "Governor and Company of the English Colony of Connecticut in New England, in America" was to consist of John Winthrop and eighteen others named in the charter, together with such others as should be "admitted and made free of the company and society." A governor (and deputy governor), twelve assistants and a representative body of two deputies from each "place, town, or city," elected by their freemen, should constitute the government and should hold a "general court" twice a year or oftener. The governor as well as the assistants was to be elected from the freemen, and might summon them at will "to consult and advise of the business and affairs" of the company. At the general courts laws should be enacted and freemen admitted; at one of them the officers should be elected. Colonists might freely be transported to the colony, should take the oath of supremacy and obedience and (with their children) should have all the liberties and immunities of natural British subjects. Goods, merchandise "and other things . . . useful or necessary for the inhabitants of the colony" might without restriction be exported thither. Courts of justice might be established by the general courts for the enforcement of laws by proper penalties and executions. Military power might be employed for the protection of the colony and martial law might be exercised when occasion should require. Rights of fishing of English subjects should be respected. The territory of the company should extend to the South Sea (Pacific Ocean) on the west.[1] In 1643 the Governor-in-chief and Commissioners of Plantations had granted to the inhabitants of the towns of Providence, Portsmouth and Newport,

"a free and absolute charter . . . to be known by the name of the Incorporation of Providence Plantations, in the Narragansett Bay, in New England . . . with full power and authority to rule themselves . . . by such a form of civil government, as by voluntary consent of all, or the greater part of them, they shall find most suitable to their estate and condition"

and to make and execute laws accordingly.[2] When later a charter was granted by Charles II., in 1663, it differed from that of Connecticut, of the preceding year, only in details. The name given was the "Governor and Company of the English Colony of Rhode Island and Providence Plantations, in New England, in America." The assistants were only ten in number. The deputies were not equally apportioned to the several towns, but Newport should have six; Providence, Portsmouth and Warwick, each four; and each other town two. The colonists should not make war on the Indians within the limits of other colonies without the knowledge and consent of the others, nor should the other colonies molest the Indians within the Rhode Island colony without the knowledge and consent of its governor and company. In matters of controversy between the colony and others in New England, it might appeal for redress

[1] Poore, vol. i., pp. 252–257.   [2] Ibid., vol. ii., pp. 1594, 1595.

directly to the king. The inhabitants of the colony, it seemed necessary to concede, might

"without let or molestation, pass and repass with freedom, into and through the rest of the English colonies, upon their lawful and civil occasions, and converse, and hold commerce and trade, with such of the inhabitants of other English colonies as shall be willing to admit them thereunto, 'they behaving themselves peaceably among them.' " [1]

The political organization contained in both the Connecticut and Rhode Island charters was a developed form and underwent no serious modification until the charters were superseded by state constitution, in Connecticut, in 1818, and in Rhode Island, in 1842. So clearly was the charter .organization recognized as a fit structure for the government of the commonwealth that when the formation of state constitutions was recommended by the Colonial Congress in 1776, it was merely enacted in Connecticut

"that the ancient form of Civil Government, contained in the Charter from Charles the Second, King of England, and adopted by the People of this State, shall be and remain the Civil Constitution of this State, under the sole authority of the People thereof, independent of any King or Prince whatever." [2]

All the charters of colonial companies heretofore considered were granted between 1606 and 1663 and followed quite closely the model of the foreign commercial company. The charter of the "Trustees for establishing the colony of Georgia in America" was not granted until 1732, and approached most nearly the type of the prevailing English charitable corporation. [3] The primary motive for granting the charter appears in the recital

---

[1] Poore, vol. ii., pp. 1594–1603.

Poore, vol. i., pp. 257, 258.   [3] *Supra*, p. 50

"that many . . . poor subjects are, through misfortunes and want of employment, reduced to great necessity, insomuch as by their labor they are not able to provide a maintenance for themselves and families; and if they had means to defray their charges of passage, and other expenses, incident to new settlements, they would be glad to settle in . . . provinces in America, where by cultivating the lands, at present waste and desolate, they might not only gain a comfortable subsistence for themselves and families, but also strengthen [the] colonies and increase the trade, navigation and wealth of [Great Britain]."

A subsidiary motive was the protection of the Carolina colonies against the Spanish and Indians on the exposed southwestern border. The corporation erected to receive, manage and dispose of contributions made by philanthropic persons was to consist of Lord Percival, James Oglethorpe and eighteen others, and such others as they should afterwards elect at annual meetings. The government was vested in a president and common council of fifteen, later to be increased to twenty-four members, elected by the corporation at annual meetings and serving during good behavior. The common council should have a chairman enjoying both an original and casting vote, and its members were to serve in rotation as chairman and president without salary. No member of the corporation should have a position of profit under it; all officers were eligible and removable by the common council, but the governor was to be approved by the crown. Annual reports of receipts and expenditures should be submitted to treasury officers of the crown, and of all "leases, grants, conveyances, settlements and improvements," to the auditor of plantations. The corporation had power to make by-laws for its own government and ordinances for the government of the colony, not repugnant to the laws of England, and to enforce them by reasonable pains and penalties; but laws for the control of the colonists were subject to the approval of the king in council. Power was given to take out settlers as colonists and the necessary military and other supplies; the rights of British subjects were preserved for the colonists and their children. For twenty-one years the power of establishing courts "for the hearing and determining all manner of crimes, offences, . . . causes and things whatsoever" should be exercised. The territory granted should extend from the Savannah to the Altamaha River and westward within the meridians of their sources to the Pacific Ocean, and should include unsettled islands within twenty leagues of its Atlantic coastline. Land might be granted to colonists, but not more than five hundred acres to each one, and none to members of the corporation; after the expiration of ten years from the date of each grant the crown should receive annually four shillings for each hundred acres granted. A militia might be formed and trained and military expeditions engaged in. Georgia should be a separate province and subject to the laws of no other colony, except that its militia should be subject to the command and direction of the governor and commander-in-chief of South Carolina. At the end of a term of twenty-one years "such form of government and method of making laws . . . for the better governing and ordering of the said province of Georgia . . . shall be established . . . as [the crown] shall hereafter ordain," and the governor and all other officers, civil and military, should be appointed by the crown.[1] After having met with only moderate success in the establishment of a colony, the corporation surrendered its charter in 1752, and its government was replaced by that of a royal province.

The purposes of the state in granting to colonial corporations charters conceding to them for their exercise such

[1] Poore, vol. i., pp. 369–377.

extensive powers over persons and property may be said
to have been five in number, though some of them are
manifestly comprehended, partly or wholly, in the others.
The purposes were as follows: (1) The colonization of
new lands; (2) The establishment and extension of commerce; (3) The extension of the dominion of the English
crown; (4) The propagation of Christianity and (5) the
relief of distressed classes of British subjects. Such purposes were shared by the companies and colonists themselves, but one other purpose frequently executed by
them was of course not endorsed by the state, (6) the
escape from political and religious oppression in England.

(1) Colonization is for the greater part inspired by purposes comprehended under succeeding heads, but there
is still a broad field within which it may be viewed as an
end distinct in itself. It was an extreme form of the
efforts of the sixteenth and seventeenth centuries to
realize what is vaguely described as the "world idea,"
the knowledge of new worlds and the desire to exploit
them. Much of the world's colonization has doubtless
been promoted not by rational plans to better the social
conditions of colonists but by the mere indefinite desire
for change and movement,—by the stimulated consciousness of individuality and an impulse to nourish it by contact with new environment, so characteristic of the period
of the Reformation. The first step in the process, the
discovery of new lands, was certainly not always taken
with the expectation of eventually deriving an economic,
religious or political advantage from it; it was prompted
most by the mere spirit of adventure. The spirit of
colonization was appreciated in England as keenly by the
king as by any subject; it never lacked royal encouragement. But the state as organized was unable to comprehend the movement; like new movements in other and
even narrower fields of social life, it was conceded a social
structure, which, while not truly a part of the state, yet

derived its strength and vigor from it. The general work of colonization, especially in the presence of a government so lacking in harmony with the political conditions surrounding it as was that of the Stuarts, was especially appropriate for corporations.

(2) The strongest particular motive for the formation of colonial companies was doubtless the economic purpose of establishing and extending English commerce. The crown found in it a larger source of revenue by reason of the increase of exports and imports and a larger body of national wealth to be taxed. Besides, from the exaggerated reports of the deposits of the precious metals, the royal reservation of a percentage of the gold and silver mined was expected to result in a direct income for the crown. The reservation in the Massachusetts charter of 1691 of all trees in the province more than twenty-four inches in diameter for masts for the royal navy, and the exaction of four shillings per hundred acres on land granted to Georgia colonists are indicative of the royal view of the colonies as a source of supplying royal needs.[1] The success of other "adventurers" in Russia, Turkey, Africa and India had encouraged the in-

---

[1] The persistence of the commercial as distinguished from the political view of the American colonies entertained by the English government is strikingly shown by the nature of the administrative bodies intended for their supervision. In 1660, two councils were created by Charles II., a "Council of Trade" and a "Council of Plantations." In 1672, they were united as a "Council for Trade and Plantations," which continued only until 1675, but was revived by William III. in 1695. Not until 1768 was the political side of the colonies distinctly recognized by the creation of a Secretary of State for the "Colonial" or "American Department," and then the Board of Trade and Plantations was allowed to exist concurrently. In 1782 both were abolished, and in the year following the "Plantation Office" was made a subordinate department of the Home Office.—H. D. Traill, *Central Government*, pp. 84–86.

The general purpose of the well-known Navigation Laws was to make the American colonies commercial feeders for English merchants and the English exchequer, without regard to political considerations.

vestors of capital in American voyages to hope for similar success. In the Virginia charter, the general purpose of colonization appears to have been even subordinated to the commercial purpose; the settlements were intended to some extent as establishments for trading with the nations; further than that the organization of the early colonies on the basis of communal holding of land was intended to facilitate the absorption by the adventurers of the economic results of the project. Even when the extension of commerce was not the primary purpose of establishing a colony, it was permitted to serve incidentally as a basis for securing the pecuniary assistance indispensable to the success of the colony. In a few cases, as in those of Connecticut and Rhode Island, the grant of powers appears to have been regarded not so much as an incentive to future economic activity as a reward for past exertions.[1] The crown was more than willing to grant such comprehensive powers to corporations that, by their exercise of them in pursuit of private gain, the royal exchequer might incidentally be benefited.

(3) "The enlargement of our own dominions" was one of the agreeable results of colonization contemplated by the crown. One reason assigned by Charles II. for granting to John Winthrop and his associates the charter of Connecticut was that the territory "or the greatest part thereof, was purchased and obtained for great and valuable considerations, and some other part thereof gained by conquest, and with much difficulty, and at the only endeavors, expense and charge of them [was] subdued and improved, and thereby became a considerable enlargement and addition of our dominions and interest there." National pride, or personal royal pride, or whatever it may be called, that, without the added hope of economic gain or other material advantage, has provided a motive for most of the world's conquests, had its influence on

[1] See quotation in succeeding paragraph.

the development of the American colonies. In order
that the new world might be settled by colonists who
should carry with them their allegiance to the English
crown, their settlements were encouraged, not directly,
but indirectly through its delegating to bodies of subjects
such powers, political, economic, military and other, as
should be necessary for the success of the enterprises.
On the other hand, the adventurers and colonists, to the
extent that they were actuated by the same sentiment,
needed only opportunity to indulge it. Extension of
dominion was a public purpose; it was accomplished to
some extent through colonial corporations by affording
to the subject through them an opportunity for an expression of his personal love of king and country. The
purpose of acquiring new dominion was sometimes thinly
veiled in the charters under the ostensibly philanthropic
purpose of reducing the savages in the new land to "civil
government" and thereby laying "a sure foundation of
happiness to all America." The frequent reservation
of the appointment of colonial officers, the supervision
of corporate action and the approval of corporate laws, as
well as the requirement of oaths of supremacy and allegiance, and the guarantee to the colonists and their de-
scendants of the rights of British citizenship, is evidence
that the crown aimed to make the extension of dominion
not merely apparent.

(4) No purpose is more uniformly mentioned in the
charters than the conversion of savages to Christianity.
The design in granting the Connecticut charter was to
have the

"people inhabitants there, . . . so religiously, peaceably
and civilly governed, as their good life and orderly conversa-
tion may win and invite the natives of the country to the
knowledge and obedience of the only true God and Savior of
mankind, and the Christian faith; which in our royal inten-

tions, and the adventurers' free profession is the only and principal end of this plantation." [1]

The Massachusetts charter of 1620 contains evidence that the purely pious purpose was sometimes confused with others more worldly, and that the attainment of it was not without serious limitations:

"For that . . . within these late years there hath by God's visitation reigned a wonderful plague, together with many horrible slaughters and murders, committed amongst the savages and brutish people there . . . in a manner to the utter destruction, devastation and depopulation of that whole territory, so that there is not left for many leagues together . . . any that do claim or challenge any kind of interests therein nor any other superior lord or sovereign to make claim thereto, whereby we in our judgment are persuaded and satisfied that the appointed time is come in which Almighty God, in His great goodness and bounty towards us and our people, hath thought fit and determined that those large and goodly territories, deserted as it were by their natural inhabitants, should be possessed and enjoyed by such of our subjects and people as . . . shall by His mercy and favor and by His powerful arm, be directed and conducted thither. In contemplation and serious consideration whereof, we have thought it fit, according to our kingly duty, so much as in us lieth, to second and follow God's sacred will, rendering reverend thanks to His Divine Majesty for His glorious favor in laying open and revealing the same unto us before any other Christian prince or state, by which means without offence, and as we trust, to His glory, we may with boldness go on to the settling of so hopeful a work, which tendeth to the reducing and conversion of such savages as remain wandering in desolation and distress, to civil society and

---

[1] Nearly the same language is found in the Virginia charter of 1609: "Because the principal effort which we can desire or expect of this action is the conversion and reduction of the people in those parts unto the true worship of God and Christian religion."

Christian religion, to the enlargement of our own dominions, and the advancement of the fortunes of such of our good subjects as shall willingly interest themselves in the said employment to whom we cannot but give singular commendations for their so worthy intention and enterprise."

To whatever extent the propagation of Christianity might be furthered it was legitimately incidental to the work of colonization and afforded a sufficient basis for grants of corporate powers.

(5) The relief of distressed classes of British subjects was the special purpose of creating one colonial corporation and must have been implied to some extent in the general purpose of colonization furthered by the creation of all the others. To whatever degree colonization may be accounted for on more general grounds, it must undoubtedly be attributed largely to the desire of the colonists to better their economic conditions. All colonial corporations, and particularly the Georgia corporation, would therefore find justification for their existence in the same social principles on which eleemosynary corporations in general are based. The colonial company was the medium through which the public purpose of disposing of surplus population or distressed classes was accomplished by giving vent to private interest, whether in the form of cupidity or philanthropy.

(6) To escape from political and religious oppression by England could hardly be recognized by the crown as a valid motive in subjects for seeking a body of corporate privileges. It was accordingly not mentioned in the charters; but it was nevertheless present in most cases, however carefully it might be concealed. The outcome of colonial and provincial history in the separation of the American colonies from England is emphatic evidence of the extent to which the hidden purpose was aided in its attainment by the granting of corporate powers for other

purposes. The social structure of corporations, like most other legally sanctioned social structures, may more or less easily be diverted from the purposes for which the state intended it, to be used for others detrimental to the state or, in extreme cases, actually subversive of it.

At first sight the colonial proprietaries appear to have differed very little from the colonial corporations. The charters by which the powers and duties of both were defined bear a strong resemblance to each other. The purposes of granting them to the proprietaries were to enable the grantees to colonize the new land, "to enlarge our English empire, and promote such useful commodities as may be of benefit to us and our Dominions, as also to reduce the savage Natives by gentle and just manners to the love of civil society and Christian religion."[1] Behind the expressed grounds for seeking the charters, the latent purpose of escaping and assisting others to escape unjust or distressing conditions in England, whether political, religious or economic, actuated many of the proprietors. In all cases but one the territory to be owned and controlled was definitely limited and constituted a separate province; in the exceptional case of Raleigh, whose charter was the earliest granted,[2] the patentee was permitted "to discover, search, find out and view such remote, heathen and barbarous lands, countries and territories, not actually possessed by any Christian prince, and not inhabited by Christian people, as to him . . . shall seem good," and "to have, hold, occupy and enjoy" them with all incidental rights and privileges; but he was conceded power to expel from the land only such persons as without his license should inhabit within two hundred leagues of places at which settlements should be established before the end of six years. In no other charters, save that of the London and Plymouth

---

[1] Charter to William Penn, 1681; Poore, vol. ii., pp. 1509–1515.
[2] Poore, vol. ii., pp. 1379–1382.

Companies, in 1606, was the control of the land dependent on actual occupancy of it, except in so far as a charter was on general principles forfeitable for nonuser in cases of absolute failure to plant colonies.

In order to enable and encourage the proprietaries to accomplish the purposes for which their charters were granted, they were empowered, like the corporations, to take out colonists and goods, to erect fortifications and otherwise use military power in the defence of their colonies by the expulsion of intruders, the resistance of attacks and the pursuit of enemies and pirates, and to enforce martial law in cases of rebellion, sedition and mutiny. The colonists and their children were to retain their rights as British subjects and not to be absolved from their correlative allegiance to the English crown. The proprietaries and their heirs and assigns had full power to "correct, punish, pardon, govern and rule " the colonists according to such laws as should seem to them to be necessary, "whether relating to the public state of the province or the private utility of individuals," with the uniform condition that they should be "consonant to reason," and not repugnant but as nearly agreeable as possible to the laws and customs of England,—and to enforce them by fines, imprisonment and other penalties. By the terms of most of the charters, notably of those of Lord Baltimore and William Penn, the laws should be made "of and with the advice, assent and approbation of the freemen of the . . . province, . . . or of their delegates or deputies . . . called together for the framing of laws " by the proprietaries; in cases of emergencies, not provided for by regularly enacted laws, the proprietaries or their representatives might use their own discretion, as conceded in the charter of Charles I. to Sir Ferdinando Gorges (1639), but such laws might not extend to persons' "lives, members, freeholds, goods or chattels." Moreover, the colonial laws were frequently

made "subordinate and subject to the power and 'regle-
ment'" of the Lords and Commissioners of Plantations,
or made approvable or voidable within a limited time by
the king in council, "if inconsistent with [his] sovereignty
or lawful prerogative . . . or contrary to the faith
and allegiance due [him]" or otherwise objectionable.

Incidentally "cities, boroughs and towns" might be
incorporated, "markets, marts and fairs" be established,
ports designated and the provinces divided into "towns,
hundreds, counties" and manors by the proprietaries.
Likewise churches and chapels might be founded and all
ecclesiastical control exercised over them, and over the
colonists in reference to them, except in so far as special
privileges should be conceded to them by the charters.
The proprietaries had power "to confer marks of favor,
rewards and honors, on such subjects . . . as shall
be well deserving, and to adorn them with titles and
dignities (but so that they be not such as are now used
in England)." Offices might be created and all officers
appointed. Courts might be erected for the hearing of
all manner of causes, civil, criminal, ecclesiastical and
marine—even courts leet and courts baron,—and view of
frankpledge might be held; but appeals were usually
permitted to the proprietary, or to his governor or other
representative, or even in cases of importance to the king
in council. Licenses to trade were issuable by the proprietary, but a percentage of the gold and silver mined
and of the profits of the pearl fishery were reserved by
the crown, and other British subjects should not be excluded from the fisheries. Ordinarily the power of taxation was not reserved by the king; in the Maryland and
Pennsylvania charters it was expressly waived, unless (in
the latter) "with the consent of the proprietary or chief
governor and assembly, or by act of Parliament in England." The proprietaries might convey lands to settlers
and lay customs and duties for their own use. "Spoiling

and robbing" other subjects and friendly aliens were prohibited on pain of outlawry if speedy compensation should not be made for the damage caused.

Thus the proprietaries were quite identical with the colonial corporations in the purposes for which unusual powers were conferred on them by the English crown, and very similar in the variety and scope of powers conferred, as far as they affected their external relations, either to the crown or to the colonists. But there was one important difference between them. The corporations had forms of organic social structure conceded to them by their charters that the proprietaries, even when more than one in number, did not possess. The relations of the members of the corporations to each other were definitely ascertained and enforced through the medium of a form of government within them; it was possible for political constitutions of colonies to be developed from them without destroying the continuity of the infra-corporate relations. The proprietaries were merely individuals. When there was only one proprietary, any development of political institutions in his colony had to come from actual delegation of his powers. Even when a plural number of proprietaries were united, as under the Carolina charter, no organization of membership was provided that could form the basis of colonial institutions; they were merely joint proprietaries, limited in number. Again, in the corporations even when their constitutions could not be converted into constitutions for their colonies, and the organization of the colonists had to be by the delegation of powers, the structure of the corporation might serve as a model for the constitution of the colony. In the proprietaries, however, if political institutions had to be provided for the colonists, there was present no constitution to serve as a model; a model would have to be sought elsewhere.

The proprietary colony was based on the English lord-

ship or county palatine; the colonial company on the
English foreign trading company. The former seemed
to derive most of their powers and duties from the ownership of the soil; the latter, from the terms of its charter.
The inference is unavoidable that it was the presence of
the land settled by a body of English subjects that caused
the growth of the double system. The great foreign
trading companies owned a commerce and controlled
only their members and servants; the feudal English lordship would have been an unsuitable structure for them;
they assumed the form derived through the London companies from the older gilds. When the newly discovered
land in America was to be settled as English domain,
with English subjects, largely through the use of commercial gain as an incentive, it is not surprising that confusion in the social form of the colonizing agents resulted,
with the English lordship and the English commercial
company side by side, each, however, having some characteristics borrowed from the other. The difference in
type of the proprietary is accountable for many minor
variations in the bodies of powers granted in the charters.
Though the corporations were to be the lords and proprietors of the soil, their provinces were not called
seigniories, as was Penn's province of Pennsylvania. The
power to incorporate cities, boroughs and towns, to
establish manors and manorial courts, to bestow titles
and dignities and to hold view of frankpledge were not
given to the corporations, though they were given to
proprietaries; such powers, in their historical development, seemed to be quite inseparable from the older
feudal conception of government based on the ownership
of the soil, and accordingly incompatible with the activity
of corporations.

The political or governmental powers bestowed on the
corporations and proprietaries, it need hardly be added,
were incidental and subsidiary to the other powers to be

exercised by them. Such of them as related to the internal organization of the corporations themselves were of course involved in their very nature as organizations of corporate groups of persons; some of them, if not expressed, would have been implied in the legal creation of the corporations. It was provided in the Connecticut charter of 1662, and in charters of other colonies, that laws should be enacted and executed "according to the course of other corporations within . . . England." The powers to be used for the control of other English subjects (not colonists) may be viewed in the same light, though they were largely negative, and not positive in operation, rather preventing others from acting than compelling them to act or imposing conditions under which they should act. The restriction of the field of colonial activity to the grantees of charters was intended not so much to afford a reward for their doing or aiding the work of colonization as to supply a necessary condition under which it might be done; they were doing work of which the major part was the legitimate work of the state and subject to all of the limitations to which the activity of the state is subject; their several fields of activity had to be exclusive. The body of powers to be used for the government of the colonists owed their delegation to the inability of the state to exercise them. Political organization of population was necessary in the American colonies,—perhaps more necessary there than elsewhere,—and if not exercised by the state, had to be exercised by some subordinate agency.

"Forasmuch as upon the finding out, discovering or inhabiting of such remote lands, countries and territories . . . it shall be necessary for the safety of all men, that shall adventure themselves in those journeys or voyages, to live together in Christian peace, and civil quietness each with the other, whereby every one may with more pleasure and profit enjoy that whereunto they shall attain with great pain and peril."

was the reason assigned by Elizabeth for granting to
Raleigh the absolute power of governing the members of
his prospective colony in Virginia. The grounds for the
original bestowal of liberal powers were equally strong for
a liberal legal interpretation of them; "these our letters
patent," was the universal promise,

"shall be firm, good and effectual in the law, to all intents,
constructions and purposes whatsoever, according to our true
intent and meaning herein before declared, as shall be construed, reputed, and adjudged most favorable on the behalf,
and for the best benefit and behoof of the . . . governor
and company."

By far the most important feature of the development
of the colonial companies was their influence on the
political institutions of the colonies. The opposition
caused by the tyrannical government of Argall in Virginia
had for its first result the appointment by the company
of a council for him. When that seemed to be insufficient and nothing short of participation by the colonists
in the government of their affairs promised permanent
relief, the liberal members in control of the company
conceded to the colonists under Governor Yeardly the
power of forming through their deputies and together
with the governor and his council a colonial legislature.
The political organization of the colony became thereby
a reproduction of that of the company itself, except as
to two features: (*a*) the independence of the governor
and council as related to the burgesses and electorate was
due to their representing the interests of the company
rather than those of the colonists; (*b*) the principle of
representation applied in the election of burgesses was
an improvement on the direct participation by members
of the company in the consideration of its affairs. The
Plymouth Company suffered a reverse development, not
only conceding no political institutions to the colonists of

New England, but itself shrinking into a mere organization of its own governing body and leaving contact with
colonists to persons not included in its membership.
Even such members of the Council for New England as
engaged in colonizing projects did so not in the capacity
of members or representatives of the company, but in
that of its grantees.   The development of political institutions in New England must consequently be sought,
not in the relations of the Plymouth Company or Council
for New England to the colonists, but in those of their
grantees to them.   The Massachusetts Bay Company, incorporated after it had received a grant from the Council
for New England, represented an advance beyond the
position of the London Company in that it did not delegate a political organization to its colony but became
actually identical with it through the admission of colonists to its membership as freemen.   The constitution of
the company became the constitution of the colony, with
its governor, elected by the freemen and advised by the
assistants, responsible for the execution of the laws, and
the deputies and assistants or councillors, likewise elected,
responsible for legislation.   The third step was taken
when by the Connecticut and Rhode Island charters the
colonies were given colonial constitutions under the guise
of semi-commercial corporations, with governments similar to that of Massachusetts Bay; but the two charters
were less in creation of new constitutions than in confirmation of older ones which had developed in imitation
of those of Massachusetts Bay and New Plymouth.   The
Georgia Company was somewhat anomalous in the colonization of America.   Its centre of force was not so
much in its colonists in America as in the philanthropists
in England that supplied it with resources; its content
was not so much colonization as the administration of
charity funds; it was quite independent, as far as its corporate life was concerned, of the social activity of the

colonists; consequently it neither generated a colonial constitution nor permitted its own constitution to become one. The colonial constitutions developed in Virginia and Massachusetts on the form of the commercial corporations contained the following elements: (*a*) The executive was a governor, either appointed by the company or elected by the colony, who was advised and assisted by a council, likewise either appointed or elected; (*b*) the supreme judiciary of the colony consisted of the governor and council; (*c*) the legislature consisted of the council and a representative body of deputies elected by the local divisions of the colony, at first deliberating in joint session but later separately, the governor having either a veto, or a casting vote in the sessions of the council.

The colonial constitutions of Virginia and Massachusetts Bay served as models for the other colonies. When settlements were made in New Hampshire, Rhode Island or Connecticut, in the north, or in Maryland or the Carolinas in the south, to a large extent by emigrants from the two older colonies, the demands for local representative institutions were met by the concession or assumption of forms of government similar to the two models. By the time when the middle colonies passed under English control, the southern colonies (except Georgia) had all conformed to the model of Virginia, and the New England colonies to that of Massachusetts. When William Penn gave form to the representation of the colonists of Pennsylvania and Delaware, as provided in his charter, the system developed in Virginia and Maryland was substantially reproduced. Even the Duke of York authorized the governor to call an assembly in New York in 1682 for the enactment of laws, which in the following year provided for a government like that of the New England colonies in response to a popular petition. In New Jersey a similar system was conceded before the colony was divided into East Jersey and West Jersey, prevailed in the separate parts and was finally perpetuated when the parts were reunited in 1702. The only material modification of the system in its developed form was found in Pennsylvania and Delaware, where the legislative body consisted of the popular representatives alone to the exclusion of the council. The prevalence of the system based on the earlier colonial corporations of Virginia and Massachusetts is perhaps the more remarkable when it is considered that all the other colonies south of New England, excepting Georgia, were proprietary colonies. The failure of Locke's "Fundamental Constitutions" in the Carolinas and of Gorges' earlier but similar scheme in Maine showed that it was impossible to successfully follow the feudal type of organization farther than it had been followed in the creation of the proprietaries.

It has been suggested [1] that corporations have usually, in history, served as temporary social structures until the activity organized within them might be absorbed by the state or co-ordinated with other activity exercised under the state. The process of absorption in the case of colonial corporations and proprietaries is represented, though imperfectly, in their replacement by provincial governments. When the process began, it was soon found that the forms of government established in the colonies under the liberal powers of the royal charters had acquired so great fixity and stability and were so nearly in harmony with the conditions of colonial society that they could not be changed. All that the crown could do in most of the colonies was to assume the appointment of the governor and council, leaving the body of popular representatives intact. Speaking broadly, the colonies had become states whose sovereignty and independence were limited only by the appointment of some

[1] *Supra*, p. 191.

of their constitutional bodies by a superior state. · In
Connecticut and Rhode Island, even the governor and
council were elected by the colonists. In Massachusetts,
the governor alone was appointed by the crown. In
Pennsylvania, Delaware and Maryland the governor and
council continued to be appointed by the proprietary. In
the remaining colonies, both the governor and council were
appointed by the crown. England, as politically organized, could do no more; later efforts to make its sovereignty over the American colonies real and effective
resulted in their revolt and eventual independence not
only of England but also of such proprietaries as still retained their powers. "The colonies formed by the Europeans in America are under a kind of dependence, of
which there is scarcely an instance in all the colonies of
the ancients, whether we consider them as holding of the
state itself, or of some trading company established in
the state."[1] The feature of corporate autonomy had
been allowed such free development in the American
colonies that England was unable to reduce them to complete organic dependence. When the colonies became
independent States they reproduced in their State constitutions the features of government with which they had
become familiar in their colonial experience. Finally,
when the Federal constitution was framed, much of the
material to which they resorted had been accumulated
during the growth of the States from colonies. The
constitution of the colonial trading company was therefore perpetuated to a large extent in the State and Federal
constitutions of the United States.

It would be beyond the province of this study to present in detail the features of the State and Federal constitutions that were derived from the original colonial
companies; it must be said in general, however, that the
constitutions of the Virginia Company and Massachusetts

[1] Montesquieu, *L'Esprit des Lois*, bk. xxi., cap. 17.

Bay Company served as foundations for the future constitutions of the colonies and of the States and Federal
state that succeeded them. The chief modifications
came from three sources: (1) colonial experience; (2)
imitation of the British constitution; and (3) the application of abstract political philosophy. The concrete
changes consisted in the introduction of the following
elements: (1) The governorship was exalted in many
colonies by its separation from the electorate due to its
representing the interests of the king, a proprietary or a
colonial corporation; even when reduced to election by
the people, the governor was an officer of far greater
power and independence than the governor of a colonial
company had been; in none of the commercial companies
of the class to which the colonial companies belonged had
the governor enjoyed a veto; in most of them he was a
mere executive officer; in some of them he degenerated
into a mere figurehead. (2) The bi-cameral legislature
had not existed in the older corporations; its existence
in the colonies was possibly due in some measure to imitation of the English Parliament, but more probably to
the representation by the council and house of representatives of opposing interests and to their exercise of
different grades of power. (3) The representation of
local communities did not exist in the commercial companies; its introduction into the colonies was a matter of
necessity; it was a refinement of representation by proxy,
which actually existed in Maryland as a stage in development between the attendance of all the freemen and their
representation by towns and other local units. (4) The
restriction of the franchise was not a feature unknown in
corporate organization; it had been applied in the East
India Company [1] and others, but not in the London Company, except to the extent that non-adventurers might
not vote; in the colonies the system was extended some-

[1] *Supra*, p. 128.

what.   (5) The separation of judicial from executive and
legislative functions that characterized the State and
Federal constitutions was never more than rudimentary
in commercial companies, largely because they judged
only infractions of their own laws, while in the colonies
a body of English common law was enforced that seemed
to be independent of the influence of the colonial legislative authorities; the theory of the existence of a body
of customary law and of "natural rights" antecedent to
the enactment of positive law by the colonial legislature
probably gave rise to the independent judiciary.   (6) The
general system of "separation of powers" and "checks
and balances" was quite foreign to the organization of
the typical trading company; it was infused into the
colonial governments just as into the English government
by the representation of conflicting social interests in
separate parts of the government.

The growth of politically organized colonies from commercial corporations was quite in harmony with the
course of development in other classes of corporations.
The political powers of the companies were the ones that
survived, while the others perished.   If the London
Company had enjoyed a longer corporate life, it might
have been expected to shrink into an organization of its
governing body, just as happened in the case of the Plymouth Company when it became the Council for New
England; as it was, its commercial importance decreased
and it became more largely a body of liberal-minded
English citizens whose aim was rather to put in force in
the company's colony a system of government in accordance with the political theories that they cherished.   The
Massachusetts Bay Company, though ostensibly organized as a trading company, readily divested itself of its
commercial attributes and expanded the political side
of its organization into a complete colonial constitution.
In the Connecticut and Rhode Island corporations, the

economic basis of the organization was hardly more than a pretext; their charters virtually conceded to the colonists political constitutions for their government. In fact, though technically corporations, they deserved the name little more than Canada would deserve it now. Self-government or political autonomy alone does not constitute a corporation, particularly when exercised by all the members of a politically organized group, and not merely by a smaller group within it. Connecticut and Rhode Island were autonomous provinces, not corporations.[1] The Georgia corporation experienced no development at all, either directly within itself or indirectly through the body of colonists subject to it. It had from its beginning a form already virtually established. No change could more easily have taken place in it than in the average charitable corporation on which it was mod-

---

[1] This view is evidently in conflict with the view presented by Herbert L. Osgood in an article on " The Colonial Corporation " in the *Political Science Quarterly* for June, 1896, the article being the first of a series of articles on the subject. Blackstone's classification of colonial governments as (1) provincial governments, (2) proprietary governments and (3) charter governments, is there criticised as follows : " (1) The term charter government, which he has employed, is loose and inexact, and the use which he has made of it increases rather than relieves the confusion. (2) Instead of three forms of colonial government there are only two, the corporation and the province." " In support of the second objection to Blackstone's classification, I shall attempt to show in this and in subsequent papers that there are but two distinct forms of colonial government in the English system, the corporation and the province. Under the corporation I include those colonies which themselves became corporations. There were three such, and only three—Massachusetts, Connecticut and Rhode Island. . . . Under the term province I include all the other colonies—those which were founded and controlled by trading companies resident in England, as well as those settled by proprietors and those which were governed directly by the king. In drawing this line of distinction, imperial control as such has been left out of sight. So far as possible attention has been strictly confined to the internal organization of the colony. In the case of the corporations this can easily be done, for they were by nature essentially independent and self-sufficing. The proprietor, and the company considered as a proprietor, were in a certain sense distinct from the colony,

elled.   In its essence it represented the governing body of
the philanthropists whose contributions it administered.
The colonists were a class dependent upon them, and
therefore normally subject to their government.

Not only were American governmental institutions
largely derived from corporations, but American conceptions of political liberty were colored by conceptions
of corporate activity.   If they were not so colored, it
may at least be said that they were given greater vigor
and effectiveness through forms of organization derived
from corporations.   The growth of political liberty in
England was hampered by the presence of feudal institutions; it has had to be developed even to the present
day under restrictions imposed on it by the necessity of
expressing itself through forms not fitted for it or of

though constituting a most important part of it, and transforming it into
the province.   They existed prior to the colony, and derived their authority
from a source outside of it " (pp. 261, 262).   It may fairly be inferred from
the statements quoted that the term " colonial corporation " is intended to
be restricted to corporations identical with colonies.   Such a restriction
would hardly be justifiable ; corporations created for the founding of colonies, even if they do not develop into identity with them, ought not to
be excluded ; the London Company and Plymouth Company, notwithstanding express terms of incorporation were not used in the charter of 1606,
were certainly corporations.   On the other hand, Massachusetts, Rhode
Island and Connecticut were hardly corporations, though the first was
evolved from one, and the second and third were expressly called corporations in their charters.   A corporation is a group of persons within a greater
body of persons politically organized in the state or a subordinate part of
it, and endowed with a particular social form of structure ; the structure is
capable of use for other than strictly corporate purposes ; when it comes
to be used, by expansion of membership or otherwise, as the political constitution of a state or of an entire subordinate part of it, its content is no
longer a corporate group.   The members of a corporation, moreover, enjoy
exceptional rights and are burdened with exceptional duties in the society
of which they are a part ; such was not the case in Massachusetts, Rhode
Island and Connecticut, for all (and not merely a part) of the colonists
(subject only to the qualifications for the franchise) enjoyed the rights and
duties described in the charters.   They may best be viewed as self-governing
provinces.

expressing itself in actual opposition to them. In America, however, the field was almost clear; feudal institutions took no firm root in the new soil. In England, corporations had been the framework within which society had made most of its progress out of the feudal organization; in America, then, where there were few remnants of feudalism, it might have been expected that corporate organization would afford the means of rapid social progress. It was the presence of the feudal element in England and its absence in America that, more than any other difference, widened the breach between the motherland and the colonies until it could not be closed again. The theory of voluntary association, with the subsequent obligation of maintaining the relations assumed until the purpose of the association is attained—the theory on which the corporation is based—is identical, when applied to the state, with the theory of the "social contract." The relations assumed by the American colonists seemed to be voluntarily assumed, but the consequences of assuming them could not be avoided; the existence of a power higher than that of the colonies, from which the latter derived its validity, obscured the element of necessity in colonial institutions, and substituted the less substantial idea of their corporate origin. A corporation is created by the state, by a higher power, before which it is strong because it may rely on it for the protection of its exceptional rights and weak because it depends on the higher power for its existence. Its strength and its weakness both demand a strict definition of its rights and duties; it must therefore have a charter. The perpetual recourse to charters taught the American colonists to value a written constitution. Corporations and colonies modelled on them did not rely for stability and certainty of rights and duties on a body of customs; when the colonies became States and later the States became part of a Federal state, the habit of relying on charters manifested itself in the formation of written constitutions.[1] The principle of the "strict construction" of constitutions, so familiar to students of American public law, is merely an application to the state of the principles applied in ascertaining the rights and duties of corporations; the theory of "implied powers," which has been partially expressed in the Federal constitution, extends no further in American public law than in the law of corporations; if a corporation be granted existence for certain purposes and the right to exercise certain powers, it is granted by implication the powers incidental to its corporate existence, powers clearly in harmony with the purposes for which it is created and the powers incidentally necessary for the exercise of its expressed powers. In truth, as far as concerns the system of public law developed in the United States, the people have simply created corporations of themselves and construe their rights and duties accordingly. Quite in harmony with their attitude towards themselves is the organization of the state behind the constitution—the state that has created corporations of itself—with a supreme court to stand between the state as state and as corporation, and to protect it in either capacity against itself in the other capacity.[2] When the

[1] As the constitution of the United States "is itself primarily a body of written law, so it is based upon successive strata of written constitutional law. . . . The general frame of government established by the [federal] constitution and the general guarantee of rights contained in it, are themselves the result of historical growth through a series of written constitutions. . . . The worship of a written constitution, which has sometimes been satirized as a sentiment peculiar to the American people, has its explanation in the fact that the genesis and growth of political liberty in this country, whether considered in the early colonial period . . . or in the later national period, have taken place in great measure within what may be called the sphere of written law."—William C. Morey, in "The Genesis of a Written Constitution," *Annals of American Academy of Political and Social Science*, April, 1891.

[2] As an illustration of the effect of the "corporation idea" on views of political institutions, the language used by Professor Franklin H. Giddings

colonies became independent States, they simply substituted the American people for the king of England as the source of political power and left themselves as politically organized where they had been before, midway between themselves as sovereign and themselves as subjects.

in his *Principles of Sociology* (p. 177) may be quoted. " In the constitution of the state the most important subordinate bodies are the public corporations. The state first *incorporates itself*, defining its territory and its membership, describing its organization and laying upon itself the rules of procedure by which it will systematically conduct its affairs. It next *in like manner* incorporates the local subdivisions of society, such as counties, townships and cities, and assigns to each certain rights, duties and powers." The expression by which the state is described as incorporating itself is plainly not used figuratively ; but the performance of such an act by the state is contrary to any sound conception of the nature of corporations or of the process by which they are created.

VII

THE LEGAL CONCEPTION OF CORPORATIONS

THE conception of an institution found in a prevailing system of law is not always identical with a sociological conception of it; it would be nearer the truth to say that such identity never exists. The system of law lingers behind society in its progress and delays to translate newly formed social relations into enforceable rights and obligations until (in many cases) long after they have been fully formed. Not only does the law negatively fail to interpret promptly and fully new social relations, but it positively preserves decadent social relations in form long after they have (in many respects) ceased to be effective in substance. Even when the point is reached at which new social relations can be no longer left without legal expression, they are expressed in terms of the existing system of law with the least possible disturbance of the principles of which it is composed; if necessary to reduce the new relations to harmony with the old in the system of law, resort will even be had to fictions—intentional assumptions of things as facts that are in truth not facts. In a perfect system of law there would be no fictions; the use of them is a confession of weakness, of the inability of the system to faithfully reflect and support social relations. The failure of a system of law to adequately express new social relations is very apparent in the United States at the present time, where the principles of equality before the law, freedom of contract and the preservation of private property seem

to be seriously out of harmony with the actual social in-
equality of individual members of society, the limitation
of the power to contract by the organization of trusts
and trades unions, and the extended modification of the
private control of physical things (private property) by
the increasing complexity of social relations. As an example of the conservation of old institutions in the law
after they have actually decayed in society, one has only
to refer to the preservation of monarchy in European
governments, in public law, or the persistent adherence
to the feudal system of land tenure until a very recent
day, in private law. No better example exists of the
use of a fiction to bring new social relations into harmony
with established law than the legal view of a corporation
as an artificial person, a *persona ficta.* As far as the
modern law of corporations is subject to criticism, it is
due to the three features suggested, (*a*) its positive conservation of obsolete social relations; (*b*) its negative
failure to recognize new social relations; and (*c*) its employment of a vicious fiction to provide an apparent harmony between an old system of law and new elements of
society.

The conception of corporations at the foundation of
the modern law of them matured in England in the
fifteenth and sixteenth centuries and found its chief ex-
pounder in Sir Edward Coke. When Sir William Blackstone wrote his *Commentaries on the Law of England,*
published in 1765, he did little more than to bring together the principles scattered through Coke's *Institutes*
and *Reports,* and to present them in a more compact and
serviceable form. The conception remained substantially
intact until after the beginning of the nineteenth century
and is still the basis of the present law of corporations,
though seriously modified by legislation and judicial decisions since 1850. The state of the law as interpreted
by Coke and Blackstone may therefore be taken as the

starting-point for a study of corporations on their technical legal side, as it was at once the culmination of previous development and the foundation of future changes;
the earlier changes had been constructive, while the modifications of the nineteenth century have been destructive in their tendencies. The elements of the law, as
somewhat unsystematically expounded in Coke's *Institutes* and Coke's *Reports* (especially the report of the
leading case of Sutton's Hospital[1]), and in Blackstone's
chapter on Corporations in his *Commentaries*,[2] may perhaps best be distributed, for the sake of clearness and
succinctness, under the three heads of (*a*) relations to the
state, (*b*) internal relations, and (*c*) relations to society.

(*a*) *Relations to the State.*— Corporations, called also
bodies politic or bodies corporate (*corpora corporata*),
were erected, with the consent of the state, by common
law, prescription or expressly by royal charter or act of
Parliament. Their erection was not dependent on the
use of express words of incorporation but might be implied in the nature of the powers granted, as the incorporation of a municipality was implied in the grant of
gilda mercatoria. Even this erection *in futuro* might be
anticipated and legalized in advance on the fulfillment of
conditions presently imposed. They might be created
by the state either directly or mediately through agents
to whom such creative power should be delegated. They
might be dissolved by act of Parliament, by the death
of all their members (in the case of corporations aggregate), by surrender of their franchises to the king or by
forfeiture of them through neglect or abuse of them.
The general purpose of creating them was to subserve
"the advantage of the public" as in "the advancement of
religion, of learning, and of commerce"[3]; the particular

[1] Coke's *Reports*, book x.
[2] Chapter xviii., pp. 466–485 (Christian's edition).
[3] Coke's observation on the creation of great companies for foreign

purposes of the creation of each corporation appeared in the body of rights and obligations confirmed to it by common law or prescription, or expressly by act of Parliament, royal charter or founder's charter. As a negative corollary, it might not be erected for illicit purposes. The chief legal quality conferred on a corporation as a means to the accomplishment of its purposes was the capacity to "take in succession." "It is impossible to take in succession for ever without a capacity; and a capacity to take in succession cannot be without incorporation; and the incorporation cannot be created without the king."[1] The accomplishment of the corporate purposes was ensured by the visitation of civil corporations by the king through the court of king's bench, of ecclesiastical corporations by the ordinary and of eleemosynary corporations by founders, their heirs or persons designated by them. On the dissolution of a corporation its lands and tenements reverted to the person, or his heirs, who had granted them to it,

" for the law doth annex a condition to every such grant, that if the corporation be dissolved, the grantor shall have the lands again, because the cause of the grant faileth. The grant is indeed only during the life of the corporation; which may endure for ever: but, when that life is determined by the dissolution of the body politic, the grantor takes it back by reversion, as in the case of every other grant for life."

(*b*) *Internal Relations.*—Corporations were sole, consisting of one person, as the king, a bishop or parson; or aggregate, consisting of more than one person, as the

commerce is of passing interest : " Here, by the way, it is to be observed, that three new things which have fair pretences are most commonly hurtful to the commonwealth, viz. . . . 3. New corporations trading into foreign parts, and at home, which under the fair pretence of order and government, in conclusion tend to the hindrance of trade and traffique, and in the end produce monopolies."—*2d Institute*, 540.

[1] 10 Coke's *Reports*, 26b.

mayor and commonalty of a city, the head and fellows of a college or the dean and chapter of a cathedral church.[1] They enjoyed "perpetual succession," the former through a succession of single persons and the latter through the maintenance of the body of members by the admission of new members to fill vacancies. Corporations aggregate might enact by-laws or private statutes for their better government, but only such as should not be contrary to the laws of the land or the statutes provided by founders. Membership in them was forfeited by infraction of the corporate statutes or of the law of the land, or might be voluntarily resigned. The corporate will was determined by vote of a majority of members. The corporation could act only thorough its organization; consequently, if an integral part of it should be wanting, the activity of the corporation was suspended until the wanting part should be supplied; thus during the vacancy of the head-ship, if one were a part of the corporate constitution, the corporation could perform no act until it had first elected a head. Nor might the head, in most matters, act without the body.

"A sole body politic that hath the absolute right in them, as an abbot, bishop, and the like, may make a discontinuance; but a corporation aggregate of many, as dean and chapter, warden and chaplains, master and fellows, mayor and commonalty, etc., cannot make any discontinuance; for if they join, the grant is good; and if the dean, warden, master, or mayor makes it alone, where the body is aggregate of many, it is void and worketh a disseisin . . ."

(c) *Relations to Society.*—In their relations to society,

---

[1] Coke subdivided corporations aggregate into two classes, (1) " either of all persons capable, or (2) of one person capable, and the rest incapable or dead in law" (On Littleton, i., 2a). The subdivision had been made necessary in order to comprehend in the classification such bodies as abbots and convents, but was of no significance after the dissolution of monasteries in the Reformation.

corporations were "artificial persons," "persons incorporate or politique created by the policy of man (and therefore . . . called bodies politique)" as distinguished
from "persons natural created by God." As such juristic
persons they were separate and distinct from the natural
persons of whom they were composed. They accordingly had to have corporatè names, in which they might
"sue or be sued, plead or be impleaded, grant or receive,"
purchase and hold lands, goods and chattels [1] "and do all
other acts as natural persons may." It was the opinion
of Coke that a corporation must also have "a place, for
without a place no incorporation can be made." "A
corporation aggregate is invisible, immortal, and rests
only in intendment and consideration of the law." As it
could not "manifest its intentions by any personal act or
oral discourse," it had to "act and speak" by a common
seal and appear by attorney. Because it could not appear in person, it could not do fealty or homage, for they
had to be done in person,—yet it could receive homage;
a corporation sole might do homage, however, and it
had been likewise possible for an abbot, because his convent had been "dead in law." Having no physical body,
a corporation aggregate could not be an imbecile, com-
mit a crime, be guilty of treason or suffer an assault or
battery; nor could it be imprisoned or suffer attainder,
forfeiture or corruption of blood; it could not be out-
lawed but had to be coerced through its lands and goods.
Having likewise no soul, it could not be bound by oath
(and consequently might not act as executor or adminis-
trator), could not be excommunicated or summoned into

[1] Corporations sole, in their corporate capacity, might not own goods and
chattels, though they might so hold lands and tenements, and corporations
aggregate might not be devisees of land by will, and could purchase land
only after having been granted a license in exemption from the provisions
of the statutes of mortmain—but those limitations did not flow from the
essential nature of corporations. They served, however, to intensify the
distinction between natural persons and corporations.

ecclesiastical courts (which could act only *pro salute animi* and punish only by spiritual censure). As the ideal personality of the corporation and the natural personality of its members were entirely distinct, "the debts of a corporation, either to or from it, are totally extinguished by its dissolution; so that the members thereof cannot recover, or be charged with them in their natural capacities," as indeed they could not while the corporation was in existence. The chief distinction between the natural persons that composed corporations and the natural persons with whom they came in contact lay in the capacity of the former to "take by succession." Those who took lands, goods or chattels by succession, whether individual persons or groups of persons, were conceived to form, together with their predecessors and successors, the ideal, immortal person of the corporation.

"As all personal rights die with the person, and as the necessary forms of investing a series of individuals, one after another, with the same identical rights, would be very inconvenient, if not impracticable, it has been found necessary, when it is for the advantage of the public to have any particular rights kept on foot and continued, to constitute artificial persons, who may maintain a perpetual succession, and enjoy a kind of legal immortality. . . . As the heir doth inherit to the ancestor, so the successor doth succeed to the predecessor, and the executor to the testator."

"Continuance of blood" in ancestors and heirs was replaced by "privity of succession" in corporations.[1]

[1] Many of the expressions found in the older law of corporations justify the query whether the lawyers would not have been more consistent if they had called a corporation an "artificial family" (in the sense of a series of generations) instead of an "artificial person"; it would at least have done less violence to the imagination. The analogy, in legal contemplation, between a family and a corporation seems to have been discovered by Sir Henry Sumner Maine. "In the older theory of Roman law the individual bore to the family precisely the same relation which in the rationale of

The core of the developed legal conception of corporations is easily discerned in the view of them as artificial persons—natural persons expanded in some directions and limited in others. When, however, an effort is made to discover the technical legal sources of the conception so fully elaborated by Coke and Blackstone, it encounters difficulties that open up a wide field of speculation. The germ of the conception was in the English law itself, but in its development it was influenced by both the Roman law and the canon law. The greatest difficulty lies in the impossibility of attributing particular changes in the English law to forces within it or to the external influences of the other two systems of law; in many cases all three systems are found to have exerted concurrent influences, which it is quite impossible to separate or compare in strength. Certain periods of English history or certain branches of English law may be designated in which it may be asserted with safety that the legal interpretation of English institutions was working itself out through the common law and supplementary statutes without external influence, or in which either the civil law or canon law was to a greater or less extent being infused into the English law; but when a particular definite change is found to have taken place in the English law, such as the recognition of the corporate nature of municipalities, it is unsafe to say that the change was due wholly to the natural evolution of English law, or to estimate the extent to which the Roman law or canon law directly or indirectly contributed to it. Outside of the field of technical law, in which legal principles may be considered

English jurisprudence a corporation sole bears to a corporation aggregate. The derivation and association of ideas are precisely the same. In fact, if we say to ourselves that for purposes of Roman testamentary jurisprudence each individual citizen was a corporation sole, we shall not only realize the full conception of an inheritance, but have constantly at command the clue to the assumption in which it originated."—*Ancient Law*, p. 182. See also Markby, *Elements of Law*, § 550.

as derived from existing systems of law, is the wider field
of social development, largely independent of the system
of law, yet also either promoted or restrained by it;
eventually, however, the system of law must inevitably be
reduced to harmony with permanent changes in society
itself. The prominent features of the evolution of the
English law of corporations may be grouped under the
heads of (1) English law, (2) Roman law, (3) Canon law
and (4) Social development.

1. *English Law.*—In the beginning the germ of the
future conception of a corporation made its way into the
English law through the recognition of the "communities" of cities and towns, and of the body of rights and
duties appertaining to residence in them. That cities
and towns and bodies of population grouped about castles
performed functions of exceptional importance, involving
exceptional rights and duties, had been recognized before
the Conquest, as appears from the records of Domesday.
William the Conqueror, however, made the recognition
sharper and more distinct. The grant of a charter to the
city of London implied the sanction, to a limited extent,
of the peculiar privileges that its citizens enjoyed. More
generally he proclaimed in his laws that "castles, boroughs and cities were founded and erected for the protection of the people of the land and for the defence of
the realm, and that therefore they ought to be preserved
in all their freedom and integrity." [1]   "If any bondman,"
moreover, "shall have remained without claim for a year
and a day in our cities, or in our boroughs surrounded
with a wall, or in our castles, from that day he shall be
made a freeman, and he shall be for ever free from the
yoke of servitude." [2]   The law crystallized at first about

[1] " Et ideo castella, et burgi, et civitates site sunt, et fundate, et ædificate,
scilicet, ad tuicionem gencium et populorum regni, et ad defensionem regni,
et idcirco observari debent cum omni libertate, et integritate, et racione."—
Laws of King William the Conqueror, Thorpe, vol. i., p. 493.

[2] *Ibid.*, vol. i., p. 494.

the term "liber burgus," but it denoted rather a medium through which the law viewed the burgess himself than a legal entity.[1] During the first two centuries after the Conquest, the twelfth and thirteenth centuries, the conception was hardly more fully developed. The next step, covering the fourteenth and fifteenth centuries, is fairly indicated by the use of the term "community" somewhat more technically, and finally, towards the end of the period, by the employment of derivatives of the term "corpus." The use of the term "corporation" at the end of the series became common in the sixteenth century. In the general use of the first term, "community,"[2] it comprehended counties, hundreds, townships, gilds, universities and monastic orders[3]; in Magna Charta it was applied even to the English nation—"tout la commune Dengleterre." When the city of London was described as a commune in 1191, it is still a matter of controversy whether the word was used generally or technically. But in 1304, in an action brought by the Abbot of St. Edmund's against some of the townsmen for usurpation of political powers, he charged "quod non habent guildam mercatoriam, nec cognitiones Placitorum ad guildam mercatoriam pertinentes, nec *communitatem*, nec sigillum commune, nec majorem . . ."[4]; the "point" of the case was whether the townsmen had a technical "community." In a charter granted by Edward III. in 1345 to the tenants of the manor of Cheylesmere in Coventry is the following concession: "dictis hominibus de Coventre tenentibus dicti Manerii quod ipsi et eorum heredes et successores Communitatem inter se decetero habeant, et Majorem et Ballivos idoneos de seipsis

---

[1] *Supra*, pp. 120, 121.
[2] Also found in the forms "commonalty," the French form "commune" and the Latin forms "communitas" and "communa."
[3] Pollock and Maitland, *History of English Law*, vol. i., p. 478.
[4] Gross, *Gild Merchant*, vol. ii., p. 34.

eligere et creare possint anneatim . . ."[1] As terms
midway between "community" and "corporation" are
found such as "communitas perpetua," "communitas
perpetua et corporata," "corpus corporatum et politi-
cum" and the like. By the charter of Henry VI. to
Kingston-upon-Hull in 1440, in which Merewether and
Stephens somewhat arbitrarily find the first grant of a
complete incorporation, the "burgesses, their heirs and
successors" were made "one perpetual corporate commonalty"[2] The Conqueror had most prominently in
mind, apparently, the physical town, with its castles
and walls and inhabitants to defend them; in the "liber
burgus" the law saw most clearly a body of tenants enjoying special privileges of land tenure, commerce and
the like, by virtue of their residence in the borough; in
the community, when the term was used generally, the
group of people was seen, though dimly, to be the subject, as a group, of legal rights and duties; when the term
was used technically or replaced by some derivative of
corpus, the organized group was clearly separated as a
legal personality from the aggregate of persons of which
it was composed. Concurrently with the emergence as
a distinct legal personality was the gradual substitution
of "successors" for "heirs" as the persons upon whom
the corporate rights and duties should devolve. In many
early grants, the powers conceded, being largely dependent on the tenure of land, were made simply to groups
of tenants, on the assumption, doubtless, that they would
descend to their heirs without express provision.[3] In
William's charter to London privileges were granted to
the citizens and their heirs. Likewise John confirmed

[1] *Ibid.*, vol. i., p. 93, note (3).
[2] *History of English Boroughs*, pp. 860–869.
[3] *E. g.*, Archbishop Thurstan, in his charter to Beverley, acknowledges
"dedisse et concessisse . . . hominibus Beverlaco omnes libertates
iisdem legibus quibus illi de Eboraco habent in sua civitate."—Stubbs,
Select Charters, pp. 109, 110.

the grant of the sheriffwick of London and Middlesex
to the "citizens of London and their heirs" to be enjoyed
by them "hereditarily." [1] In later charters to other cities
and boroughs heirs and successors were mentioned together, as in the charter of Richard II. to the men of
Basingstoke, in which it was conceded "hominibus ville
predicte quod ipsi, *heredes et successores* sui unam Communitatem perpetuam de seipsis et unum Commune
Sigillum habeant imperpetuum . . ." [2] When the
conception of the corporation was complete, the successors alone should theoretically enjoy corporate rights
and perform corporate duties. The transformation was
apparently never fully accomplished. In both towns
and gilds heirs of townsmen and gildsmen were accorded
special consideration, in the former even until the nineteenth century, in the latter, as long as they existed.
Even in the early centuries, when the heirs of townsmen
appeared formally to be the only persons to enjoy their
rights after them, it had been almost universally possible
for the status of burgess-ship to be acquired by outsiders,
as in the familiar case of villeins that had escaped from
feudal manors.

The coming into distinctness of the conception of the
community as a legal entity separate from its individual
members was accompanied by the more formal concession
of the element of perpetuity. In few cases had corporate
privileges been bestowed on groups of tenants or burgesses for limited periods. The group had been reasonably considered perpetual and its enjoyment of a privilege
presumptively unlimited in time. When the body of
privileges came to be viewed as inhering in a technical
"community," a medium through which burgesses enjoyed the privileges rather than an aggregate of them,
when the burgesses were said to *have* a community rather

[1] *Historical Charters and Constitutional Documents of the City of London*,
p. 16.　　　　　　　[2] Gross, *Gild Merchant*, vol. i., p. 94, note (3).

than to *be* one, then the element of perpetuity seemed an attribute of the artificial community to be expressly attached to it rather than an inherent quality of its nature. The "limited liability" so much considered in modern corporations had an origin similar to that of the element of perpetuity—in the legal separation of the community or aggregate of members from the members themselves. In a rough way, the members of mediæval gilds and municipalities were held jointly responsible for the debts of members, whether incurred in personal transactions, or in transactions relating to matters of common concern; it was only when the process of separating the members from the community in thought and action and legal rules was complete, in the fifteenth century, that the well-known principle of the civil law, "Si quid universitati debetur, singulis non debetur, nec quod debet universitas, singuli debent,"[1] became applicable in England. A common seal appears to have been used by groups of population, such as counties, that never attained the status of corporations; on the contrary it seems not to have been used by many bodies that might properly be considered corporations; in some cases the private seal of an officer was attached to corporate documents; in fact, hardly a statement can be made of the use of seals before the fourteenth century that would not have to be guarded with many exceptions. It is sufficient for the present purpose to say that during the fourteenth century the grant to a community of the privilege of using a common seal became one of the usual features of corporate charters. It was undoubtedly one of the manifestations of the evolution of the community as a distinct legal personality, and afforded Blackstone, in the eighteenth century, a technical justification for the statement that a corporation must "act and speak" only by its common seal.

---

[1] *Digest*, iii., 4, 7, § 1.   See p. 225, *infra*.

The classes of corporations (in the general sense of the term), other than municipalities, affected by the development of the law of corporations before the sixteenth century were the ecclesiastical corporations (with the allied educational and eleemosynary corporations) and the gilds. The former came into contact with the English system of law largely through their landholding capacity; for the most part the conception of them was derived from the canon law, the law of the Church; as far as the temporal law sought to interpret them, it must have sought to appreciate and reflect a conception of them that had already matured within the organization of the Church. As far as the gilds were concerned, they were easily fitted into the conception already formed with relation to the municipalities. They undoubtedly accentuated the personality of the towns in which they flourished and thereby aided the legal conception of corporations to an earlier and more vivid realization, but by the time the conception was approaching fullness, the gilds were in decay. It was to only a limited extent that the gilds, as such, appeared as parties in litigation. On the whole they were subordinate to the towns, especially during the fifteenth century, when the legal conception of a corporation was crystallizing. The gilds of London appear to have been exceptional, for London was so large and had such varied separate interests that it never attained the distinct personality characteristic of many smaller cities and towns; the gilds were consequently nearer to the conception of a corporation than the city itself and continued in existence long after gilds in the rest of England had virtually disappeared.

2. *Roman Law.*— In attempting to estimate the influence exerted on the conception of a corporation in the English law by the conception of it in the Roman law, one comes almost at the outset upon a remarkable similarity in the bodies of corporation law in the two systems.

The similarity, close as it must be conceded to be, is far too easily accounted for by the assumption that "the [English] conception [of a corporation] has been taken full-grown from the law of Rome,"[1] though it has been made by many writers.[2] Two serious obstacles are encountered by the assumption: (*a*) The most prominent feature of the conception in the English law is wanting to that in the Roman law, and (*b*) the occasion or medium of the absorption by the English law of the particular branch of Roman law cannot be shown from the historical facts.

(*a*) In the *Corpus Juris Civilis*, the developed body of Roman law with which the English system came in contact, corporations were not regarded as "artificial persons."[3] Contrasted with *singulares personæ* were *societates*, *collegia*, *universitates* and *corpora*. The *societas* corresponded closely in general to the modern *society*, neither encouraged nor forbidden by the state, except as its purposes should be positively unlawful; but the term was also applied to associations formed for farming the taxes or other public revenues, or for working gold, silver and salt mines,[4] the latter being apparently intended as an indirect source of public revenue. Social-religious organizations

---

[1] *Encyclopædia Britannica, sub verbo* "Corporation."

[2] The view is somewhat modified in Pollock and Maitland's *History of English Law*, vol. i., p. 469. "Every system of law that has attained a certain stage in its development seems compelled by the ever-increasing complexity of human affairs to add to the number of persons provided for it by the natural world, to create persons who are not men. Or, rather, to speak with less generality and more historical accuracy, a time came when every system of law in western Europe adopted and turned to its own use an idea of non-human persons, ideal subjects of rights and duties, which was gradually discovered in the Roman law-books."

[3] This view is expressed with some degree of hesitancy because the weight of authority is clearly opposed to it. See Sohm, *Institutes of Roman Law* (Ledlie's translation), p. 101; Sheldon Amos, *History and Principles of the Civil Law of Rome*, p. 118. H. O. Taylor (*Private Corporations*, chapter on Corporations in the Roman Law) is apparently the only authority that supports the position taken in the text.   [4] *Digest*, iii., 4, 1.

quite similar to the social-religious gilds of mediæval England were usually formed on the basis of some community of interest, as tenancy on estates of land; as political purposes were sometimes secretly combined with those strictly social or religious in character, such organizations were always the cause of more or less anxiety and apprehension to the government. Corresponding to the English craft gilds were the Roman *collegia* of fellow-artisans or fellow-workmen, such as bakers, smiths, fishermen and mariners.[1] Later monastic convents, cathedral chapters and chapters of collegiate churches were anticipated in the *collegia* of priests attached to temples. Even some departments of the government, as the treasury, *fiscus*, were viewed as being subjects of rights and duties, and approached the status of later English "corporations sole." But the most fruitful sources of corporation law in Rome, as later in England, were the subordinate political communities, *civitates, municipia, coloniæ, vici*, comprehended under *universitates;* the body contemplated by the law appears to have been sometimes the whole community, sometimes only the governing body. The term *corpus* was the technical legal term implying the recognition and sanction of the *collegium* or *universitas* by the state, but *universitas* was frequently used synonymously with it, and *collegium* was also used with the presumption that it was a legal *corpus*. As in English law so in the Roman law the relation of the state to the formation of corporations ranged from no restriction at all, except for purposes declared to be illegal,[2] to absolute prohibition, except with the express license of the state.[3] *Collegia illicita* were dissolved and their common property divided

---

[1] *Digest*, iii., 4, 1.

[2] "Sodales sunt, qui ejusdem collegii sunt . . . His autem potestatem facit lex, pactionem, quam velint, sibi ferre, dum ne quid ex publica lege corrumpant. . . ."—*Digest*, xlviii., 1, 22, 4.

[3] *Digest*, iii., 4, 1 ; xlviii., 1, 22, 1 ; xlviii., 1, 22, 3, § 1.

among their members.[1] Serfs might not be admitted to
membership in some colleges without the consent of their
masters.[2] A person might be a member of only one
collegium at one time; if he should belong to more, he
was required to choose the one to which he should adhere
and leave the others.[3] At least three members were
necessary to constitute a *collegium* or *universitas*,[4] though
it should not cease to exist by its reduction to a membership of one.[5] Corporate action was determined by vote
of a majority,[6] though it appears that (at least in municipalities) two thirds of the corporation or governing body
had to be present.[7] The *universitas* could act in litigation
and dealings with the world only through its agent, its
syndicus (permanent representative) or its *actor* (agent for
a particular purpose or occasion). Debts due to a corporation or owing by it were payable neither to nor by
its individual members.[8] Things (*res*) were of five kinds:
(1) *communes* (as the air); (2) *divinæ* (*res nullius*, things
belonging to "nobody"), including (*a*) *res sacræ* (temples),
(*b*) *religiosæ* (burial-places) and (*c*) *sanctæ* (city walls)[9]; (3)
publicæ (rivers, ports, streets, public edifices); (4) *res
universitatis* (corporate things, theatres, race-courses,
public slaves)[10]; and (5) *singulæ* (private things). In contemplation of law the member of the corporation appeared

[1] *Digest*, xlviii., 1, 22, 3.

[2] *Digest*, xlviii., 22, 3, § 2.

[3] *Digest*, xlviii., 1, 22, 2, § 1.

[4] *Digest*, l., 16, 85.

[5] "In Decurionibus vel aliis universitatibus nihil refert, utrum omnes
iidem maneant, an pars maneat, vel omnes immutati sunt. Sed si universitas ad unum redit, magis admittitur, posse eum convenire et conveniri,
quum jus omnium in unum recederit, et stet nomen universitatis."—*Digest*,
iii., 4, 7, § 2 ; l., 16, 85.

[6] "Quod major pars curiæ effecit, pro eo habitur, ac si omnes egerint."—
Digest, l., 1, 19.

[7] *Digest*, iii., 4, 3.

[8] *Digest*, iii., 4, 7, § x. See also p. 221, *supra*.

[9] *Digest*, i., 8, 6, § 2.

[10] *Digest*, i., 8, 6, § 1.

to sustain the same relation to the corporate property that the citizen sustained to the property of the state.[1] As the municipalities emerged in Roman history, and forced themselves in between the citizen and the state, the political powers that were detracted by them from the state lost their standing in the *jus publicum* and became subjects of *jus privatum*. The evolution was not at all dissimilar to that experienced by English cities and boroughs. Moreover, the point was reached at which the property of the corporation could be viewed as not the property of the members, and not even to be used by them in common.[2] But the Roman law never reached the point in development at which the corporations were included in the category of "persons."[3] The only expression from which it may be inferred that the conception of "personality" was entertained is found in the provision relating to succession by inheritance: "Mortuo reo promittendi et ante aditam hereditatem fidejussor accipi potest, quia *hereditas personæ vice fungitur, sicuti municipium, et decuria, et societas.*"[4] There, apparently for the purpose of illustration and comparison, the body of rights and duties eventually to be attached to some person by virtue of the possession of the goods comprised in the inheritance are likened to the body of rights and

---

[1] "Quibus autem permissum est corpus habere collegii, societatis, sive cujusque alterius eorum nomine, proprium est *ad exemplum Reipublicæ* habere res communes, arcam communem, et actorem sive syndicum, per quem *tanquam in Republica*, quod communiter agi fierique oporteat, agatur, fiat."—*Digest*, iii., 4, 1, § 1.

[2] "Servum municipum posse in caput civium torqueri, sæpissime rescriptum est, quia not sit illorum servus, sed reipublicæ. Idemque in ceteris servis corporum dicendum est, nec enim plurium servus videtur, sed corporis."—*Digest*, xlviii., 18, 1, § 7.

[3] The view of corporations even appears, from some parts of the civil law, to have reached the opposite extreme of a denial of corporate personality. "Hæ autem res, quæ humani juris sunt, aut publicæ sunt, aut privatæ; quæ publicæ sunt, nullius in bonis esse creduntur; ipsius enim universitatis esse creduntur."—*Digest*, i., 8, 1.   [4] *Digest*, xlvi., 1, 22.

duties attached to a corporation and not exercised by its
particular members. When commentators write of "juristic persons" in the Roman law, they use their own expression to describe what the Romans themselves did not
recognize as persons.

(*b*) What was the occasion or medium of the absorption
of the Roman law of corporations into the English law?
It is quite universally conceded that from the time of the
conquest of Britain by the Anglo-Saxons in the fifth
century until the discovery of the Justinian *Corpus Juris
Civilis* at Amalfi in 1130 and the revival of the study of
Roman law at Bologna, a period of about seven hundred
years, the Roman law exercised no influence on the English law. The influence so extensively felt on the continent did not penetrate to England. After the Norman
Conquest and even before Vacarius lectured on the civil
law about the middle of the twelfth century, some indirect influence may have been exercised through the large
number of ecclesiastics that came to England with the
Norman kings, but it is said that even they applied themselves to the study of the common law. The use of
Norman-French in the courts would have facilitated the
absorption of foreign elements; but if there was any such
movement, except as some principles of Norman law
were imported, its effects must have been slight, for no
evidence of them is to be found. In the reign of Stephen,
however, when Theobald was made Archbishop of Canterbury, he brought to England with him Vacarius, an Italian
priest, who began to lecture (at Oxford, it is said) on the
civil law in 1149. The revival of the study of the civil
law was one feature of the "twelfth century Renaissance"
and the inauguration of the lectures of Vacarius may be
taken as the beginning of its influence on English law.
Stephen at first prohibited by proclamation the study of
the civil law in England, but his opposition was either
soon withdrawn or disregarded. Under his successor

"those [civil] laws were, with more safety, cherished
here, and held, at least by some, in much greater esteem
than before." [1] From the middle of the twelfth century
to the beginning of the reign of Edward III., in the first
half of the fourteenth century, the civil law enjoyed its
greatest influence on the law of England. The judges,
court officers and lawyers were ecclesiastics,[2] all learned
in the Roman law. The kings, favoring the Imperial
principle of the Roman law, "quod principi placuit legis
vigorem habet," may be assumed not to have been averse
to its use in England, though they may have opposed its
teaching and interpretation by the Roman Catholic
Church.[3] The common law itself was not a settled system [4] and lacked the strength of a body of written law in
an age when a written text was accorded the presumptive
weight of tradition.[5] During the period a state of hostility between the laity and clergy is said to have resulted from their rivalry in the support, respectively, of
the Common law and Civil law. The establishment of
the court of common pleas permanently at Westminster
in accordance with the terms of Magna Charta, and the
founding of the Inns of Court—the "University of the
Common Law"—are represented as preserving the common law from being overwhelmed by the Civil law.
Henry III., in 1235, certainly issued an order to the
mayor and sheriffs of London "ne aliquis scholas regens
de legibus in ea civitate de cætero ibidem leges doceat,"
which, whether it referred to the Civil law alone [6] or to

[1] Selden, *Fleta*, cap. viii., sec. 1 (p. 187 of Kelham's translation).

[2] "Nullus clericus nisi causidicus" is the frequently quoted comment of
William of Malmsbury, *De Gestis Regum Anglorum*, lib. iv., p. 369 (Rolls
Series).

[3] Green, *History of the English People*, vol. i., p. 252.

[4] English law as a *system* is somewhat indefinitely said to have originated
between the reign of Henry II. and that of Edward I.—Heron, *History of
Jurisprudence*, p. 237.

[5] Maine, *Ancient Law*, p. 79.

[6] Selden, *Fleta*, cap. viii., sec. 2 (p. 200 of Kelham's translation).

both the Civil law and Common law,[1] must have given greater importance to the work of the Inns of Court. In the following year, when all the influence of the Church was exerted to secure the incorporation in the English law of the civil law rule (enforced in the ecclesiastical courts) for the legitimization of bastard children by future marriage of the parents, "all the barons and earls with one voice answered, that they would not change the laws of England, which have hitherto been used and approved."[2] In 1164 Pope Alexander III. had forbidden monks to teach either medicine or the Civil law outside of their monasteries; later Innocent IV. forbade the clergy to read the Common law, "because its decisions were not founded on the Imperial constitutions, but merely on the customs of the laity."[3] It might reasonably be inferred that many features of the Roman law would be found in the English law as the result of the contact, but of Glanvil's compendium of the law, written in the reign of Henry I., it is said by a competent authority that

"though it bears traces of his acquaintance with the Roman law, and adopts in some few cases its terminology, [it] is otherwise entirely free from Roman influence and shows the almost complete purity of the English law at the end of the twelfth century from Roman elements."[4]

The common law, though an undigested mass of court-sanctioned customs, had remarkable vitality because it

---

[1] Coke, 2d *Institute*, Preface.

[2] Statute of Merton, c. 9, 20 Henry III.   A century later " the nobility declared 'that the realm of England hath never been, unto this hour, neither by the consent of our lord the King and the lords of parliament shall it ever be ruled or governed by the Civil Law.'"—Heron, *History of Jurisprudence*, p. 241.

[3] Blackstone, *Commentaries*, Introduction, vol. i., p. 20.   See also letter of Innocent IV. to scholars in 1254 with relation to legal studies, Matthew Paris, *Chronica Majora*, vol. v., pp. 427, 428 (Rolls Series).

[4] Scrutton, *Influence of the Roman Law on the Law of England*, p. 77.

was in so great harmony with the actual conditions of the English people; its lack of systematic arrangement was perhaps an indication of its greatest virtue; it was unsystematic because society was not systematically organized. The attainment of a perfectly formed system of law may be an indication of social decadence, for social progress is always uneven and is reflected in incoherence in laws and branches of law; it is true at least that the Roman law did not attain symmetry and formal perfection until Roman society was in decay; likewise the feudal system of law was attaining the virtue of a system only when feudalism was beyond the first stages of disintegration. Moreover, the principles of the public law of Rome, favoring imperialism and monarchy, must have been odious to the English baronage and common people (as far as the latter participated in political life) and even to the Church at a time when it was asserting its superiority over emperors and kings; and the odium of the public law was perhaps imparted to the private law as part of the same system.

Bracton's *De Legibuset Consuetudinibus Angliæ*, written in the reign of Henry III. after the middle of the following century, contains much that was taken directly from the *Corpus Juris Civilis* (or the *Summa* of Azo), but it is very questionable how far the portions relating to corporations were applicable to existing English corporations. The jurisdictional privileges of cities and boroughs and of citizens and burgesses were recognized[1]; and of royal charters, some were said to be private, others common and others for a corporation (*universitatis*)[2]; thus far, evidently, no resort was had to Roman sources.

" Things belong to corporate bodies (*universitates*) and not to individuals, which are in cities, such as theatres, stadia,

[1] Vol. vi., p. 247 (edition of Sir Travis Twiss).
[2] Vol. i., p. 109.

and such like, and if there are any things in cities which are common . . . these things are said to belong to corporate bodies as regards both the dominion and the use. But the use of things is said to belong to corporate bodies, not as regards their [actual] use, but as regards their dominion and products, such as land and serfs, which are said to belong to cities, because they so belong to all the citizens as not to belong to any one person by himself "[1]; "a thing cannot be the subject of donation, which cannot be the subject of possession, as a thing which is sacred or dedicated to religion, or is, as it were, so, as a thing which belongs to the public treasury, or things which are, as it were, sacred, such as the walls and gates of a city; . . . of sacred things some are not holy but sacred, such as the walls and gates of a city, and they are sacred on that account that they have been sanctioned by kings or by citizens abiding in them; for capital punishment is appointed for those, who with rash audacity overleap the walls or gates of a city; likewise of tenements, some are neither sacred nor holy, but public, of some body, to wit, a corporation, or of a commune (*universitatis, communionis*) or of all and not of any one private man or a single person, such as are theatres and stadia or public places, whether they are in cities or outside of them."[2]

The portions quoted are plainly taken bodily from the Roman law, and they are as plainly inapplicable to contemporary cities and towns in England. There were no theatres and stadia in English towns; gates and walls were not regarded as sacred; no theory of public municipal property had been worked out; corporations owned no serfs. If the portions of Bracton's work taken from the Roman law and clearly inapplicable to existing conditions be disregarded,[3] it contains no evidence of the

[1] Vol. i., p. 59. [2] Vol. iii., pp. 369-371.

[3] "That an English writer of the time of Henry III. should have been able to put off on his countrymen as a compendium of pure English law a treatise of which the entire form and a third of the contents were directly borrowed from the *Corpus Juris*, and that he should have ventured on this

absorption by the English law of the Roman law of corporations. The same may be said of the abridgments of Bracton's work in the reign of Edward I., that of Thornton, the *Fleta*, the *Mirror of Justices* and the work bearing the name of "Britton."

The beginning of the reign of Edward III. (1327) may be taken as the date when the direct influence of the Roman law on the law of England ended. Earlier the Year Books contain records of the use of the Roman law as accepted authority, either to support a principle of English law or to supply it when wanting;

" where an express rule was wanting in [the English] law, recourse might then be had to the rule of the Civil law, as far as grounded on reason, and when both laws were conformable to each other, . . . then the matter in debate was in some measure confirmed or explained by the words of the Imperial law." [1]

But after that time the Year Books were void of citations of Roman law as authority, English lawyers boasted of their ignorance of it and judges were inaccurate in their interpretations of it.[2] Judges and lawyers were no longer chosen from ecclesiastics. For the future its influence was to be due to its value as a systematized body of law, evolved from the experience of centuries of Roman history. It was studied by the judges, lawyers, statesmen and churchmen. The universities taught it. It was a prominent part of a liberal education. It remains to-day the greatest monument of analytical legal reasoning. Its influence was therefore subtle and impossible to estimate,

experiment in a country where the systematic study of the Roman law was formally proscribed, will always be among the most hopeless enigmas in the history of jurisprudence."—Maine, *Ancient Law*, p. 79.

[1] Selden, *Fleta*, cap. iii., sec. 5, p. 49 (Kelham's translation).

[2] See an account of the attitude of a lawyer named Skipwith in 1347, given by Selden (*Fleta*, cap. viii., sec. 5).

but it must nevertheless have been considerable. If it failed to manifest itself in its recognition as authority in the adjudication of cases, it was felt perhaps hardly less in moulding the thoughts of judges and lawyers and giving them form and system. It was the source of a body of maxims, recognized as having weight because founded on reason.[1] It contributed likewise a mass of legal terms. But no more in the particular field of the law of corporations than in the general field of English law can the extent of the influence be estimated. Remarkably enough, the date of the end of the direct influence of Roman on English law is just the date at which the "communities" of English municipalities begin to emerge in technical distinctness from their individual members. If it may be said that during the period of the greatest influence of the Roman law none of its principles of corporation law were absorbed by the English law, so it may be said that during the period in which the English law of corporations was attaining technical perfection the Roman law had the least appreciable influence on it. During the fourteenth and fifteenth centuries and the first half of the sixteenth century, the principle of artificial personality, with all its material deductions and corollaries, was completely evolved; yet at no step in the evolution may the law of Rome be shown or reasonably assumed to have been used as a model.[2]

[1] Broom, *Legal Maxims*, preface, p. vii.

[2] Compare the statement in the article in the *Encyclopædia Britannica* (*sub verbo* " Corporation ") to which reference has already been made. The position there taken is not at all peculiar; on the contrary, it is fairly representative of the body of literature dealing with the history of the law of corporations, or of corporations on their technical legal side, and is here referred to for that reason. The " Roman conception of a corporation was kept alive by ecclesiastical bodies. When English lawyers came to deal with such societies, the corporation law of Rome admitted of easy application. Accordingly, in no department of our law have we borrowed so copiously and so directly from the Civil law. . . . The introduction of corporations into cities and towns does not appear to date farther back

The use of the principles and procedure of the Civil law,
or of the Canon law modified by it, in the ecclesiastical
courts and in those of the universities may be readily
traced to the influence of the Church and its predilection
for the Civil law. The king's chancellor, from whom
emanated the body of adjudications to correct and supplement the Common law, was an ecclesiastic. Masters
and scholars were clerics and subject to the jurisdiction
of the courts of the Church; when the courts of the
chancellors of the universities took their place, the Civil
law remained the basis of their procedure and adjudications. The use of the Civil law in the Marine or Ad-
miralty courts and in the Court of Chivalry was probably
due to the fact that the rights of foreigners often came
before them, and seemed to demand the application of
the Civil law for the same general reason for which it has
contributed so largely to the body of International law.[1]
But for the matter under consideration, it must be said
that it would be very difficult to show any positive influence on the law of corporations from the use of the
Civil law in those courts.

The truth is that the Roman law and English law
passed through parallel courses of development, corresponding to parallel courses of development in the states
whose social relations they registered and interpreted.

than the reign of Henry VI., although they had long possessed what may
be called a quasi-corporate character. By that time the corporate character
of ecclesiastical and educational societies, and even of gilds, had been
recognized, and the great convenience of corporate powers was, no doubt,
the reason why they were demanded by the commonalties of towns."

[1] Selden was of the opinion that even in the universities the Civil law
prevailed largely because some scholars were foreigners,—"because the
study of that law had flourished among them; [and] that it might appear
that equal justice was distributed to foreigners, who studied in those universities, as well as to our own countrymen, when any differences arose among
them."—*Fleta*, cap. viii., sec. 4, p. 221 (Kelham's translation). Blackstone,
following Fortescue, believed that the use of Latin in the universities was
accountable for their adherence to the Civil law (!).

The English law reached the point of development indicated in the *Corpus Juris Civilis* towards the end of the fifteenth century and passed beyond it in the following century to a point that the Roman law had not attained. The development of the English law no doubt proceeded in a more orderly and systematic course, and unfolded its successive conceptions in greater distinctness through the influence of the Roman law, as an elaborated system, on the minds of the men who gave it form and system. The close similarity of the two systems in the department of corporation law remains as a basis for the inference that the intangible influence of the Roman law was exerted in somewhat greater strength on that than on other branches of English law, but it is far from conclusive evidence of a direct "borrowing" or "taking" of the one by the other.

One other avenue through which the Roman law reached the English law and undoubtedly modified it in both form and substance may be anticipated. The Canon law, the system of law built up by the Roman Catholic Church, was in most respects based on the Civil law of Rome and derived its methods and maxims from it. Each was permitted, on principle, to supplement the other in its application.[1] The inclination of the canonist was to apply the Civil law, rather than the Common law, in the field of temporal rights and obligations, if the Canon law could not be extended to comprehend it. As far, therefore, as the Canon law influenced the law of England, to such extent it must be conceded that the Roman law exercised an indirect influence.[2]

" It is obvious that the republication of the Canon law could not but operate as a fresh recognition of the lasting validity

---

[1] Selden, *Fleta*, cap. vi., sec. 5, pp. 137, 138. Sheldon Amos, *History and Principles of the Civil Law of Rome*, pp. 433, 434.

[2] Selden, *Fleta*, cap. vii., sec. 1, p. 141. Blackstone, *Commentaries*, Introduction, vol. i., p. 18 (Christian's edition).

within its own limits, of the Roman Civil law, while the language and forms of the new Canon law codes tended to reproduce and preserve the ancient legal phraseology and logical forms of thought." [1]

After the reign of Stephen the Civil and Canon law were so "inseparably interwoven with each other" [2] that their effects could not be separated.

3. *Canon Law.*—The Canon law exercised a peculiar influence on English law, quite in harmony with the general influence of the Church on the social organization of the Middle Ages. Broadly speaking, the Roman Catholic Church performed for Europe the inestimable service of preserving the organic framework of decaying Roman institutions during the shock of the barbarian conquests until it might again serve as the framework of society after its reorganization. As a part of the service the Church built up within itself a form of government and a body of law modelled on those of Rome. The Canon law was the law of Rome modified and tempered by the teachings of the fathers of the Church and the religious doctrines of Christianity. As a vague presumption of universality attached to the government and laws of Rome, the presumption that inspired the dream of the mediæval empire, so the claim of the Church to be universal afforded a basis for the claim that its laws were universally applicable in spiritual matters, which gave to the *Corpus Juris Canonici* all the strength that it enjoyed. [3]

The earliest corporations were those of the Church, the monasteries and cathedral chapters. Their internal relations as well as their external relations to the Church were the product of Canon law and subject to its regulations. If at first the bodies of mediæval masters and

---

[1] Sheldon Amos, *History and Principles of the Roman Civil Law*, p. 431.
[2] Blackstone, *Commentaries*, vol. i., p. 18.
[3] Sir Matthew Hale, *History of the Common Law*, p. 92.

scholars assumed the form of gilds after their separation from the direct control of the Church, they were later reorganized in educational colleges that abjectly followed the ecclesiastical type, while their members remained *clerici*. The hierarchical feature of the organization of the Catholic Church and Catholic Christianity was reproduced in the corporations, both ecclesiastical and educational; as a matter of legal interpretation, accordingly, the monks were "dead in law" and their personality was absorbed in that of their abbot. The English lawyer might liken dean and chapter to husband and wife, and say that the chapter was *covert* of the dean, but the temporal law, for the most part, merely accepted the interpretation of ecclesiastical institutions adopted by the Church, and enforced it with the least modification necessary to ensure harmony with the Common law.[1] If the Church corporation owned land, it was vested in the bishop or abbot, not because it was demanded by the principles of the Common law, but because the view held by the Church in its law was accepted by the state when the corporation came in contact with the temporal side of society. The doctrine of the absorption of corporate powers by the head of the corporation, favored by the Church on account of its veneration of authority and the hierarchical form of its government, was partly accountable for the exaggeration in temporal corporations of the importance of the headship of the mayor or alderman. The conception of the submergence of the personality of the individual in that of the group was especially favored by the Church; it is frequently found expressed in the Scriptures,[2] the patristic writings and the literature of monasticism; the bond of religious unity was so close that the conception was often reflected in the life of the early social-religious gilds.

[1] Blackstone, *Commentaries*, book i., p. 469.
[2] I Corinthians xii., 12–27; Romans xii., 4, 5; Ephesians iv., 4, 16.

Yet, after all, what the Canon law borrowed from the Civil law was largely its form and structure, its system, terminology and procedure; though its substance was also largely absorbed, yet the rights and obligations recognized and enforced by the Canon law were derived to a great extent from the thought and literature of the Church. There was nothing in the corporation law of Rome that favored the doctrine of the legal absorption of the group in its headship; that was a doctrine evolved from Christianity as an interpretation of the social relations of men; when the English law enforced it, as it did to a great extent, it was not borrowing from the Civil law of Rome, but from the Canon law, the ecclesiastical system of interpreting and enforcing social rights and duties.

When the relations of corporations to their members and to society came to be subjected to the test of philosophy, it was the scholastic philosophy, the philosophy of the monastic and cathedral schools, that was first applied. It was the speculative canonist and the scholastic philosopher that invented the mystical "personal" elements in the conception of the corporation; it was they that described it as a *persona ficta* long before it was adopted by the English lawyers as the basis of a system of corporation law. Innocent IV. earned the title of "the father of the modern learning of corporations" by giving formal sanction to the results of their quibbling analyses. If the source of the conception of a corporation as an artificial person is to be found, it must be sought among the speculations of the canonists and scholastics of the thirteenth century,[1] not among the interpretations of Roman or English jurists. The conception, moreover, was most promoted in its development by ideas and thoughts drawn from the literature of the Church.

4. *Development of Society.*—Whatever may have been

---

[1] Pollock and Maitland, *History of English Law*, vol. i., p. 477.

he capacity of the English law to expand, or to absorb
lements of the Roman and Canon law, so far as to even-
ually evolve a complete system of corporation law, the
volution was greatly influenced by this fundamental
haracteristic of the Common law: It was based on the
ndividual as the unit of society.   It cannot be said with
:ntire truth that it *expanded* so as to comprehend cor-
iorations; the body of principles apparently necessary
or the regulation of their relations have been *attached* to
he main body of English law by means of fictions, as-
umptions of things as true that are not true.   For that
eason it has always been necessary for the historian or
urist, in writing of the states of western Europe and
he United States, or of their systems of laws, to supple-
nent the main body of his work at intervals with addi-
ional chapters on corporations.   If the purpose was to
inalyze the organization of the state, corporations were
ound outside of the scheme of districts, counties and
ownships; if the purpose was to study the grouping of
:itizens, bodies of individuals enjoying exceptional rights
hat had crystallized in corporations were found outside
he scheme and had to be accounted for in supplementary
:hapters or apologetic footnotes.   It has always been a
]uestion whether they were public or private in nature,
ir whether they were divisions of the state or associa-
:ions of citizens—a matter of importance in technical
inalysis; and whichever view was taken, it had to be
:xpressed with more or less qualification.[1]   Chapters on

---

[1] Sheldon Amos evidently encountered the difficulty.   "Corporations
whether instituted for municipal, ecclesiastical, educational or eleemosyn-
iry purposes] might appear rather to be claimed by the chapter dealing
vith laws directly relating to the constitution and administration of the
.tate, if not by that dealing with laws of contract.   The corporate bodies,
iowever, here under contemplation, differ at once from purely govern-
nental institutions and from industrial or mercantile associations.   They
:ombine, in a manner peculiar to themselves, a public and a private char-
icter.   They may have originated in special historical circumstances, or

"Corporations" always give the impression that they have been "tacked on."

Both the later Roman law and the Canon law were like the English law in holding the individual in legal contemplation as the social unit, but in both of them the full elaboration of individual relations was impeded by the unpropitious nature of the media through which they had to be interpreted and enforced—imperialism in the state and hierarchy in the Church. Both the Roman and English law had early been based on an aggregate social unit, the family or clan; the rights and duties that they had enforced were those that inhered in men by virtue of their participation in the social life of a composite unit. It was due in both of them to the inability to perfect the transition from the composite unit to the individual unit that left a large number of semi-public, semi-private corporations between the state and the private citizen; other bodies and even individuals were brought within the comprehension of the term, but hardly for any reason than that they resembled corporations in some important particulars. The defect of Roman civilization was apparently that it had not a content of individual life capable of further development. Imperialism in form is not necessarily subversive of individual liberty; it is imperialism in *substance* that is fatal to it; just as formal democracy may be only a mask for tyranny. When a society is progressing from the condition of a federation of composite units to that of a nation of individual citizens, the system of law must be developed on the side of rights rather than on the side of duties. When the transition has been completed, the system of law normally seeks an adjustment of rights and duties that leaves neither exaggerated

even in the more or less eccentric exercise of individual wills. But, starting from these beginnings, they have progressively allied themselves with the general objects of national policy."—*A Systematic View of the Science of Jurisprudence*, p. 281.

in comparison with the other. But a system of law, however highly developed on the side of rights, can hardly be promotive of liberty unless the subjects to whom it is applied are capable of development. The decay of personal life caused the downfall of Rome; what the invasions of the Germanic tribes contributed to the society of Europe was assertive individuality—or "personal independence," as Guizot described it. But the first effect of the sudden injection into the semi-Romanized life of western Europe of the unassimilated life and customs of the Germanic races was the feudal system—a negative product—not so much an end as a beginning—a state to which society retrograded until it might resume progress. The problem of civilization thereafter, on its legal side, especially in England where the subfoundation of Roman institutions was wanting, was to evolve a system of principles, rules and procedure through which the element of assertive individuality might be permitted orderly and harmonious development.

The social unit under feudalism was the manorial village. The relations of villeins of one manor to villeins of another, if they may be conceived to have enjoyed such relations, had to be sustained through the lord of the manor; even within the manorial group many of the relations of fellow-villeins had to be sustained through the feudal lord, though enough of them found a medium in the communal organization of the villeins themselves to afford a sound basis for their self-government after the loss of control by the feudal lord. The departure from the feudal system, it is hardly necessary to suggest, was accomplished largely through a chaotic mass of exemptions of subjects from feudal obligations. The unevenness of the development of exemptions, combined with the inability of the state to absorb the political powers lost by the feudal nobility—in other words, its inability to substitute, until after centuries of development, a

national state for an aggregate of feudal manors—left
here and there bunches of political powers vested in communities that were afterwards viewed as technical corporations.   The work of the English law, during the twelfth,
thirteenth and fourteenth centuries, as far as the promotion of liberty was concerned, was largely to construe
and enforce the mass of exemptions.   The jurist comprehended the nature of individual rights and obligations
by comparing or contrasting them with normal rights
under the decaying feudalism; from that point of view,
all (or nearly all) individual rights and obligations were in
a sense exceptional.   But the exception became the rule
when with the passing away of feudalism the system of
law reached the level of the individual and interpreted
his rights and obligations directly, rather than by contrasting them with a prior status, even though it continued to
use in describing them the obsolescent terminology of
feudalism.   The communities to which clusters of powers
had been transferred were now compared, not with the
feudal lords by whom the powers had been conceded, but
with the normal English subject.   While formerly members of communities, in legal view, had been merely members of a larger society, enjoying exemptions, *like* their
fellows, they now occupied, by virtue of their communities, an exceptional status in the society, *unlike* their
fellows.   *The law recognized no technical corporations
until it had reached the basis of the individual as a social
unit.*   Only when the background of individual rights
and obligations became plain to the eye of the English
law was it able to see corporate rights standing out in relief against it.   There was no place in the system of law
for the bodies of citizens (as units) enjoying corporate
powers, especially when the powers were translated into
common property in lands or goods or the exclusive right
to perform political functions.   The extreme individualistic tendency of the law prompted it to insist on finding

a person, natural or other, to stand for the scattered powers, unabsorbed by the state, that were left over from the feudal period. The Roman law was able to view property as belonging to the State, Church or corporations, or when contrasted with the property of individuals, as that "of no one" (*nullius*); but in the English law such property must belong to the king, a lord, bishop, abbot or some other *person*, though in Bracton's day the churchmen might be said to hold property "in right of " the Church. The result was the fiction of corporate personality. The maturity of the conception was in the fifteenth century, the century of transition between the older feudal order and the new national order.

If the history of English law were to be divided into periods, they might be as follows: (I.) The feudal period, ending in the middle of the twelfth century. · (II.) The post-feudal period, until the end of the fifteenth century, during which the English system was slowly evolving itself from the feudal system through a mass of exemptions from its principles. (III.) The first individualistic period, the sixteenth and seventeenth centuries, during which the elaboration of the system on the basis of the individual was impeded by the absolutism of the Tudors and Stuarts. (IV.) The modern system of law, dating from the last quarter of the seventeenth century, based on the individual and afforded nearly complete development through democratic government. During the first and second periods the personality of corporations was not recognized by the law, except imperfectly at the end of the second period. In the third period, the soil of absolutism in the state proving very fertile for the legal conception of corporations, it matured fully. In the fourth period, at least until after the beginning of the nineteenth century, the conception has undergone no change, having apparently become firmly established as a part of the law.

The maturity of the conception of corporations in the English law was undoubtedly facilitated by the development of the corporations themselves. It was not entirely fortuitous that the conception of corporations as artificial persons was nearly coincidental with the completion of the process of "shrinkage" of corporations from entire communities to smaller select bodies within them. The close bodies in gilds and municipalities were crystallizing during the fourteenth and fifteenth centuries. It was when they ceased to derive their life from the communities themselves and appeared to enjoy an existence independent of them, not in harmony with them but rather in opposition and contrast to them, that their distinct "personality" emerged. Moreover, the development facilitated the substitution of the private for the public view that might be expected to be taken of the communities. The close bodies, as well as the rest of the community, regarded the powers reposed in them largely as sources of private advantage; the state was accordingly much more readily inclined to assign them to the department of private law than to that of public law. The nearer they approached the plane of private persons in their activity, the easier it was for the jurist's imagination to impute personality to them.

The Canon law, under the influence of the hierarchical organization of the Church, was able to partially avoid the difficulty experienced by the Common law, through the principle of "the absorption of the corporate group in the headship," if the expression may be used. One is at first surprised in examining the bulky *Corpus Juris Canonici* to find no mention of ecclesiastical corporations, though he finds much of ecclesiastical persons and of the requirement that bishops and abbots be elected by chapters and convents and act in many respects only with their consent. For a time the English law would accept the view and enforce laws in accordance with it, but it was

fundamentally out of harmony with its system and soon
or late dean and chapter and abbot (or prior) and convent
had to be included in the category of artificial persons
with other corporations. The monasteries were swept
away by the Reformation before the view that monks
were "dead in law" and their legal personality absorbed
in that of abbot or prior could be reconciled to the principles of English law; they remained long enough, however, to trouble Coke in his analysis of corporations.

The peculiar manner in which a system of law is erected
is accountable for much of the confusion that has entered
into the conception of a corporation and the heterogene-
ous mass of principles and rules collected about it. The
judge and lawyer, in classifying institutions, have regard
rather for the social effects of their analysis than for the
generic qualities of the institutions. Certain social effects
are desired, or already settled in accordance with a standard approved by custom or public opinion. The purpose
of analysis and classification is to obtain the desired
practical effects, and institutions and men are grouped
accordingly. If the regulation of the relations of dean
and chapter is desired, and the merging of the personality
of the latter in that of the former seems expedient to
accomplish it, it would not be surprising to find deans
called artificial husbands and chapters artificial wives.
If it is in substantial harmony with ideas of justice that
sleeping-car companies be held liable for the security of
goods taken into sleeping-cars by their occupants, they
may be found classified with either common-carriers or
inn-keepers. In the system of English law true corporations have found themselves in strange company; their
name has been extended to comprehend other bodies and
persons to the manifest confusion and inconsistency of
the law, as one feature or another has been exaggerated
and made the basis of classification. Corporations are
associations; therefore the State, the Church, the county,

the township and the family are corporations, and the tendency of the present century is to view partnerships as closely akin to them. Corporations are created by the state; therefore legalized societies and private clubs as well as bodies of public officers, like boards of regents of universities, are corporations. Corporations may endure forever and take property in succession for public purposes; therefore bishops, abbots and rectors are corporations sole, because their corporate property is inseparable from their offices, which may be perpetual. In each case the person or group brought within the definition is wanting in some essential attribute of corporations other than the one used as a test.

A great change that is still not without its effect on the law of corporations took place, or more properly, culminated in the sixteenth century. The standpoint from which all institutions were viewed was shifted from society as a whole to the individual. Social forces were conceived as moving from below and not from above. The destruction of tradition and the elevation of reason was one phase of the change. To be sure, the view was not to find full expression in philosophy until the eighteenth century, but the Reformation was a practical application of it. Private contrast largely superseded status in the determination of social relations. Corporations were viewed not so much as *divisions of society* as *associations of individuals*.[1] They were now enlarged individuals,

---

[1] The great majority of modern writers (except recent writers on sociology) begin their treatment of corporations from the standpoint of the individual, though it is not always remembered that, as a matter of social organization, the corporation has derived its form, historically, from groups which were regarded from the opposite standpoint. As an illustration, the words of Sheldon Amos may be quoted: "As society progresses, it is recognized that it is not sufficient to accord rights to, and impose duties upon, determinate and individual human beings. The necessity of coöperation and combination for purposes of industry, trade, the public service, and social intercourse, as well as the importance of preserving a continuity of

not reduced societies.   The legal theory of artificial personality was in such complete harmony with the view of
society and the individual from the shifted standpoint
that it acquired great permanence in the course of the
sixteenth century.

right and duty, which shall be independent of the accidents of human life,
lead to the enlarged conception of legal persons, which expresses itself in
such artificial unities as gilds, colleges, universities, corporations, and the
like."—*History and Principles of the Civil Law of Rome*, p. 118.

VIII

MODERN CORPORATIONS

WHEN the field of modern corporations is entered, the feature of it that first attracts the attention of the investigator is the absence of the older corporations, or their presence in such a modified form or under such exceptional conditions that he may leave them out of account without doing serious injustice to the subject. Most of the corporations considered in earlier chapters have gone out of existence; some of them have been so remodelled by the state that they have virtually lost their corporate identity by becoming administrative organs of the state; only a few of them remain as obsolete survivals of a past state of society. Modern corporations seem to be substantially new bodies, modern not only in time but also in the nature of their activity. So great is the change from the old to the new that a superficial view of the subject almost justifies a doubt whether a study of old corporations is profitable as a preparation for the study of modern corporations. A second thought, however, is convincing that the corporate element in the organization of society is substantially the same. Society has changed, both in structure and activity, but, the service performed by corporations as a part of the structure within which some of its activity takes place is unchanged. Social progress may demand that new definitions be found for the terms "public" and "private," but, when a group of associated individuals is confirmed in its character as a group for the accomplishment of a public purpose through the pursuit by the group of private interest, the group is as much a corporation under the new definitions as it would have been under older ones.

Of the corporations included in Class I. and described as Local-Internal Corporations,[1] those of the Church that survived the Reformation in England have become hardly more than administrative units of the national Church (or State); their activity is conditioned and regulated by ecclesiastical commissions and similar bodies of a supervisory nature to so great a degree that they would hardly be recognized as corporations at all if it were not for the demands of an obsolete system of land tenure. In the United States, in general, no such bodies have existed in the Protestant churches; their organization has been effected, though without absolute uniformity in the several States, on the basis of societies regarded by the law as purely civil in nature, and hardly more justly to be regarded as corporations than the residents of an English parish; the only bodies in them that resemble corporations are the boards of trustees in whom are vested the title and management of the property of the church, but they are merely elected representatives of the church society, no more corporate in character than the legislature of a state. Even the organization of the Roman Catholic Church, with its greater regard for tradition, has been so expanded and amplified that the religious orders have become substantially component parts of it, rather ranks inside of it than autonomous groups outside of it. The English municipalities, with the glaring exception of metropolitan London, were reformed during the early part of the nineteenth century until they became self-governing divisions of the state; if the term "corporations" is still applied to them, as to cities and towns in the United States, it is in disregard of the nature of the

[1] *Supra*, vol. i., pp. 90–91.

changes that have taken place. The mediæval gilds have passed away entirely, except in so far as they are perpetuated in the clearly anomalous London companies; modern trades unions are not the successors of the older gilds, much as they resemble them in many respects. Educational and eleemosynary corporations, identified with universities, colleges, schools, hospitals, almshouses and the like, have been greatly modified by the state through its administrative, legislative and judicial organs; for the most part, especially in the United States, the plain tendency has been in the direction of replacing them by institutions maintained by the state itself; in England many have been merged in public institutions, others have been reduced to a similar condition through the regulation of the appointment of members, and all are so closely supervised by governmental departments and commissions that they lack genuine corporate autonomy. Even the venerable Universities of Oxford and Cambridge, the most conservative of corporations, have been subjected to the influence of the prevailing tendency, while their colleges have been reduced nearly to the status of departments in them; the later institutions, such as the University of London, bear plainly the stamp of state initiation and control. In the United States, state universities, colleges and schools, and those under the control of religious denominations, administered by representatives of large social groups, have very generally taken the place of the semi-monastic foundations familiar in English history, though several of the older institutions approximate the latter type.

Of the corporations included in Class II. and described as National-External Corporations,[1] even fewer remain as a part of the organization of the society of the twentieth century. The Regulated Companies passed away with the expansion of the international political organiza-

[1] *Supra*, vol. i., pp. 90–91.

tion of modern states; the functions of their officers, as far as they have not been entirely dispensed with, are now performed by officers of the state; their control and protection of individual merchants in their foreign trade, to such extent as they are still enforced, find expression through the medium of administrative departments of the state. The Regulated-Exclusive Companies shared the fate of the Regulated Companies, differing from them only in the element of exclusiveness that has been perpetuated in modern commercial companies. The great Joint-Stock Companies of the type of the East India Company have passed away, except as they are used to a limited extent in Africa and a few other places in which England is still seeking to "expand"; the enduring product of the East India Company is found in the political machinery through which England governs her Indian possessions; history may reasonably be expected to repeat itself in Africa. Even the United States has had an Alaska Commercial Company in the present century to which it has virtually delegated the duty of regulating the seal fishery of the Pribiloff Islands. But the monopolistic joint-stock company, wielding political powers, is an institution of the past and confessedly exceptional in present society; the Hudson's Bay Company, denuded of its monopolistic trading privileges, is easily classified with modern commercial companies. The Colonial Companies, short-lived as they were, existed long enough to contribute through transformation or imitation a large part of the political foundations of American Colonies and States and of the United States; they have not been used as models for subsequent corporations.

The great fact of the history of the old corporations is that the state has wholly or partially absorbed their powers. To such extent as the social activity of the surviving corporations has been supplemented in response to greater public demands, it has been done almost entirely through the medium of new institutions, created, maintained and administered by the state, and not through new corporations. The absorption of the powers of a corporation by the state does not imply merely the resumption of powers previously granted by it; some of the powers may have been inoperative, when granted, from lack of subject-matter on which to have effect; on the other hand, it does not follow from the absorption of corporate powers by the state that the state continues to exercise them as the corporation has previously done; they may be allowed by the state to lie dormant under the influence of political theories repugnant to their exercise. The Local-Internal Corporations were not so much the means through which the State and Church accomplished the transition from an agglomeration of local units to a national or even (in the Church) to a world unit, as the measure of their inability to readily complete the transition. Likewise, though in a different field, the National-External Corporations did not so much provide the means through which the states of modern Europe expanded, as they represented their inability to readily accomplish the great movement. In both cases, as nationality was gradually perfected (the parallel movement in the Roman Catholic Church was not so successful) the *raison d'être* of the corporations ceased. Modern corporations, though they exercise their activity in a field somewhat different from that of their predecessors, are evidence of the same lack of ability on the part of the state (society politically organized) to fully comprehend and correlate the social life of its citizens. The plane of corporate life has been depressed, in a sense, to a lower level. The purpose of the modern corporation is less plainly to contribute to national development and is apparently confined, to a large extent, to the amplification of the individual. The view of the subject is obscured by the fact that society is now working from a different standpoint, from that of the individual instead of from that of the state. The result can hardly fail to be the same—an eventual disintegration of corporations, an absorption of their political elements by the state and the relegation of the remaining elements to the individual. As contrasted with earlier corporations, modern corporations are national, not local, in the scope of their activity, and aim at the perfection of the infra-national relations of men. They resemble each class of their predecessors in one respect and differ from each of them in another respect. There is a sense, to be sure, in which some modern corporations are local in the extreme, but it is in respect of the subject-matter of the activity and not of the individuals organized; on the other hand, many modern corporations are international in character, but not so much in respect of the subject-matter as of the component individuals; thus they are contrasted with earlier corporations in their exceptional phases, for the Local-Internal Corporations, as far as they were more than local, were so on the side of their activity rather than on that of their membership, and National-External Corporations, as far as they were international, were likewise so on the side of their activity rather than on that of their membership.

A classification of modern corporations is quite sufficient in itself to indicate the wide difference in nature, but in activity rather than in form, by which they are separated as a class from the two classes of older corporations. The most serviceable basis of classification is doubtless the "public" element in them; they will be arranged in order, therefore, according to the degree of distinctness in which their activity is recognized as public in the opinion of society. An exception will be made of the division of Economic Corporations, however, and they will not be classified on the basis selected; but their subdivisions will be so arranged. For the purpose of making the divisions and subdivisions more distinct, corporations excluded from them will be contrasted with such as are included in them.[1] Incidentally such comments will be added as limited treatment will permit.

III. Modern Corporations are so called because they are an integral part of modern society, of the society that originated in the sixteenth and seventeenth centuries, distinguished by individualism in general, but more particularly by democracy in the state, and by the destruction of tradition and the elevation of reason in religion and science. They might be described, in contrast with earlier corporations, as National-Internal Corporations, because generally restricted in scope to national limits and tending to perfect the relations of individuals within it rather than to extend their political or economic influence without it. From another point of view they might well be described as Individualistic Corporations, because more distinctly regarded as groups of individuals than were earlier corporations; by the use of such a term, however, they would not be clearly distinguished from the National-External Corporations, though not improperly contrasted with the Local-Internal Corporations, which might well be called Socialistic Corporations, as approaching the ideal of totally organized social groups. Modern Corporations may be divided as follows:

1. Political Corporations, such as the numerous Societies for the Prevention of Cruelty to Children, and to Animals, including only such as actually exercise political powers through their agents by arresting law-breakers, assuming custody of children by force, seizing unlicensed private property (especially dogs) and destroying it. Some Civic Associations would be included, because they assume some of the functions of city government (though only permissively on the part of the state) such as the

[1] It must be suggested that the classification to be given will be largely tentative, hardly more than provisional; more extended study would probably justify some alterations.

cleaning of streets and the maintenance of the sanitary condition of public and private property. At least one penitentiary in the United States is maintained and conducted by a "private" corporation, but as the motive is private gain, derived from fees from the State and its counties and cities and from the United States, the corporation would probably have to be included in "Economic" Corporations. Many similar organizations, such as Law and Order Leagues, wield no political powers directly, but frequently seek to procure the enforcement of laws for the regulation of the traffic in intoxicants and for the suppression of vice by gathering evidence and "arousing public opinion"; such corporations could hardly be classed as political, but would have to be placed under the head of Scientific Corporations, as aiming to promote the formation and enforcement of more correct public opinion. For reasons that have appeared in preceding pages—but which will probably appear inadequate to those who have adopted the conception and classification of corporations found in most legal treatises—counties, cities, towns, school-districts and the like are not included in political or other corporations. At the risk of unnecessary repetition it is again insisted that they are departments of the state, and bear the name of corporations only by virtue of traditional usage.

2. Eleemosynary Corporations, such as maintain and conduct hospitals, asylums, infirmaries, public libraries and like institutions, and administer the funds for their support. The field of such corporations is characterized by the extent to which the state and its subdivisions have encroached on it through their own institutions from one direction, and the extent to which, from another direction, such corporations have ceased to be autonomous and have become merely representative bodies of large divisions of society based on religious, racial or other bases. Such of them as still possess sufficient autonomy

to be called corporations date as a class from the fifteenth and sixteenth centuries, the period of the destruction of gilds and monasteries, the chief organized agencies of charity in the Middle Ages. It need hardly be added that in the category of such corporations would not be included the governing bodies of state institutions, appointed or elected officers serving merely in a representative capacity; some hesitancy would be justified in including even similar bodies appointed or elected by religious denominations.

3. Educational Corporations, such as the "close" bodies maintaining or conducting universities, colleges, training schools, technical schools, seminaries and "institutes" of many kinds. Much that has been said of eleemosynary corporations is applicable to such corporations. Their field of activity has been even further encroached upon by the state (especially in the United States), religious denominations and other large and more or less indeterminate groups of citizens. If the English universities and colleges of the ecclesiastical type be omitted, the class may be said to date from the sixteenth century. Boards of regents and other governing bodies of state universities would not be included.

4. Scientific Corporations, such as the Royal Society, the American Musical Association, and many of the numerous other associations for the advancement of literature, politics, science and the arts, and, more generally, for the promotion of culture and morality in society. Not all such associations could be properly considered corporations, even if legally "incorporated" for the purpose of holding property or some similar purpose. The grounds on which many of them would be excluded are most frequently the want of responsibility attaching to membership, indefiniteness of membership, incapacity to enforce "group will" either on members or non-members and want of continuity of organization.

A few such associations antedate the nineteenth century; the great majority of them have originated in very recent years.

5. Religious Corporations, such as the boards of trustees of some churches, or more properly the bodies of communicants themselves, of which the boards of trustees serve as governmental organs. The chief difficulty in classifying such bodies arises from the fact that they are usually only subdivisions of a large class in society, to be viewed in the same light as a social order. For many purposes, however, they are considered to be separate and distinct, especially in contemplation of the law, which regards them as merely civil societies. Some recent organizations subsidiary to the churches have sustained relations to them very similar to those sustained by corporations to the state, with some similar unfortunate consequences. Some such societies as the Young People's Societies of Christian Endeavor, encouraged in their religious zeal by the churches, have formed national organizations largely independent of the churches, and have thereby excited apprehensions that they would get beyond their control.

6. Social-Fraternal Societies, such as the Knights of Pythias, Odd Fellows, Redmen, Foresters and many similar bodies. They would have to be regarded in almost the same light as the religious corporations, organizations of very large social groups, composed of many smaller groups in many respects distinct and independent, especially in legal contemplation. In their present state of development, bar associations, medical associations, trades unions, boards of trade and even stock exchanges would have to be included in the class. The meaning of the term "fraternity" is not unduly extended if it be used to comprehend the element of mutual fair dealing infused into the mercantile life of stock-brokers by their organization in exchanges.

7. Economic[1] Corporations, of which there are many
kinds, but all distinguished from other corporations by
being a part of the machinery of society for producing,
exchanging and distributing wealth. They may be subdivided, in the order in which their functions are most
distinctly recognized as "public," as follows:

(*a*) Improvement Companies, such as are organized for
the reclamation and improvement of large tracts of un-
occupied land, establishing town-sites, building towns,
(*e. g.*, Pullman, Illinois), "booming" new settlements
and incidentally developing mines, ranches and other
economic projects.

(*b*) Transportation Companies, for the transmission of
persons, goods and intelligence, including railway, stage,
toll-road, canal, ferry, express, messenger, telegraph,
telephone, gas, electric light, water, irrigation and drain-
age companies. Associations of pilots would probably
have to be included in the class. Hardly a single kind
of the companies mentioned existed before the beginning
of the nineteenth century, many of them not until after
1830; many of them have originated during the past
twenty years; they are essentially the product of conditions peculiar to the nineteenth century.

(*c*) Banking Companies, ranging from the great bank
which serves as the financial agent of the state, such as
the Bank of England and the historical Bank of the
United States, through the present national and State
banks of the United States, to the so-called "private
banks." If the great "state banks" be left out of account, banking corporations may be said to be peculiar
to the nineteenth century. The Bank of England stands
in classification near the line that separates the great

---

[1] The term "economic," as used in the text, is confessedly unfortunate.
For want of a better term, its use for the purpose of describing corporations organized and maintained for the acquisition of pecuniary gain may
not be unpardonable.

national-external companies from the infra-national economic corporations. The East India Company and South Sea Company were both holders of government loans; in the latter, commercial activity was merely incidental to the loaning function, but it was connected with foreign trade; the Bank of England was very similar to them, except that the commercial privileges, attached as a kind of bonus to its holding of government debt, had to do with the infra-national economic relations of citizens, and promoted rather internal national development than external national expansion.

(*d*) Insurance Companies, including fire, life, marine, accident, cyclone and other insurance companies, as well as the several kinds of guaranty companies, and ranging in form from the compact "old line" companies to the individualistic Lloyd's companies. Some of the mutual companies would have to be included under the head of social-fraternal corporations; that they would be properly so included seems to be confirmed by the recent growth of "insurance departments" as adjuncts of the Masonic and other fraternities. As a class, insurance companies date their origin from the end of the seventeenth century, though they have had their greatest growth in the nineteenth century.

(*e*) Trust and Investment Companies, representing a differentiation of the capitalist and investor's agent from the banker. Most savings banks would have to be included in the class. Many insurance companies, moreover, apparently make the business of insurance hardly more than collateral or incidental to that of an investment company.

(*f*) Commercial Companies, if the term "commercial" may be used broadly enough to include corporations for mining, agricultural, manufacturing and trading enterprises, and narrowly enough to exclude corporations previously described. The term "private corporations" is commonly used to describe them.   The varieties are almost innumerable; some of them are difficult to distinguish in form from the kinds of modified partnerships known as "limited companies."   It is in this class, moreover, that the corporate form of social structure has been abnormally developed and subjected to most abuse in application.   A few of them are found in the history of the eighteenth century, but they were almost universally monopolistic in character, formed by individuals and sanctioned by the state for the purpose of protecting or promoting the use of improved processes or inventions, or to encourage the development of the natural resources of localities.   With a few such exceptions, all of the class belong to the nineteenth and twentieth centuries and have multiplied most rapidly since 1850.

With the exception of several educational and eleemosynary corporations, a few scientific associations, banking corporations, insurance companies and monopolistic "patent" companies, the class of corporations described as essentially modern are products of the nineteenth century.   In the United States only a few corporations of any kind are found before the beginning of the century; they were of slight importance to society, though the historical facts relating to them are full of interest.   The charters of some of the old American universities indicate that they were intended to some extent for the conversion of the heathen (Indians) to Christianity and for the dispensation of charity; the bodies of some of them were modelled closely on the prevailing ecclesiastical type of the English university college.   In South Carolina a corporation very similar to the English "incorporated gild" was created, with the power, among others, of maintaining a school; remarkably enough, the corporation is still in existence.   Since the beginning of the nineteenth century, however, the multiplication of corporations has proceeded with great rapidity.   In the absence of trustworthy statistical or other data it is impossible to state with a reasonable degree of exactness how many have been created or are now in existence, or to otherwise estimate the extent to which they have entered into the social life of the century, but it cannot be denied that the growth of corporations in western Europe and the United States signifies nothing less than a social revolution. Though the great change cannot be fully accounted for at the present time, as well because it is still in progress and has not yet accomplished itself, as because the requisite data are not at hand for the purpose, a few general considerations may be offered as at least a partial explanation of it, under the heads of (1) economic conditions, (2) political conditions and (3) the reaction of economic development on society.

1. *Economic Conditions.*—The growth of modern corporations has been most largely on the economic side of society. As far as their growth has taken place on the other sides of society, it has been due almost entirely to the reaction of economic on political and religious conditions. The nineteenth century was the century of economic development as former centuries have been distinguished by their development in politics, religion or some other department of life. The last half of the seventeenth and the first half of the eighteenth century were remarkable for the small addition of corporate structure to that already in existence. The only legitimate field for corporations was apparently the exploitation of new foreign lands. Even when several corporations were designed by the Stuarts for the field of foreign commerce, they proved abortive, because they were given control of trade already established instead of trade to be created by them in new lands. There was little room for further extra-national expansion. In the internal economic relations of England and America, there was no growth of corporations during the period for the

general reason that there was no growth on the economic side of internal national life.   One is almost surprised to find in the literature of the seventeenth and early eighteenth centuries so much evidence that England was considered to be over-populated and that the colonization of America was regarded as necessary to relieve it of its surplus people.   Such expansion of economic life as took place was extensive rather than intensive; the aim was to utilize the forces of nature by reaching them at more points, not by exploiting them more vigorously at given points.   The existing structure of society was sufficient for the economic activity organized within it; no new structure was needed and new corporations were consequently not brought into use.   Even the creation of the Bank of England at the end of the seventeenth century was hardly exceptional; its privileges, or such of them as concerned the relations between citizens, were hardly more than a premium on the public services performed by it as a lender of money to the state.   In the second half of the eighteenth century, however, what Arnold Toynbee described as an industrial revolution took place. The great inventions of the period increased the control of men over the forces of nature and presented to them the possibility of a greater economic development than they were able to organize in existing social forms.   The first effect of the movement on the creation of corporations was very similar to the effect so manifest in the early history of the great companies for foreign trade. As the body of "adventurers" that discovered and developed a "new trade" in foreign lands were considered entitled to the exclusive enjoyment of it because they had discovered and developed it, so now in domestic trade the discoverers of inventions and the promoters of new industries (whether based on inventions or not) seemed to be entitled to the exclusive enjoyment of their fruits.   As such advantages had in earlier centuries been under the control of gilds, now, since their decay, they were subject to a large extent to the control of close municipal bodies, the "corporations" of whose restrictions Adam Smith complained. Such advantages might be enjoyed, in some degree, in the new municipalities, free from the restrictions of the older ones, but in general incorporation was necessary. They depended negatively on exemptions from the control of existing social organs, and needed positively powers of control over industry similar to those wielded by existing corporations. Moreover, in the incorporation of such bodies, the state could not undeceive itself that it was incorporating the entire groups of persons engaged in the industries, capitalists, masters, workmen and all, though it reserved the effective powers of control for the exercise of limited interior groups which deserve to be considered the real corporations. Such corporations as the London companies seem to have served as models. When the enterprise in view was a unit in itself, as a bank, insurance office, canal or railway, instead of an industry requiring a body of artisans, or when the factory system became firmly established, concentration easily took place, resulting in the incorporation of the owners alone. The movement by which regulated companies developed into joint-stock companies in the foreign commerce of England was paralleled in domestic trade by the incorporation of the unit of industry instead of the whole industry.

The purpose of the state in so granting corporate powers was, of course, to give to society the benefit of the possibilities opened to it by developing industry; in order to do so, it was necessary to confer upon groups of citizens the powers of organization incidental to the control of the new activity, especially in the presence of the restrictive social organization with which they came in contact. In the light of the development of earlier corporations, it can hardly be said that the movement was at all extraordinary. In an unusual development of any side of society the existing organization of the State (or Church), unable to accommodate it, if it is not actually restrictive of it, concedes it an organization in the form of corporations. Three factors, therefore, only the last of which has since become inoperative, appear to have entered into the growth of corporations at the end of the eighteenth century: (a) The possibility of an absolute growth of industry itself, (b) the desire of the state to promote it by affording it necessary and appropriate organization and (c) the presence of restrictive social organizations, whether governmental or corporate, with which new industries came in contact. It is often assumed at the present day that all modern industrial corporations have owed their existence to the necessity of "massing capital"; that would account, to a slight extent, for the feature of association in them before the beginning of the nineteenth century, but would be wholly inadequate to account for the corporate form of organization or the semi-political powers with which they were endowed. The massing of large amounts of capital in industries was one of the effects of the factory system of industry and the opening of wider markets through the development of improved facilities of transportation. Modern corporations in their early stages were merely organizations that enabled men to gain a reward for giving to society the benefit of inventions and new industries, with slight reference to the amount of capital employed.

2. *Political Conditions.*—If it is true that corporations are in general social organizations midway between the state and the individual, owing their existence to the latter's need of organization and the former's inability to supply it, their prevalence must be largely dependent on political conditions, the nature of the state and the degree of perfection and stability attained by it. The attitude of society to its political institutions during the

seventeenth and eighteenth centuries was essentially destructive. The attainment of nationality in the sixteenth century had been expressed in an exaggerated monarchy; no sooner was nationality accomplished than the infranational relations of individuals demanded increased attention. Under existing conditions the effort to establish individual liberty was necessarily destructive in its effects on political institutions. It seemed to be necessary first to deprive them of their strength, to reduce the monarchy to an institution of comparative insignificance, to materially modify the aristocratic element in the organization of the state. The constructive process, the formation of political institutions that would be harmonious with theories of individual liberty, was only slowly working itself out and was to wait for its completion until the nineteenth century, though it was long anticipated in America. While the work of disintegration was in progress, the state, viewed as identical with the parts of society that actually wielded political powers, was more or less justifiably considered as something apart from the mass of citizens, something to be opposed, at best little more than an unavoidable evil. Individual liberty was reflected on its legal side by an exaggeration of rights. While the monarchy based itself on divine right, the people went to the opposite extreme in maintaining that government was based on the consent of the governed. Philosophy eventually systematized the prevailing thought and explained not only the political organization of society, but finally its entire organization by the assumption of contracts between individuals. It seemed inevitable that in thought society should suffer disintegration before it could again be harmoniously organized.

The importance of the fact in a study of corporations lies in the denial of expansion of activity to the state. The mercantile system was the first stage in the liberation of industry from control by the political organization of

society. The standpoint was not yet wholly changed.
The development of the nation was still consciously the
goal, but it was not identified with the development of
the individual; the individual was to be regulated in his
activity so as to contribute by it directly to the development of the nation; even more narrowly, in practice, the
political interests of the state as organized had to be subserved; if a new trade was to be discovered or established
or new lands colonized, it had to be so done as to extend
the dominion of the English crown and swell its revenues.
It is significant that the mercantile system was applied
most fully in matters relating to foreign commerce; it
could not have been extensively applied in domestic trade,
as became plain from the opposition aroused by the "monopolies." When the time came for the industrial revival
at the end of the eighteenth century, the theory was that
the "wealth of nations" was best increased by giving to
the individual the greatest possible freedom to increase his
own wealth. All local and national restrictions might
best be removed; the first form in which such restrictions
were removed was in bodies of exemptions contained in
charters of incorporation. Moreover, if a social function
was of recognized public importance, it was safer for society that the state delegate to groups of individuals the
power to perform it than for it either to perform it itself
or to closely supervise its performance. That was the
difference (not always easy to discover) between the general liberation of the industry of individuals from political
restrictions and the creation of corporations; when the
individual was liberated, it was considered that his interest was identical with that of society and that he would
subserve the latter by pursuing the former, if merely permitted to do it; when the corporation was created, its
work was recognized as of public importance but it was
considered that it would not perform it without encouragement by the removal of restrictions or oftener by the

positive delegation of public powers. In further contrast
with the liberation of the individual, corporations were
given a social form, an organization, that in earlier history had been found capable of serving as constitutions
for semi-autonomous colonies, and that, even in industry,
might expand so far as to menace the social integrity of
the individual. Distrust of the state as organized caused
the accumulation of political powers in the hands of minor
states, corporations, which excited no apprehensions because they were democratically organized and did not
seriously conflict in their activity with established industrial relations; moreover, were they not based substantially on individual contract and was not "freedom of
association" one element of liberty? If the entire state
had been formed and organized like the corporation,
would not philosophers and political theorists have had
to confess that it was an ideal state?

After the experience of a century the distrust of the
state has not ceased to be a potent factor in the organization of industry. The constitutions of the United States
and of the several States were constructed on the principle that government is hardly more than a necessary evil,
the less of which is had, the better for the citizen. The
less responsibility imposed on congresses, legislatures
and councils and on national, State and municipal ad-
ministrations, the more their ability to discharge their
functions has decreased, just as the physical member
withers from lack of use. If railways, lines of telegraph
and other public enterprises were to be maintained, the
state should delegate its power of eminent domain, its
public lands, its highways and streets, and renounce its
power of taxation to corporations, so that the individual
might be protected against the state in the contest of
"man vs. the state." But there is much evidence that
the true nature of corporations is gradually becoming
plainer, though least in the system of law. When the

workman finds his wages determined by the corporation
that controls the business employing his labor, and seeks
refuge in a trade union that deprives him of his individuality, when the farmer finds his connection with a
market dependent on the regulations of a railway company, when the business-man finds the volume of credit
and currency subject to the curtailment or expansion of
banking, trust and investment companies, when the small
investor finds his only avenue of investment in savings
banks and trust and investment companies, when the
citizen finds his social intercourse conditioned on membership in church organizations and social clubs, when the
scientist or professional man finds that he cannot bring
his efforts to bear on society except through the medium
of associations,—they all begin to realize that they are
governed more by corporations than by the state, that
they are the major part of the mechanism of government
under which they live.   But the distrust of the state still
exists in a large measure; corporations, it is said, must
be controlled by the state through commissions—the
state must not absorb them and cannot be trusted to
control them directly.

The principal source of the increase of corporations,
which might be included under either "economic conditions " or "political conditions," has been the internal
economic development of western European nations and
the United States (especially the latter) in the presence
of political institutions and political theories by which the
activity of the state has been strictly limited.   The demand for canals, railways, banks, telegraph and telephone
lines, water-works, electric light and gas plants and the
many other factors of modern economic progress, has at
times approached the condition of a "craze."   It has appeared in the minds of men to justify prodigality in the
concession of public powers to corporations.   The past
century has witnessed greater economic expansion than

any previous century in the world's history. Nations, states, cities and geographical sections have competed with one another in the extension of encouragement to corporations for the development of their natural resources. Early in the century it was not considered justifiable to create corporations for any purpose not clearly public in nature; each application was considered by itself, and if favorably was followed by a legislative act of incorporation. Not only was it always difficult to distinguish between public and private, but the view that individuals should have the freest possible opportunities to create wealth encouraged the presumption that every business was of public importance in the respect that it might increase the aggregate wealth of society. Not only was the work of legislatures simplified by the passage of "general incorporation" laws for special classes of corporations, but justice between individuals in different occupations seemed to demand that the laws should comprehend successive classes of enterprises lower in the scale between public and private; the climax was reached in some states when general acts were passed permitting the incorporation of associates "for any lawful purpose." Thus the innumerable "private corporations" came into existence. The period of expansion has been followed by one of organization. The vine has been stimulated to attain its full growth; now it is found in need of training and pruning. In periods of expansion society develops irregularly and unevenly; when they are at an end, the incongruous new social structure in which the expansion has taken place is reduced to a greater or less degree of conformity with the rest of the structure (political and other) of society, usually with accompanying modifications in the latter. The second process is always disquieting in its effects, involving always the readjustment of the relations of indviduals, and not infrequently the disturbance of "vested interests."

3. *The Reaction of Economic Development on Society.*—
The most manifest reactionary effect of industrial development on society is what might be called a form of
materialism, with some limitations on the common use
of the term. Under the domestic system the tool was
an adjunct of the man. The workman's skill was part of
him. The element of skill has been largely transferred
to the machine. The workman has become an adjunct
of the machine, which he controls by wheels and levers.
Since the sixteenth century, when capital in the modern
sense became a factor in industry, the relation of the
capitalist to industry had been of the same nature as
that of the workman under machine industry. Capital is
merely the accumulated products of past labor devoted
to the production of new wealth. The capitalist does
not produce directly; he merely controls the production
of others through the ownership of capital. Under the
gild system masters (from whom capitalists afterwards
developed) were little different from journeymen or workmen; both engaged directly in production side by side.
In both classes the general relation to industry has
changed from the actual performance of the work to the
control of its performance by machinery. The evolution
in the broad field of industry has been parallel with that
in the evolution of corporations themselves. Corporations are instruments of control, of social organization,
just as machines are instruments of men's control over
the forces of nature; corporations are social machines to
which the individual has become almost as completely an
adjunct in his relations to men as he has become a mere
adjunct of the machine in his relations to nature. Nor
is it at all remarkable that the highest developed form of
corporation has become the social structure of capital.
For is not social control the essential feature of the
capitalist class? Does property in physical things confer
any benefit on their owner (beyond the advantages of

consumption) except as they be made the basis of controlling others in the production of new things? The historical growth of corporations has been in complete harmony with such a conception of capital. The mediæval gilds, originally the organizations of classes of persons engaged in industry or trade, became quite generally restricted, by the sixteenth century (the date of the appearance of a distinct class of capitalists), to the class of employers within them. The great foreign companies of the succeeding centuries carried the development forward from the point it had reached in the gilds, purified of all but capitalistic elements; they were purposely and consciously restricted to the social class to which the gilds had become restricted after four centuries of history. Both in the relations of men to nature under machine industry and in the relations of men to each other under the system of capitalistic production, the corporation appears from its historical development to be a fit and appropriate social organization.

Through the extension of the use of machinery and the development of transportation the individual has been removed to a greater distance in both time and space from the forces of nature on which he depends. His contact with nature is more effective, but it is less direct. He has become far more dependent on the artificial physical element (machines, factories, railways) and the human element (organized society) than on nature itself. The category of public industries is accordingly extending itself so as to cover industries formerly viewed as private in character. The early stage-coach was hardly more than a private industry; the modern railway is one of the most familiar examples of a public industry. As an industry becomes more public in character, it is elevated in popular estimation above the owners of it and in a sense separated from them,—it is idealized or personified. It appears to have rights and duties in itself, distinct from those of its owners. Is not that the same movement that resulted (in a somewhat different field) in the development of the legal conception of the "ideal personality" of municipalities? The law regards the capital invested in it as "clothed with a public trust," by virtue of which its owners have only a limited control of it; its patrons are regarded as entitled by law to the benefit of its services in return for a reasonable compensation. It is the increased dependence of men on physical things, grouped in great units such as systems of railway, telegraph and water works, that has contributed in a large measure to the growth of corporations.

A very conspicuous result of the industrial development of the nineteenth century has been the enlargement of the physical unit of greatest industrial efficiency beyond the capacity of the individual. Under the gild system the unit was the tools of the man with his strength applied to them; human capacity, capital and market were all limited. Under the domestic system the unit was increased to the co-operating family of the master with the few workmen added to it and made virtually a part of the household; human capacity and capital were increased, while the market remained substantially unchanged. Under machine industry the machine with its operator was the unit, increased to a factory full of machines and operators when the market was so widened through improved transportation as to permit localization of industries. In transportation the unit has grown from the single vessel or stage-coach to the fleet of vessels and system of railways covering thousands of miles. The individual capitalist was undoubtedly incapable of engaging alone in industries organized in such large units; association of capitalists was the necessary result. As far as association enabled capitalists to attain the unit of greatest efficiency the movement was undoubtedly beneficial to society. But the movement has divided in two directions with generally unfortunate results. The individual has been increasing in capacity so rapidly during the past few decades that most corporations find themselves in the control of small interior bodies of stockholders with large holdings of stock, the remaining stockholders being relegated to the status of mere creditors of the corporations, with no effective voice in the management of their affairs; in some railway companies stock is issued with the reservation of the recipient's proxy, his voting capacity. The other direction in which the movement of association has been diverted from the line of greatest benefit to society is in that of exceeding the unit of greatest efficiency. A factory of a certain size or a railway of a certain length is proportionally more efficient than one either larger or smaller than the former or longer or shorter than the latter. Where association exceeds such a unit, it is arbitrary and results in what are now generally known as "trusts." Association is not peculiar to corporations, however, but differs from association in other forms because of the peculiar conditions under which it takes place and is maintained. Corporate association has reference rather to the corporate property or industry than to the persons associated. The physical element is exaggerated, the human element is depressed. The purchaser of stock considers that he is acquiring an interest in an enterprise, not so much that he is assuming common relations with the numerous other stockholders; for the most part, he does not know them and does not take the pains to learn who they are; if he "knows the property" and by what directors it is administered, he is satisfied. It is the social separation of men, the disintegration of society in its personal phases, and the consequent participation of men in society through the medium of institutions, clubs, societies and the like, that raises corporate association into something extra-personal, unsympathetic, apparently the product of necessity; it is the same characteristic that is found in the association of citizenship in which the personal relations are depressed in the presence of a state embodying grand political and ethical aims. The subject is more appreciatively a citizen of his state than a fellow-citizen of his neighbor; so the stockholder looks upon himself rather as a participant in the corporate enterprise than as an associate of his fellow-stockholders.

After a so confessedly imperfect review of the causes of the unprecedented growth of corporations in the nineteenth century, a brief consideration of the most prominent present tendencies in their development may not be out of place. The most remarkable change in public sentiment is in relation to the functions of the state. It cannot be denied that a strong reaction against the destructive, "dispersive" philosophy of the eighteenth century is in progress. The effects of the change are more marked in England than in the United States because its political organization is more fully adapted to reflect and respond to such a change in public sentiment. The "scattering" of sovereignty, the limitation of governmental powers, was too fully translated into political institutions in America to permit a rapid expansion of the activity of the state. In the United States the end of the Civil War (1865) may fairly be taken as the date of the beginning of the reaction. To what extent the extraordinary activity of the state demanded by the exigencies of the war, certainly extended in many cases beyond the limits imposed by constitutions, may have laid a basis for the enforcement of the change in public sentiment may well be questioned. Undoubtedly the people became accustomed during the four years of war to a greater latitude of state action than had ever before been sanctioned by public opinion, but the extension of it to comprehend the field occupied by corporations was due to other causes not so closely connected with the Civil War. The internal development of the country had been greatly restrained by the unsettled political relations of the opposing sections. When the restraint was removed by the termination of the war, the course of development was resumed with extraordinary vigor, and chiefly through the instrumentality of corporations. During the decade succeeding the war and even before the war was ended, the United States and the several States, as well as counties, cities and towns, were scandalously prodigal of concessions to corporations. Unfortunately the development has recently come to a somewhat abrupt end with the virtual exhaustion of its geographical area, and the field of corporate enterprise has been transferred from unsettled or growing communities to places in which the stage of settlement and growth has been passed; the society in which corporations now have to act is one in which social progress is rather intensive than extensive, consisting more in the regulation of old relations than the establishment of new ones; public thought, for example, is concerned more with the government of established cities than with the foundation of new ones. The change in the character of social progress has suddenly revealed to the people the immense volume of public powers that have been reposed in corporations, and the dangerous extent to which corporate structure has shown itself capable of expansion beyond the activity legitimately organized within it. Trusts and industrial combinations are more or less justly identified with corporations, because the same social structure has in experience proved so readily adaptable to their purposes. Under such conditions the extension of governmental powers, to which the people became accustomed during the war and the period of corruption that followed it, presents a ready remedy for the evils of government by corporations and finds the people taught by experience not to fear its use. State ownership of railways, telegraphs and other industries confessedly public in nature is openly advocated now, though even a decade ago such advocacy would have met with only modified approval. The masses of the people have heretofore opposed the extension of the activity of the state because it might encroach on their own; confusing corporations with themselves as individuals, grants of public powers to them have seemed to accord with their opposition to encroachment by the state on the liberty of the individual. But now the same classes are clamoring for the extension of the activity of the state to protect the individual against the corporation. It is beginning to be recognized that more government is necessary under the developed conditions now attained by society than under the comparatively simple conditions prevalent a century ago,—and that such increased government has actually been provided, not by the state but by corporations. The plain tendency in corporate life at present, in its relations to the state, is in the direction of subjection and submission to close supervision. In history the state has never been satisfied with the mere supervision of corporations by commissions or otherwise; it would be against the teachings of history to expect that now the state will stop short of the complete absorption of the governmental features of corporations. The work of absorption has already progressed far in the fields of political, eleemosynary and educational corporations; the economic corporations have been disturbed but little. The scientific and social-fraternal associations have hardly passed beyond the "permissive" stage, in which they are merely recognized as of public importance and permitted to own property and otherwise act as organized groups; there are some slight indications that a few of them are entering the stage in which they are encouraged by the state to exist, and in which the state eventually depends upon them for the supplementing of its organization of its citizens.

In their relations to each other corporations exhibit the

tendency to combination that in earlier centuries resulted in the domination of the mediæval Catholic Church by the monastic orders, that gave the class of burgesses a predominant influence in the English House of Commons, that makes metropolitan London even to-day hardly more (politically) that a federation of livery companies, as other English cities and towns have only recently ceased to be. If corporations have been afforded free development, they have never failed to evolve a higher organization, which they have sometimes succeeded in substituting for the organs of the state themselves. In the light of the history of corporations there is nothing astonishing in the growth of Charity Organization Societies, associations of college presidents,[1] the National Society of Christian Endeavor, Amalgamated Trades Unions, the grand lodges of fraternal organizations, joint traffic associations, pools, trusts, clearing houses and the like,—they are the parliaments and congresses of corporations, phenomena perfectly familiar to the student of the history of corporations. Such consolidation has never proved to be permanently independent; it has either served as a medium of absorption by the state, or has had to be destroyed with such exhausting efforts of the superior organization of society as was involved in the dissolution of the Society of Jesus.

Within the corporations the process described in earlier chapters as "corporate shrinkage" is found to be accomplishing itself. In the political, eleemosynary, educational and religious corporations, the process is almost complete; what is regarded as the corporation, both in law and in popular estimation, is the governing body, the council, board of trustees or board of managers. Even in scientific associations, an interior body called in some

---

[1] Many of the scientific associations are so thoroughly dominated by university influences that they may almost be considered as organizations of federated universities rather than associations of individuals.

of them the council or senate, and in a greater or less degree independent of common members, is the repository of the actual powers of the associations; the membership is largely indeterminate, many of the members being such only for the purpose of securing publications or bulletins of information issued by the associations. In the social-fraternal organizations membership has a more definite meaning, though even in those of an industrial nature membership has come, during the past few years, to confer rather a license to follow a trade than a right to participate in the social life of the group. The somewhat independent status of "walking delegates" is one of the evidences of the change. It is beyond denial that trades unions have shown a tendency to become closer bodies controlling some of the conditions of branches of industry instead of organized associations of the men engaged in the industries; in that respect they have more nearly approached the status of true corporations. In economic corporations attention need hardly be called to the virtual exclusion of the small stockholder from participation in the corporate activity; one could not consider him responsible for corporate misdoings. The frequent resort to the issuance of bonds has had the same effect, to relegate the mass of persons (both bondholders and stockholders) interested in corporate enterprises to the status of creditors of the smaller and closer bodies that are the real corporations. The retention of proxies by rings has also had a restrictive influence. The result of all the influences has been the virtual shrinkage of most economic corporations to small interior bodies, in some cases members of a single family or of a group of allied families. In one sense the movement is in the direction of an exaggerated individualism; under the "new feudalism" the baronage will consist of the small bodies to which corporations have shrunk, exercising as "private rights" the public powers of corporations that have so shrunk.

All that may be said of the relations of corporations to individual members of society is implied in what has already been said of them. The present tendency is for them to become less organizations for the self-government of industries than organizations for the imposition of the conditions under which industries shall be prosecuted —essentially governmental bodies. The tendency of corporations to expand into monopolies, if not originally created such, elevates them above the level of the individual, whose normal industrial condition is one of competition with his fellows; though their interests were identical a few years ago, they are at variance now. Yet the corporate or semi-corporate organizations of society are so numerous and so pervasive of all kinds of social activity that the individual citizen, trying to attain the ideal of personal independence venerated in the theory of the political institutions of his country, finds every avenue under the control of some kind of an association in which he must acquire membership or to whose regulations he must submit. If he is suspected of failure to support his children a Society for the Prevention of Cruelty to Children takes them from him and places them in an "institution" in contempt of his right to be heard in his own defence and to be held innocent until he is proved guilty. If he fails to pay for a license to keep a dog, a Society for the Prevention of Cruelty to Animals, entitled to receive the license-fee, takes away his animal summarily and deprives him of the benefit and protection of the courts that he is taxed to support. He is not permitted to dispense charity indiscriminately and according to his own judgment; even if he embodies his charity in an institution, its management must be submitted to the supervision of a Charity Organization Society, or suffer the penalty of adverse criticism. His self-education is almost out of the question; as far as his education is not regulated by the state, it is regulated, in quantity and quality, by the religious denominations and corporations in control of the universities and colleges. As a scientist he cannot make himself an efficient factor in society except through the medium of associations. As an artist, his work must receive the commendation or approval of some academy or similar body. As a lawyer or physician he is subject to the rules of bar associations or medical societies. In social intercourse with his fellows he finds societies, clubs, circles, lodges and churches indispensable. The conditions of the town in which he lives are possibly the effects of the policy pursued by the improvement company that is "booming" it, regulating the architecture of the dwellings in it and imposing upon the inhabitants many other restrictions. The success of his business may be absolutely dependent on the treatment accorded him by transportation companies. He may be wealthy and honest and yet fall into bankruptcy through the refusal of banks to supply him with "credit." His loss by fire and the loss suffered by his family by his death entitle him and them to nothing but sympathy from others; relief should have been provided for through insurance companies. His range of investments outside of those reached through trust and investment companies is comparatively small. If he aspires to a public office, he finds a successful opponent in a fellow-citizen having more extended membership in fraternal organizations, trades unions and church societies. He discovers, in fine, that citizenship in his country has been largely metamorphosed into membership in corporations and patriotism into fidelity to them.

APPENDIX

IN an attempt to represent cartographically the areas of activity of the corporations and sub-classes of corporations included in Class II. and described as National-External Corporations, several difficulties are quite impossible to overcome, and limit somewhat the usefulness of the accompanying map.

1. The descriptions of territories found in charters manifestly cannot be taken as a basis for the representation in the map of the areas of the companies' activity. Some of the descriptions applied to territories that existed only in the imagination; the Hudson's Bay Company was expected to discover a passage from Hudson's Bay to the Pacific Ocean and was granted the commerce tributary to it and to the streams that flowed into it. Again, some of them were extremely indefinite, as the territory of the East India Company, which was to extend beyond the Cape of Good Hope to the Straits of Magellan. In some cases the company's commerce was to extend to all lands not already occupied by other subjects of the King of England or the subjects of other Christian princes.

2. It would appear plain that only territories actually occupied by the companies ought to be represented on the map. But even if one company did not occupy all the territory conceded to it, other companies were, in general, debarred by its grant from occupying it. The

territory actually occupied would consequently not be a perfect measure of its influence.

3. It is a question whether the activity of some of the companies ought to be represented as occupying *territories*. The Merchants of the Staple and Merchant Adventurers did not occupy territories, but rather staple-towns and market-towns in them. The grants of foreign sovereigns to English companies, as to the Russia and Turkey Companies, were usually in the form of concessions to have their factories in certain cities. For some purposes, then, it would more nearly represent the truth to indicate the activity of the companies rather by dots standing for their staple-towns, market-towns and factories, than by lines standing for the boundaries of geographical areas. Again, the territorial range of activity was often described with reference to routes of transportation. Notably in the case of the Hudson's Bay Company, it should have all the commerce tributary to Hudson's Bay, the rivers flowing into it and other bodies and streams of water. Would its area of activity be better represented by indicating the bodies and streams of water by reference to which it was determined?

4. The commerce conceded to some of the companies was conditioned on its being reached by them through certain channels of transportation. The Eastland Company enjoyed only as much of the trade with Norway, Sweden, Denmark and other of the Baltic countries as it might reach through the Sound; its merchants might apparently not have access to Norway directly by its west coast. Likewise the Russia, Turkey and East India Companies engaged to a considerable extent in the same trade, but were confined respectively to the routes by way of Archangel, the Mediterranean and the Cape of Good Hope. The trade of the South Sea Company with the west coast of North and South America was restricted to the route of the Straits of Magellan, so as not to inter-

fere with the East India Company. Such features of the territorial distribution of the commerce of the companies, important as they certainly were, cannot well be represented on the map; to that extent the map is an imperfect medium of expressing the truth.

5. The colonial companies and proprietaries were so closely related in their work of colonization that the territories occupied by them need hardly be separated. Moreover, they were small in comparison with those of other companies and so frequently overlapped each other that it would be difficult to represent them separately. The entire territory occupied by the colonial companies and proprietaries is accordingly represented without division on the map. The extension of many grants from ocean to ocean is probably best left out of account.

6. It must be borne in mind that many of the companies were intended for the discovery not of new lands and trade but of new ocean passages, such as the northeast passage and the northwest passage, and for the development of fisheries. Such "areas of activity" would have to be represented as covering quite indefinable (or even suppositious, expanses of the surface of the ocean.

Under the limitations implied in the foregoing suggestions, the accompanying map may be of service by exhibiting graphically some of the features of the corporations described in the chapters respectively devoted to them.

INDEX